JOURNAL FOR THE STUDY OF THE NEW TESTAMENT SUPPLEMENT SERIES
132

Executive Editor
Stanley E. Porter

Sheffield Academic Press

Imperial Cult and Commerce in John's Apocalypse

J. Nelson Kraybill

Journal for the Study of the New Testament
Supplement Series 132

Copyright © 1996 Sheffield Academic Press

Published by Sheffield Academic Press Ltd
Mansion House
19 Kingfield Road
Sheffield S11 9AS
England

Printed on acid-free paper in Great Britain
by Bookcraft Ltd
Midsomer Norton, Bath

British Library Cataloguing in Publication Data

A catalogue record for this book is available
from the British Library

ISBN 1-85075-616-3

'...all shipmasters and seafarers, sailors and all whose trade is on the sea, stood far off and cried out as they saw the smoke of her burning, "What city was like the great city?" And they threw dust on their heads, as they wept and mourned, crying out, "Alas, alas, the great city, where all who had ships at sea grew rich by her wealth!"' (Rev. 18.17-19)

Frontispiece: An ancient mosaic from Ostia, port of imperial Rome. It depicts a merchant ship with a corn measure (*modius*) on each side, indicating grain was the normal cargo. The inscription reads, *NAVICUL[arri] ET NEGOTIANTES KARALITANI* ('Shipowners and Merchants from Cagliari [Sardinia]').

CONTENTS

PREFACE

Not long after I began the following study, I had the opportunity to give a series of lectures on Revelation at the *Centro de Estudios* of the Mennonite Church in Uruguay. A few students in the class had suffered abuse or torture, for their religious or political convictions, at the hands of a dictatorship supported by the government of my own country. 'Coins of the United States say "In God We Trust"', ventured one student, 'but actually your leaders trust in their guns and their dollars.' Those students helped their North American teacher see that issues of empire, economics and idolatry are as real today as they were when John of Patmos condemned Babylon (Rome) for injustice, oppression and blasphemy.

Back in Virginia, where I was a student, newspaper headlines were full of references to empire and allegiance over the next few years. The Soviet empire collapsed; the American empire extended its own economic and political influence. Wars fueled by religion, nationalism or ethnic hatred festered in several parts of the globe. International arms merchants literally made a killing, a blasphemous business that feeds the economies even of nations that call themselves Christian.

There is virtually no comment on these modern events and concerns in the following pages. I have tried to view Revelation from the perspective of a *first-century* reader. John of Patmos had the Roman empire in mind when he wrote, not people of the twentieth century. However, if we can understand why John saw loyalty to Jesus as being in tension with loyalty to Rome, then we will have a valuable reference point for similar analysis of domination systems today. Empires and nations of every generation make demands that raise critical questions of allegiance and obedience for followers of Jesus.

Although I believe Revelation is instructive for weighing the political and economic choices of Christians today, it is important to recognize the limitations of drawing too heavily from just one book of the Bible in making our own ethical choices. By any conventional standards, John of

Patmos was a politically powerless and marginalized person. If he had not already suffered abuse at the hands of the state, he expected Christians soon would do so. Either by choice or by force of circumstances, he was isolated on an island, filled with rage about the prevailing political power of his day. We need to balance John's bitter assessment of Roman power against the cautious optimism of Paul the apostle and other early Christians who had more positive encounters with Roman power.

Particularly in democratic societies, in which governments fulfil a wide range of productive and healthy roles, Christians cannot simply adopt John's stance of categorical condemnation. Sectarian withdrawal from society is not a valid option if the church can actively 'engage the powers' to speak or act for justice and truth. Yet John's keen insight into spiritual dimensions of political power might help us see that even the best of governments sometimes make choices or demands that followers of Jesus must challenge. Christians in economically and politically powerful nations, in the terminology of Revelation, live more in Babylon than on Patmos. From our position of relative security and comfort it may be difficult to hear or accept John's radical critique of imperial power, a critique that seems logical to many people in the two-thirds world.

I am grateful to mentors and other scholars who helped me understand the message of Revelation. Paul J. Achtemeier, of Union Theological Seminary in Virginia, was my advisor for a doctoral thesis that laid the foundation for this book. His knowledge of biblical scholarship, his love of the scriptures, and the quality of his own research set a high standard. Others helped by responding critically to all or part of my work. These include Stanley E. Porter, Martin Hengel, Peter Lampe, Millard Lind, Alan Kreider, Richard Bauckham, Christopher Rowland, Larry Kreitzer and Justin Meggitt. Gerald Nussbaum and A.T. Fear kindly helped me decipher a few Latin inscriptions. Trisha Dale did proofreading, and my colleagues at the London Mennonite Centre conspired to allow me time for research. Steve Barganski of Sheffield Academic Press skillfully managed the final editing and publication. I am indebted to each person named above, aware that any errors or shortcomings are my own responsibility. Most of all, I am indebted to my wife Ellen for her loving support.

Highgate, London
Advent, 1995
J. Nelson Kraybill

LIST OF FIGURES

ABBREVIATIONS

AB	Anchor Bible
AE	*L'Année Epigraphique*
AJA	*American Journal of Archeology*
AJJS	*Australian Journal of Jewish Studies*
ANRW	*Aufstieg und Niedergang der römischen Welt*
AUSS	*Andrews University Seminary Studies*
BAGD	W. Bauer, W.F. Arndt, F.W. Gingrich, F.W. Danker, *Greek–English Lexicon of the New Testament*
BCH	*Bulletin de Correspondance Hellénique*
BDB	F. Brown, S.R. Driver, and C.A. Briggs, *Hebrew and English Lexicon of the Old Testament*
BMC, I and II	H. Mattingly, *Coins of the Roman Empire in the British Museum*, I and II (2nd edn, 1976)
BR	*Biblical Research*
CBQ	*Catholic Biblical Quarterly*
CIG	*Corpus Inscriptionum Graecarum*
CII	*Corpus Inscriptionum Iudaicarum*
CIL	*Corpus Inscriptionum Latinarum*
CRev	*Classical Review*
CTM	*Concordia Theological Monthly*
HBD	P.J. Achtemeier (ed.), *Harper's Bible Dictionary*
HTR	*Harvard Theological Review*
IDB	G.A. Buttrick (ed.), *Interpreter's Dictionary of the Bible*
IDBSup	*IDB*, Supplementary Volume
I. Delos	*Inscriptions de Délos*
I. Eph.	*Inschriften von Ephesos*
IG	*Inscriptiones Graecae* (1873–)
IGR	*Inscriptiones Graecae ad Res Romanas Pertinentes* (1906–27)
ILS	*Inscriptiones Latinae Selectae* (1892-1916)
Int	*Interpretation*
JANESCU	*Journal of the Ancient Near Eastern Society of Columbia University*
JEH	*Journal of Ecclesiastical History*
JBL	*Journal of Biblical Literature*
JQR	*Jewish Quarterly Review*
JR	*Journal of Religion*

JRS	*Journal of Roman Studies*
JSOT	*Journal for the Study of the Old Testament*
JTS	*Journal of Theological Studies*
LCL	Loeb Classical Library
MAMA	*Monumenta Asiae Minoris Antiquae* (1928-39)
Nestle-Aland	E. Nestle, K. Aland *et al.*, *Novum Testamentum Graece*, 26th edition
NTS	*New Testament Studies*
ODCC	*Oxford Dictionary of the Christian Church*, 2nd edn
OGIS	*Orientis Graecae Inscriptiones Selectae* (1903-5)
OTL	Old Testament Library
OTP	J.H. Charlesworth (ed.), *Old Testament Pseudepigrapha*, 2 vols.
P W	Pauly–Wissowa, *Real-Encyclopädie der classischen Altertumswissenschaft*
REG	*Revue des Etudes Grecques*
SBLSP	SBL Seminar Papers
RSV	Revised Standard Version
SEG	*Supplementum Epigraphicum Graecum* (1923–38)
SIG	*Sylloge Inscriptionum Graecarum* (1915-24)
SNTSMS	Society for New Testament Studies Monograph Series
TDNT	G. Kittel and G. Friedrich (eds.), *Theological Dictionary of the New Testament*
TynBul	*Tyndale Bulletin*
ZNW	*Zeitschrift für die neutestamentliche Wissenschaft*

INTRODUCTION

> Fallen, fallen is Babylon the great! It has become a dwelling place of demons... For all the nations have drunk of the wine of the wrath of her fornication, and the kings of the earth have committed fornication with her, and the merchants of the earth have grown rich from the power of her luxury... And all shipmasters and seafarers, sailors and all whose trade is on the sea, stood far off and cried out as they saw the smoke of her burning. (Rev. 18.2, 3, 17)

Why does John of Patmos, in a book written for Christians living under Roman rule, turn his attention to merchants, shipmasters and sailors at the climactic moment of Babylon's (Rome's) demise? A thorough answer to this question takes a student of Revelation beyond the haven of early Christian communities into open seas of the Graeco-Roman world.

John himself serves as guide and interpreter for this journey into a first-century Empire. It is a dangerous passage. A dragon, wounded and sulking from defeat in heaven, stalks the faithful people of God (Rev. 12.3-18). A hideous beast rises from the sea to claim illegitimate sovereignty over every living creature (13.1-10). A second beast emerges from the earth, forcing humanity to worship the first and threatening with death those who refuse to comply (13.11-18). John, of course, refuses to comply. A renegade against the powers of darkness, he sets his own course through deep spiritual waters full of symbols and figures that seem to represent very real characters in his world.

In Revelation 18, John turns his attention to a convoy of merchant ships streaming toward Babylon (Rome), laden with dainties to gratify the insatiable beast. Spiritual symbol merges with historical reality: From his vantage point on the island of Patmos, along a major trade artery, John describes the steady flow of commercial vessels that pass by each day on their way to Rome and other imperial ports.

1. Christians Lured by the Beast

Just before his first mention of maritime trade, John portrays Babylon (Rome) as a drunken whore (17.1-18). It is not surprising, then, that the dirge in Revelation 18.1-24 goes on to condemn entrepreneurs who sail to the great city as wanton and compromised. Who are the people engaged in this maritime trade, and why does John in his vision take time for them in the terrible hour of Rome's demise? Could there have been fellow disciples of Jesus Christ at the helm of merchant ships, at the loading docks, or in the guild halls of export industries?

The following essay argues that Christians had ready access to the ships, docks and guild halls that serviced Rome's enormous appetite. We do not have sufficient first-century data to demonstrate that large numbers of Christians used commercial networks of the Empire to advance their own social or economic status; our best evidence for Christian involvement in international trade comes from the second century. Already in the first century, however, some believers moved frequently among traders and business people; others were small entrepreneurs themselves. Some first-century Christians had wealth or social connections that would have enabled them to move in circles of political and economic influence.

John of Patmos had the perception to see that Rome's political and economic grandeur was attractive to some followers of Jesus. Undergirding his Apocalypse is a conviction that arrogant Rome, drunk with luxury and full of blasphemy, soon would collapse. In light of this belief, Revelation 18 is more than a poem about the fall of a foe; it is a clarion call for Christians to sever all economic and political ties with an Empire that had sold out to injustice, idolatry and greed.

The following study highlights allusions to finance and commerce throughout John's Apocalypse, using Revelation 18 with its 'kings... merchants...shipmasters and seafarers, sailors and all whose trade is on the sea' as a focal point. John contemptuously labels Rome as 'Babylon' (14.8; 16.19; 17.5; 18.2, 10, 21). He borrows traditional language of the Hebrew prophets to cry, 'Come out of her, my people, so that you do not take part in her sins...' (18.4; cf. Isa. 48.20; Jer. 51.45). John was aware of economic matters and wrote Revelation to Christians in a busy trade region. I will argue that he intended his 'come out' warning as practical pastoral instruction: if Christians had (or were tempted to have) dealings with Rome through maritime trade or other commercial ties, they should withdraw immediately or they would share both in Rome's guilt and her punishment.

This study explores the nature of trade networks in the Roman Empire and the evidence of Jewish or Christian involvement in them. Various sources provide clues to the meaning of images that John uses to describe

Rome and her allies. John's use of particular Old Testament passages, for example, indicates he was concerned about the interplay of idolatry, military power and commerce. Soundings from other apocalyptic literature of the era reveal that John was not alone in his bitter condemnation of Rome and his concern that trade was sometimes a slippery slope of spiritual and moral compromise. Rabbinic writings illustrate that some Jewish teachers advocated cautious involvement in many areas of Roman society, while others pressed for radical withdrawal. Several New Testament and early Christian authors speak of idolatry and finance in the same breath, giving us insight into economic issues debated by the early church. Recent studies on patronage in the Roman Empire illuminate the kind of socio-economic relationships that John apparently had in mind when he spoke of 'fornication' with Rome. Archaeological evidence from Roman port cities helps explain how commerce and religion blended in ways that John found objectionable.

Insights from all these avenues of study point to the conclusion that John of Patmos was not against commerce and trade in themselves, as if they were intrinsically evil. Rather, *John warned Christians to sever or to avoid economic and political ties with Rome because institutions and structures of the Roman Empire were saturated with unholy allegiance to an Emperor who claimed to be divine (or was treated as such).* True to its name, Revelation reveals lofty propaganda of the Roman Empire to be a sham, and calls Christians to give allegiance to an alternative society in the New Jerusalem.

The raw blasphemy of late first-century Emperor worship was deeply offensive to John and other devout monotheists. In the hierarchical structure of Roman rule, idolatry and greed at the top meant cooperative allies or subordinates far across the Empire could be drawn into a web of complicity. Getting a full view of Roman corruption was an 'unveiling' (ἀποκάλυψις, Rev. 1.1)[1] to John's spiritual eyes. He glimpsed the *Gestalt* or fundamental form of Empire looming murkily in the mist of the Mediterranean world; it was a seductive and dangerous beast. He saw through imperial glamor to the naked arrogance and spiritual narcissism of Rome, and urgently wanted to share his perceptions with fellow Christians who could fall prey to the charms of power, wealth and social acceptability.

---

1.   In Rev. 1.1, the immediate source and object of the unveiling is Jesus Christ. The title ἀποκάλυψις also is an appropriate description for the unmasking of Rome and her allies throughout Revelation.

2. On the Shoulders of Giants

The following study would have been impossible without the work of many earlier scholars who helped solve the riddle of the Apocalypse. A century ago, biblical exegetes first began to look seriously at the ancient political and cultural context of the book of Revelation.[2] Scholars such as Hermann Gunkel[3] and Wilhelm Bousset[4] identified the first beast of Revelation (13.1-10) as the Roman Empire and 'Babylon' (18.1-24) as ancient Rome. Images in the book of Revelation, they said, were symbols familiar to its first readers. The book portrays people and institutions of the author's own era, not events of a far distant future. A generation of scholars built upon this insight, and produced monumental commentaries that explored in depth the Jewish, Graeco-Roman and Near Eastern milieu of the Apocalypse.[5]

Recent scholarship has applied to Revelation a full range of exegetical tools, from further historical-critical research to redaction criticism and literary analysis.[6] While differences persist among interpreters, most

2.   Most exegetes from the second century to the nineteenth either spiritualized Revelation into timeless concepts about the nature of God and the cosmos, or read it as a cryptic allegory portraying events leading up to their own time. Victorinus (d. c. 304 CE), author of the earliest extant commentary on Revelation, made a few passing references to the work's original setting: 'The time must be understood in which the written Apocalypse was published', he said. Victorinus interpreted the seven kings of Rev. 17.10 as Otho, Vitellius, Galba, Vespasian, Titus, Domitian and Nerva. However, even he spiritualized most of the book, viewing the seven churches named by John as each a 'class, company or association of saints' rather than as literal congregations. Victorinus, *Commentary on the Apocalypse* 3.1, 7.10. Eusebius represents the school of interpreters who saw Revelation as a timetable for events in their own day. He believed the Church of the Holy Sepulchre, built by Constantine in Jerusalem, was the New Jerusalem foreseen by John (Rev. 21.2). *Life of Constantine* 33.

3.   H. Gunkel, *Schöpfung und Chaos in Urzeit und Endzeit* (Göttingen: Vandenhoeck & Ruprecht, 1895), p. 336.

4.   W. Bousset, *Die Offenbarung Johannis* (Göttingen: Vandenhoeck & Ruprecht, 1906), pp. 358-65, 418-26.

5.   Outstanding among these are I.T. Beckwith, *The Apocalypse of John: Studies in Introduction* (New York: Macmillan, 1919), and the classic by R.H. Charles, *A Critical and Exegetical Commentary on the Revelation of St. John* (Edinburgh: T. & T. Clark, 1920).

6.   For a succinct summary of modern scholarship on Revelation, see E.S. Fiorenza, 'Revelation', in E.J. Epp and G.W. MacRae (eds.), *The New Testament and its Modern Interpreters* (Philadelphia: Fortress Press, 1989), pp. 407-27.

scholars[7] accept major conclusions drawn by R.H. Charles and other early twentieth-century exegetes: John of Patmos was an otherwise unknown Christian prophet of Jewish origin.[8] Late in the first century[9] he wrote to seven congregations in Asia Minor with whom he personally was acquainted.[10] He encouraged his readers to be faithful to Jesus Christ despite increasing pressure to participate in the Roman imperial cult. He awaited the imminent demise of Rome and the triumphant reign of Christ with the saints.

See also 'Recent Theories about the Social Setting of the Book of Revelation', in L.L. Thompson, *The Book of Revelation: Apocalypse and Empire* (New York: Oxford University Press, 1990), pp. 202-10.

7.   Fiorenza says the majority of modern commentaries agree that Revelation reflects a political-religious conflict with the Roman Empire and a persecution of the church in Asia Minor under Domitian. She cites the works of Swete, Charles, Loisy, Beckwith, Allo, Carrington, Wikenhauser, Bonsirven, Behm, Brütsch, Féret, Boismard, Lohse, Cerfaux-Cambier, Caird, Visser and Kiddle-Ross. See, 'Apocalyptic and Gnosis in the Book of Revelation and Paul', *JBL* 92 (1973), p. 565.

8.   In contrast to most recent scholars, J.M. Ford argues that Revelation emanated from the 'circle' of John the Baptist and his disciples (*Revelation* [AB, New York: Doubleday, 1975], pp. 28-37). Her view rests on a few general thematic affinities between Revelation and the message of the Baptist as presented in the Gospels. Without compelling evidence, her argument does little more than construct an improbable possibility of such authorship. Slightly more convincing is the notion of a 'Johannine school' of writers who shared certain symbols and Christology in common, and who wrote both Revelation and the fourth Gospel. For a summary and criticism of this hypothesis, see Fiorenza, *The Book of Revelation: Justice and Judgment* (Philadelphia: Fortress, 1985), pp. 85-113. It is noteworthy that only Revelation and the fourth Gospel refer to Jesus as the Lamb (ἀρνίον), and the Gospel seems to share some of Revelation's conviction that fidelity to the Emperor is incompatible with faithfulness to Jesus (see Jn 18.36; 19.12, 15). However, the fourth Gospel's realized eschatology contrasts so starkly with Revelation's apocalyptic expectations that the two books have little in common and are unlikely to be from the same 'school'.

9.   The earliest known statement regarding the date of Revelation comes from Irenaeus. There is no good reason to question his assertion that John received the vision late in Domitian's reign, about 95–96 CE. Irenaeus, *Adv. Haer.* 5.30.3. It is plausible that John may have drawn from earlier sources for part of his Apocalypse.

10. For a thorough discussion of Revelation's date and authorship see A.Y. Collins, *Crisis and Catharsis: The Power of the Apocalypse* (Philadelphia: Westminster Press, 1984), pp. 25-83.

3. Recent Sociological Interpretation

Several recent interpreters have used sociological analysis as a way to build on historical-critical research of an earlier generation, and their work provides a foundation for the following study.

Adela Yarbro Collins, in *Crisis and Catharsis: The Power of the Apocalypse*, describes the social setting of churches in Revelation as 'perceived crisis'.[11] Some Christians of Asia Minor found themselves in conflict both with Jews and Roman authorities. This conflict flared up at a time of general tension in Asian society between rich and poor. Collins explores the ideology and relative power of various ancient social groups, and explains part of the anger in Revelation as class resentment. In her treatment of shippers and merchants (Rev. 18), for example, Collins mentions the 'new class of wealthy provincials who made their fortunes' in commerce under Flavian rule.[12] The power of newly rich provincials provoked resentment among marginalized people and fomented discontent toward Rome as well. 'The combination of hostility toward the local elite and toward the Roman authorities is not surprising,' she says, 'since they cooperated with and supported one another.'[13]

The most thorough sociological treatment of Revelation is a recent work by Leonard L. Thompson, *The Book of Revelation: Apocalypse and Empire*.[14] Thompson builds on sociological analysis of the New Testament by scholars such as Gerd Theissen, Wayne A. Meeks and Abraham Malherbe. His study focuses on Christian communities in the province of Asia. He also explores Jewish life in that province and traces the outlines of 'social, economic, and political life in the cities where Christians lived and worked'.[15] Thompson rejects the argument of class conflict, and argues that most Christians were not being singled out for persecution in Asia Minor. Rather, John believed the political order of Rome was wholly corrupt, and voluntarily separated himself from it. He was hostile to both Jews and Christians who accommodated in any way

11. Collins, *Crisis and Catharsis*, pp. 84-110. Cf. A.Y. Collins, 'Early Christian Apocalypticism: Genre and Social Setting', *Semeia* 36 (1986), pp. 1-12.

12. The Flavian family of Emperors consisted of Vespasian (69–79 CE) and his sons Titus (79–81 CE) and Domitian (81-96 CE).

13. Collins, *Crisis and Catharsis*, p. 123.

14. L.L. Thompson, *The Book of Revelation: Apocalypse and Empire* (New York: Oxford University Press, 1990).

15. Thompson, *Revelation*, p. 116.

to idolatrous practices of Roman imperial society.

Like Collins, Thompson explains the crisis mentality of Revelation as springing more 'from John's perspective on Roman society...than from significant hostilities in the social environment'.[16] Neither Collins nor Thompson implies the crisis in Revelation was imaginary. There were real power groups and real institutions with whom the author found himself in conflict. Yet many Christians (and Jews) in Asia got along well under Roman rule, and did not experience or expect the kind of alienation from society reflected in Revelation. Thompson notes that John includes the economic order of the Roman Empire as an integral part of a corrupt realm. 'The peace and prosperity of Roman society is, from his point of view, not to be entered into by faithful Christians.'[17]

Although not primarily a sociological study, a recent commentary on Revelation by Christopher Rowland builds on political, social and economic studies of the ancient world to give penetrating insight into the book's message.[18] Rome's economic oppression, idolatrous religious claims and beguiling facade as benefactor all play a prominent role in Rowland's interpretation. Whereas my own study focuses almost entirely on the first-century context of the Apocalypse, Rowland examines the original setting of the book and goes on to make cautious application of John's vision to the modern world. 'It is the Beast and Babylon, not Rome and Caesar, which are the vehicles of John's message,' Rowland says. 'As such they have a wider appeal than a narrowly focused political analysis rooted in particular events.'[19]

Rowland reminds us that many symbols in Revelation have psychological and spiritual meaning that transcends immediate circumstances of the first century CE. The book is rife with imagery that already had a long history in Jewish or pagan tradition before John applied it to the Roman Empire of his day. Likewise, generations of readers since the first century have used symbols of Revelation to interpret political

---

16. Thompson, *Revelation*, p. 175.

17. Thompson, *Revelation*, p. 174. The 'Index of Ancient Sources' in Thompson's book (pp. 263-64) lists no references to Revelation 18—the chapter that speaks of prominent socio-economic groups in the Roman Empire. This is surprising in a book that emphasizes sociological exegesis, but is typical of the way many scholars have given scant attention to the 'dirge' over Babylon.

18. C. Rowland, *Revelation* (Epworth Commentaries; London: Epworth Press, 1993).

19. Rowland, *Revelation*, p. 24; cf. p. 31.

or religious realities of their own era.[20]

The following study explores the meaning key symbols in Revelation *already* had when John wove them into his book. It does not, however, make more than passing reference to the meaning of Revelation for Christians today. While application of John's message to modern realities is beyond the scope of this work, it is necessary and urgent for Christians to venture such interpretaton. Where, in our world today, do governments and economic institutions act in ways that demand idolatrous allegiance? Which are the Empires, large and small, that build their own security at the expense of defenseless people? What should modern Christians do when governments seek our personal or financial support for acts of violence or nationalistic self-interest?[21] What ideology or pseudo-religion do political and economic powers use to justify their deeds? How are Christians tempted to take part or benefit?

4. *Socio-Economic Analysis*

Despite prominent references to commerce and trade in Revelation, no modern exegete has attempted a thorough economic study of social groups represented in the Apocalypse. However, Richard Bauckham does examine economic data in Revelation 18, and states in brief an argument that reinforces the central thesis of this study. After reviewing the dirge over Babylon, with its categories of commercial products and groups with interest in trade, Bauckham asks,

> Why then does John give us the perspective of Rome's collaborators in evil: the ruling classes, the mercantile magnates, the shipping industry? Part of the reason may be that, although the perspective was certainly not John's, it could rather easily be that of some of his readers. If it is not likely that many were among the ruling classes, it is not unlikely that John's readers would include merchants and others whose business or livelihood was closely involved with the Roman political and economic system... And for such readers, it is of the utmost significance that, prior to the picture of the mourners, comes the command: Come out of her my people...[22]

20. One noteworthy recent example uses Revelation to interpret marginalization and suffering in South Africa: A. Boesak, *Comfort and Protest: Reflections on the Apocalypse of John of Patmos* (Edinburgh: St Andrew Press, 1987).

21. For an outstanding study of Christian attitudes toward power and its abuse, see W. Wink, *Engaging the Powers: Discernment and Resistance in a World of Domination* (Minneapolis: Fortress Press, 1992).

22. R.J. Bauckham, 'The Economic Critique of Rome in Revelation 18', in L. Alexander (ed.), *Images of Empire* (Sheffield: Sheffield Academic Press, 1991),

Bauckham recognizes that Revelation 18 probably addresses not only a distant imperial society ('them'), but also fellow Christians within John's faith community ('us'). If John in fact had this immediate pastoral concern in mind, a thorough socio-economic analysis of Revelation 18 is indispensable for understanding the overall message of the book.[23] My study is an attempt to meet that need.

Socio-economic analysis simply provides one perspective from which to examine the meaning of John's vision; it cannot explain the whole. The point is not that John wrote Revelation because he was poor and socially marginalized. Rather, it is more likely he *identified with* the poor and marginalized because he believed Christians no longer could participate in an unjust commercial network thoroughly saturated with idolatrous patriotism. This study examines how commerce and the imperial cult blended in the first-century Roman world, and how John of Patmos thought followers of Jesus should respond.

pp. 47-90; reprinted in Bauckham, *The Climax of Prophecy* (Edinburgh: T. & T. Clark, 1993), pp. 338-83. Cf. Bauckham, *The Bible in Politics: How to Read the Bible Politically* (London: SPCK, 1989), pp. 97-100; and Bauckham, *The Theology of the Book of Revelation* (New Testament Theology series; Cambridge: Cambridge University Press, 1993), pp. 14-17.

23. Bauckham points out that the literary unit of the passage under examination runs from 18.1 to 19.8. 'The Economic Critique', pp. 46-51. My study, however, focuses largely on chapter 18 since it contains the bulk of allusions relevant to socio-economic analysis.

Chapter 1

A DWELLING PLACE OF DEMONS

> Babylon…has become a dwelling place of demons, a haunt of every foul
> and hateful bird, a haunt of every foul and hateful beast (Rev. 18.2).

Late in the first century CE, on the small island of Patmos, a Christian
prophet named John looked out across the Mediterranean world and
declared an end to the greatest power on earth: 'Fallen, fallen is Babylon
the great!' he cried (Rev. 18.1). There were no signs that Rome—or
'Babylon' as he called it—was about to fall when John of Patmos made
this claim.[1] Throughout his Apocalypse, though, runs a theme that the
city already was full of demons. The Empire based in Italy drew its
power from Satan and blasphemed God, he declared. It made war on
the saints and caused all inhabitants of earth to worship it (13.1-8).

For playing this arrogant and perverse role John was certain Rome
would pay a terrible price. With the unwavering confidence of a prophet
inspired, John looked ahead to the day when 'God remembered great
Babylon and gave her the wine-cup of the fury of his wrath' (16.19). In
John's vision an earthquake unmatched in human history split the city in
three. The earth moved and huge hailstones fell from heaven until suf-
ferers cursed God (16.20-21). These vivid images lead up to Revelation
18 and a survey of the smoldering ruins. An angel descends from heaven
to proclaim a dirge over the ghastly scene (18.1).[2] Hideous creatures

---

1. The first episode involving Babylon (בבל) in the canonical Hebrew Bible is
the Tower of 'Babel' (בבל) incident, in which inhabitants of the city arrogantly
attempt to build a tower 'with its top in the heavens' in order to 'make a name' for
themselves. Gen. 11.1-9; cf. 10.10.

2. Whether Revelation 18 is a 'dirge' or a 'taunt song' depends on the speakers'
attitude toward the fall of Rome. Do the various groups cited mourn or celebrate?
Clearly friends of 'Babylon' grieve (18.15-19), while God's people rejoice (18.20).
Chapter 18 contains a complex interplay of grief and jubilation. Yet it ends soberly,
recognizing there is much good in Rome that will come to a violent end—including

inhabit the abandoned capital (18.2). Rome is like a proud queen burned with fire (18.7-8).

Woven in with these unforgettable scenes are mundane references to economic and political realities in the first-century Mediterranean world. In quick but vivid strokes John portrays kings, merchants and shippers who satiated their greed by an unholy alliance with the imperial city. A cargo list enumerates the luxury items—from gold to slaves—that maritime merchants of the first century hauled to Italy (18.11-13). For the first time in the Apocalypse, we get a clear view of commercial relations with Rome as a central concern of the author.

1. *Economic Aspect of John's Vision*

If this were John's only mention of economic matters, we might conclude business and finance were of little concern to Christians in Asia Minor. Instead, we find allusions to economic (and related social) status at key points throughout the Apocalypse. The socio-economic status of any Christian church John mentions seems inversely related to the book's level of approval toward it. Christ encourages the impoverished congregation at Smyrna (Rev. 2.8-11), for example, while berating its wealthy counterpart at Laodicea (3.14-19). The Christian community at Philadelphia has 'but little power' (3.8), yet wins divine approval.[3] Faithful believers now suffering poverty and powerlessness some day will enjoy wealth and safety in the New Jerusalem (21.9-27). Beyond such explicit references to Christians, John makes the general observation that people who refuse to wear the mark of the beast cannot 'buy or sell' (13.17). He highlights the fact that merchants of the earth who trade with Rome 'have grown rich from the power of her luxury'

music, crafts, milling and marriage (18.21-23). Collins reviews how major interpreters have understood the emotional pitch of this chapter. See 'Revelation 18: Taunt Song or Dirge?' in J. Lambrecht (ed.), *L'Apocalypse johannique et l'Apocalyptique dans le Nouveau Testament* (Gembloux: Leuven University Press, 1980), pp. 185-87.

3.   Collins says John's approval of impoverished Christians is related to a 'traditional element of the reversal of fortunes, which seems to play a role throughout Revelation'. She cites Lk. 1.51-53 and 6.20-26 as other examples of the same motif. 'Persecution and Vengeance in the Book of Revelation', in D. Hellholm (ed.), *Apocalypticism in the Mediterranean World and the Near East* (Tübingen: Mohr, 1983), p. 745. The reversal of fortunes tradition may have shaped some of John's language, but I will argue that larger issues of idolatry governed his evaluation of the churches.

(18.3). These repeated references to socio-economic matters suggest that John saw participation in the imperial economy as an important discipleship issue for people who confessed Jesus as Lord.[4]

Imperial Cult as a Pivotal Concern

In Revelation 18 John highlights the triad of kings, merchants and seamen that controlled practical aspects of economic life in the Mediterranean world. What was the character of the relationship between these three categories of people? Did merchants and seamen, in order to attain financial success, have to espouse a particular ideology or religious orientation?

Our examination of these questions starts with the majority opinion of modern scholarship that pressure from the imperial cult lies at the center of John's concern. The two beasts, which loom so large in John's symbolic world, provide the key to understanding Revelation as a whole. The first beast (13.1-10) seems to represent either the Roman Empire or the Emperor himself.[5] The second beast (13.11-18) probably is the priesthood of the imperial cult, the elaborate institution that flourished in Asia Minor and accorded divine honors to the Emperor.[6] The cult so

---

4.   Undoubtedly A.H.M. Jones is correct to write that 'in most of the cities of the Empire, trade and industry played a minor role' in the economy. Yet in certain cities, including Carthage, Aquileia, Ephesus, Alexandria and Palmyra, 'a large proportion of the population lived by trade and wealthy merchants were included in the local aristocracy', in P.A. Brunt (ed.), *The Roman Economy: Studies in Ancient Economic and Administrative History* (Totowa, NJ: Rowman & Littlefield, 1974), pp. 29-30. John of Patmos wrote to Christians in an exceptional region where international trade was a major factor.

5.   The first beast is a composite creature, with features drawn from four beasts that appeared in the vision of Dan. 7.1-28. Commentators now virtually agree that these four beasts represent the Empires of the Babylonians, the Medes, the Persians and the Greeks.

6.   The classic presentation of this view is by Charles, *Commentary,* I, pp. 345-67. Among earlier expressions of the same are Bousset, *Offenbarung,* pp. 358-74, and W.M. Ramsay, *The Letters to the Seven Churches of Asia* (New York: Hodder & Stoughton, 1905), p. 97. More recent exponents include G.B. Caird, *A Commentary on the Revelation of St. John the Divine* (New York: Harper & Row, 1966), pp. 170-73; E.S. Fiorenza, *Revelation: Vision of a Just World* (Minneapolis: Fortress Press, 1991), pp. 84-87; and many others. Some recent interpreters emphasize that we should not *limit* symbolism in Revelation to specific entities in John's own day. See, for example, O. O'Donovan, 'The Political Thought of the Book of Revelation', *TynBul* 37 (1986.61-94), p. 68. My own view is that John adapted traditional symbols

threatened Christians that John thought some soon would die for refusing to participate (20.4; cf. 6.9-11).

There is little doubt that Rome—the actual city where Paul went as prisoner (Acts 27, 28)—is the focus of John's concern. John identifies the 'harlot' with whom kings of the earth have 'fornicated' (Rev. 17.2; 18.3, 9) as the 'great city that rules over the kings of the earth' (17.18). Only Rome fit that description in the first century, and John reinforces his point with other allusions.[7] The beast upon which the harlot sits has seven heads, which also are 'seven mountains' and 'seven kings' (17.9). Here the familiar ancient epithet of Rome as the city of 'seven hills'[8] makes the object of John's condemnation transparent.[9] It probably is not coincidence that the most explicit references to Rome in the entire book come immediately before the injunction to 'Come out of her, my people' (18.4). This practical directive is too urgent to allow any possible misunderstanding.

During the reign of Domitian, cultic presence of Rome in Asia Minor became especially prominent with the establishment at Ephesus of a new provincial cult of the Emperors.[10] A series of dedicatory inscriptions at Ephesus, sponsored by other cities of the province, commemorates a

to describe actual circumstances of his day. However, he wrote in a typological fashion that makes Revelation a useful paradigm for reflecting on the Christian's response to idolatry and the abuse of power in any generation.

7.   Cf. Tertullian, who says 'Babylon, in our own John, is a figure of the city of Rome'. *Adv. Iud.* 9.

8.   Cf. *Sib. Or.* 2.15-18, and 11.109-117. As early as the reign of Servius Tullius, sixth king of Rome, people called the city the *urbs septicollis*. Among many ancient authors who thus refer to Rome are Vergil (*Aeneid* 6.782), Martial (4.64), and Cicero (*Ad Atticum* 6.5).

9.   Ford argues that Revelation 17 and 18 deal primarily with Jerusalem rather than Rome. *Revelation*, pp. 276-307. So also A.J. Beagley, *The 'Sitz im Leben' of the Apocalypse with Particular Reference to the Role of the Church's Enemies* (Berlin: de Gruyter, 1987). Proponents of this view are in the awkward position of having to explain how Jerusalem rather than Rome was the 'great city that rules over the kings of the earth' (17.18). When Beagley discusses the merchants of chapter 18, he asserts that Rome 'was not, in any case, a major trading city or sea-port'. *The 'Sitz im Leben'*, p. 108. Technically he is correct, since Rome was a few miles up the Tiber River from the sea. Yet Jerusalem, much less of a trading city, was located far from any body of water.

10.   See S.J. Friesen, *Twice Neokoros: Ephesus, Asia and the Cult of the Flavian Imperial Family* (Leiden: Brill, 1993), pp. 41-49. Previous cities to attain this honor were Pergamum, Smyrna and Miletus.

new 'Ephesian temple of the Sebastoi'.[11] A terrace for the new structure occupied valuable land in the city center, a visible reminder to any resident or visitor of devotion to the imperial cult. Archaeological remains reveal the temple was impressive, with a base that measured thirty-four by twenty-four meters.[12] A huge image of an Emperor (either Titus or Domitian) towered nearly eight meters above worshippers inside the temple.[13] This major new center of pagan worship, and the popular enthusiasm that supported it, may have been the catalyst that heightened John's concern about Rome's idolatrous influence on Asian society.[14]

Evidence from inscriptions suggests that Ephesus formally inaugurated the provincial cult sometime in 89/90 CE.[15] The city celebrated its new religious status by hosting Olympic games, and by issuing a coin which assimilated the likeness of Domitian to that of Zeus Olympios.[16] At the harbor residents constructed the largest building complex in Ephesus, a bath-gymnasium that measured 360 by 240 meters. Steven Friesen dates completion of this project to 92/93 CE, and concludes that the 'reason for the construction of these immense facilities was to provide the buildings necessary for conducting the Ephesian Olympics instituted in honor of Domitian'.[17] If Friesen's chronology is correct, a

11. *I. Eph.* 232-42; 1498. Philadelphia inscription, 2.236. The Roman Senate damned the memory of Domitian after his death, and Domitian's name has been removed from all these inscriptions. See S.R.F. Price, *Rituals and Power: The Roman Imperial Cult in Asia Minor* (Cambridge: Cambridge University Press, 1984), pp. 198, 255. For a chronological chart of the dedicatory inscriptions see Friesen, *Twice Neokoros*, pp. 46-47.

12. Friesen, *Twice Neokoros*, pp. 63-75. Friesen (p. 73) notes that architecture of the temple shows little sign of Italian influence. 'The assumption that the Emperor, or someone else in Rome, designed or approved the facade is groundless', he concludes. Even the architecture underscores the indigenous nature of commitment to the imperial cult in Asia Minor.

13. Price estimates the statue measured seven or eight meters to the top of the spear in Domitian's hand. *Rituals and Power*, p. 187.

14. The following inscription, from 89/90 CE and found at Ephesus, is typical of the effusive adulation showered upon Domitian: 'The demos of the Aphrodisians, devoted to Caesar, being free and autonomous from the beginning by the grace of the Sebastoi, set up (this statue) by its own grace because of its reverence toward the Sebastoi and its goodwill toward the neokorate city of the Ephesians...' Friesen, *Twice Neokoros*, p. 33.

15. *I. Eph.* 232-42; 1498. See discussion by Friesen, *Twice Neokoros*, pp. 41-49.

16. Friesen, *Twice Neokoros*, pp. 119-21.

17. Friesen, *Twice Neokoros*, pp. 122-23.

colossal new monument in service to the imperial cult dominated the harbor at Ephesus late in the first century when John probably wrote the book of Revelation.

Intersection of Cult and Commerce
The Roman imperial cult provided people in the provinces with a vivid and evocative expression of loyalty to the Emperor.[18] The cult pervaded many levels of society and presented Christians with practical dilemmas as they engaged in business or social relations. The cult, for example, gradually penetrated shipping lines and merchant guilds of Rome and the East during the first century CE.[19] Since the seven cities of Revelation were in an important industrial and commercial region, Christians there had regular contact with international institutions of finance and trade. If there were Christian entrepreneurs among the seven churches (as I will argue in Chapter 2), they would have needed to decide how far they could let business interests carry them into relationship with a pagan power.

John became convinced that Rome, with her arrogant claims to sovereignty and divinity, had stepped beyond the legitimate role of government. From Rome emanated demonic power that flowed through political, social and economic tentacles of her Empire. John was adamant that disciples of Jesus Christ must withdraw from exchange with Rome on every level, including trade.[20] When he gives a full treatment of economic issues in Revelation 18, John implies that Christians entrepreneurs were among those linked to Rome: 'Come out of her, my people,' he says, 'so that you do not take part in her sins' (18.4).[21] For this

18. For a thorough analysis of why people in Asia Minor participated in the imperial cult, see Price, *Rituals and Power*, pp. 234-48.

19. See pp. 123-41.

20. Tertullian understood Rev. 18.4 as a call for Christians to distance themselves from Rome: 'From so much as a dwelling in that Babylon [Rome] of John's Revelation we are called away'. *De Cor.* 13.

21. Cf. Jer. 51.45, 'Come out of her, my people, save your lives...' Jeremiah directed this call to Jews intimately involved with Babylon. Similarly, John seems to evoke the message of Jeremiah to address Christians intimately involved with the 'Babylon' (Rome) of his day. It would be possible to construe John's message in Rev. 18.4 as a warning to Christians who have not yet made a moral compromise with Rome: 'Come out of her, my people, so that you do not take part in her sins'. At minimum, though, John's language suggests Christians are in venues where idolatrous compromise is likely.

stance of radical separation from the greatest of human powers, believers must prepare to pay with their lives (13.10).

2. *A Comfortable Church with a Few in Trouble*

A boycott of relations with all Roman institutions could have left Christians economically destitute. However, there is little evidence from late in the first century that many believers perceived themselves to be in conflict with Rome or to be threatened with poverty. Some believers, such as those at Laodicea, were wealthy and self-sufficient (Rev. 3.17). This picture of social and economic security is reinforced by recent sociological studies of the early church. Wayne Meeks, in his examination of Pauline churches, concludes early believers came from all but the extreme top and bottom of Graeco-Roman society. In Pauline communities—including those of Asia Minor—the 'typical' Christian was a free artisan or small trader. Some even had slaves, property, ability to travel and other signs of wealth.[22] Early Christian churches competed with the Jewish synagogue for socially prominent adherents. Paul's preaching at Thessalonica persuaded Jews and 'a great many of the devout Greeks and not a few of the leading women'. Luke states that this provoked the Jews to jealousy (Acts 17.4-5; cf. 17.12, 13.50).

Paul's letters suggest that some Christians in the East were not economically deprived during the fifth and sixth decades of the first century. The apostle noted that some (but 'not many') members of the church at Corinth were 'wise', 'powerful' or 'of noble birth' (1 Cor. 1.26). Explicit mention of wealthy Christians appears elsewhere in letters

22. W.A. Meeks, *The First Urban Christians: The Social World of the Apostle Paul* (New Haven: Yale University Press, 1983), p. 73. See also E.A. Judge, *The Social Pattern of Christian Groups in the First Century* (London: Tyndale Press, 1960), pp. 49-61; A.J. Malherbe, *Social Aspects of Early Christianity* (Baton Rouge, LA: Louisiana State University Press, 1977), pp. 29-32; and M. Hengel, *Property and Riches in the Early Church* (London: SCM Press, 1974), p. 37. Philemon at Colossae had a house large enough for church meetings and a guest room for Paul; he owned at least one slave (Phlm. 2, 10, 22. Cf. 'house of Tavia' at Smyrna, Ign. *Pol.* 8.2). G. Theissen notes that scholars have expressed widely divergent views on the social status of early Christians: A. Deissmann places early believers in the lower social strata, while E.A. Judge says Christians came from a socially pretentious section of the big cities. 'Both opinions are probably correct', Theissen argues, since churches in cities such as Corinth were 'marked by internal stratification'. *The Social Setting of Pauline Christianity* (Philadelphia: Fortress Press, 1982), p. 69.

attributed to Paul: 'As for those who in the present age are rich, command them not to be haughty, or to set their hopes on the uncertainty of riches, but rather on God' (1 Tim. 6.17). The mention of both slaves and masters within the church (Eph. 6.5-9) suggests some Christians enjoyed a comfortable level of economic and social status. The book of James indicates wealth and concern for social position created tensions in the faith community (Jas 2.1-7). In his letter to Emperor Trajan about Christians in Bithynia, Governor Pliny (c. 112 CE) notes Christians came from 'all ranks and ages' in society.[23] Ignatius of Antioch, on his way through Asia Minor (c. 115 CE) as a prisoner of Rome, stayed with or knew Christians who held a comfortable station in life. He writes of a Christian woman married to a 'Procurator' (steward of a Christian household?),[24] and sends greetings to the 'house[hold] of Tavia'.[25]

Identity and Circumstances of the Author
Contrary to early church tradition that John the apostle wrote Revelation,[26] most scholars now believe the author was an otherwise unknown itinerant prophet (Rev. 10.11; 22.9) familiar with the churches in the province of Asia.[27] He probably was Jewish by birth and had lived for some considerable time (if not from childhood) in Palestine.[28] He was

23. Pliny, *Ep.* 10.96.
24. Ign., *Pol.* 8.2.
25. Ign., *Smyrn.* 13.2.
26. Justin Martyr describes John of Patmos as 'one of Christ's Apostles', *Tryph.* 81. Irenaeus refers to the author of Revelation as 'John, the Lord's disciple', *Adv. Haer.* 5.35.3. Cf. Tertullian, *Adv. Marc.* 3.14, 24. Belief that the author was an apostle was the deciding factor for Revelation being listed in the Muratorian Canon. Dionysius of Alexandria, in the third century, was the first to mount a sustained argument against apostolic authorship. Eusebius, *Hist. Eccl.* 7.25.1-27. See Charles, *Commentary*, I, pp. xxxviii-l, and W.G. Kümmel, *Introduction to the New Testament* (Nashville: Abingdon, rev. edn, 1975), p. 499.
27. See Charles, *Commentary*, pp. xxxviii-l, and Caird, *Commentary*, pp. 4-5. There is considerable evidence that John was familiar with local circumstances of his readers. See C. Hemer, *The Letters to the Seven Churches of Asia Minor in their Local Setting* (Sheffield: Sheffield Academic Press, 1986).
28. Scholars are virtually unanimous that John was a Jew. Charles, for example, cites ubiquitous Hebrew idioms imbedded in the Greek text, as well as John's broad knowledge of the Hebrew scriptures, *Commentary*, I, pp. xliii-xliv. Ford says John was 'a Jew who was firmly grounded in the prophetical tradition of Israel', *Revelation*, p. 28. D.E. Aune says 'it is certain he was a Jewish Christian who may have been an apocalypticist before his conversion', 'Revelation', in J.L. Mays (ed.),

trilingual (Greek, Hebrew and Galilean Aramaic).[29]

Several factors indicate the author was not the apostle John to whom the church for many centuries ascribed the fourth Gospel: (1) Revelation differs from the fourth Gospel both in vocabulary and style; (2) John of Patmos never implies or gives indication that he knew the earthly Jesus and does not claim apostolic authority; and (3) The era of the apostles apparently is past, since the author sees names of the twelve apostles written in the New Jerusalem (Rev. 21.14). It is unlikely a living apostle would include his own name in a vision of the eschatological city.

Apparently John related to a small minority within the church of Asia Minor that came into serious conflict with local powers. His knowledge of local circumstances at seven named congregations (Rev. 2, 3) suggests he had visited or otherwise related personally to members of those churches. He writes with the passion of a prophet and the heart of a pastor, keen to exhort and encourage his flock during a time of testing.

While the majority of Christians in Asia Minor apparently were functioning well in society, a few were in trouble. John himself is on the island of Patmos 'because of the word of God and the testimony of Jesus' (1.9). Some recent interpreters have challenged the traditional view that John was either a prisoner or in exile.[30] Yet the fact that John mentions persecution (θλῖψις),[31] patient endurance (ὑπομονή)[32] and

Harper's Bible Commentary, p. 1300.

29. See G.C. Jenks, *The Origins and Early Development of the Antichrist Myth* (Berlin: de Gruyter, 1991), pp. 231-32.

30. Eusebius, citing Irenaeus as his source, says John was 'condemned to live in the island of Patmos for his witness to the divine word' (*Hist. Eccl.* 3.18). A key verse for understanding John's legal status is Rev. 1.9, where the author says he was at Patmos διὰ τὸν λόγον τοῦ θεοῦ καὶ τὴν μαρτυρίαν Ἰησοῦ. Charles argues that διά in Revelation always means 'because of' or 'in consequence of' rather than 'for the sake of'. That is, John's ministry resulted in him suffering on the island; he did not go there in order to preach (Charles, *Commentary*, I, p. 22). So also K. Wengst, *Pax Romana and the Peace of Jesus Christ* (Philadelphia: Fortress Press, 1987), p. 221. Thompson disagrees, declaring that the word διά 'designates a very general relationship of cause, occasion, or even purpose'. John could have visited Patmos voluntarily on a preaching mission. *Revelation: Apocalypse and Empire*, p. 173. Two factors speak in favor of viewing John as a prisoner or in exile: (1) Repeated references in Revelation to persecution or martyrdom suggest the author himself was in trouble; (2) Eusebius records the tradition of the early church that John was imprisoned at Patmos, *Hist. Eccl.* 3.18.

31. θλῖψις does not necessarily mean 'persecution' in Revelation, but it does imply suffering and hardship. Believers at Smyrna experience θλῖψις that includes

the island of Patmos all in one sentence (1.9) suggests he was an unwilling resident.

There are other signs that *some* readers of John's Apocalypse face social or political trouble. At Pergamum a believer named Antipas already has been killed as a 'witness' and 'faithful one' of Jesus Christ (2.13). It makes little difference whether lynch mobs or government authorities carried out the execution.[33] In either case it was possible for Christians to be killed for their belief or practice, and the government apparently made no move to protect them. Under the altar in heaven are people 'who had been slaughtered for the word or God and for the testimony they had given' (6.9-10; cf. 20.4). These references to capital punishment indicate that John understood himself (and other faithful Christians) to be in a volatile, life-threatening position in society.

Date of Composition
A composition date after 70 CE seems likely because John uses the epithet 'Babylon' for Rome—a sardonic equating of the two great powers that each destroyed the Jewish temple in Jerusalem (587 BCE, 70 CE).[34] Writers of the early church who date Revelation place it in the last years of Domitian's rule (95–96 CE),[35] and a majority of modern scholars accept this tradition. Some recent scholars have marshaled worthy

---

slander and will lead to imprisonment or martyrdom (2.9-10). Those who commit adultery with the heretical prophet Jezebel will be incapacitated by θλῖψις sent from God (2.22). As John uses the term, it means more than 'distress'. The early church associated θλῖψις with torture, martyrdom and exile (Mk 13.19; Mt. 24.9, 21). Paul's imprisonment constituted θλῖψις (Eph. 3.13; cf. 4.1).

32. John exhorts readers to ὑπομονή in 13.10, immediately following a reference to captivity and death by sword. In Lk. 21.19, a call for ὑπομονή follows Jesus' words about arrest, persecution and martyrdom. Paul uses the term to mean perseverance in the face of suffering (Rom. 5.3 and 2 Cor. 6.4).

33. Fiorenza suggests Antipas died under a 'lynch-law exercised by the citizens' rather than a general persecution. 'Apocalyptic and Gnosis', p. 570 n. 29. Collins argues the term μάρτυς, as applied to Antipas, has a 'basically forensic' meaning. That is, Antipas gave true testimony in a trial setting, 'Persecution and Vengeance', p. 733.

34. Other Jewish and Christian literature contemporary to Revelation also referred to Rome as Babylon. See 1 Pet. 5.13; *2 Bar.* 11.1-3, 67.7; *Sib. Or.* 5.143; and *4 Ezra* 3.2, 28-31.

35. Irenaeus dates Revelation 'toward the end of Domitian's reign', *Adv. Haer.* 5.30.3. Victorinus says John received Revelation while 'in the island of Patmos, condemned to the labour of the mines by Caesar Domitian', *Commentary* 10.11.

arguments favoring a date late in Nero's reign or immediately after his alleged suicide, during tumultuous days of revolt in Jerusalem and civil war in Rome (66–70 CE).[36]

I accept the majority opinion of early church writers and modern scholarship that Revelation reflects circumstances of the last decade of the first century. It is possible, of course, that John (or someone else) wrote parts of Revelation under Nero (54–68 CE) and completed the work under Domitian (81–96 CE). In any case, the exact date of author-ship has little bearing on major arguments of my essay. I will argue that John was deeply concerned about penetration of the imperial cult into social, political and economic institutions of the Mediterranean world. Already during the reign of Nero, that religious and ideological pheno-menon had metastasized like a cancer throughout the Roman world. Whether Nero or Domitian held the scepter of power, John would have counseled his readers to sever all relations with people or institutions that treated a human ruler as divine.

Persecution Not Widespread

The fact that Antipas is the only martyr named in Revelation suggests that lethal persecution was possible but still not common for Christians in Asia Minor. Although John expects widespread persecution soon to strike (3.10), he does not believe it will affect all Christians equally. 'The devil is about to throw *some of you* (ἐξ ὑμῶν, a partitive genitive) into prison,' he says; 'Be faithful until death...' (2.10).

There is little evidence in Roman sources for widespread persecution of Christians in Asia Minor—or anywhere in the Empire—during Domitian's reign.[37] The conventional portrait of Domitian as a bloodthirsty tyrant

36. C. Rowland, for example, cites circumstances of the Jewish War and the 'apparent break-up of the Empire' in 69 CE as a likely time when John of Patmos feared 'those in authority would take the unusual step of insisting that all, irrespective of the religious sensibilities, would be compelled to worship before the statue of the Emperor'. C. Rowland, *The Open Heaven* (London: SPCK, 1982), p. 413. Cf. Jenks, *Origins and Early Development*, pp. 233-34.

37. Until recently most modern scholars felt Revelation reflected a situation of intense persecution. Kümmel, for example, says the 'book's own testimony indicates that it originated in the province of Asia in a time of severe oppression of Christians', when 'the whole of Christianity is threatened with a fearful danger', *Introduction*, p. 467. Beginning in the second century, some Christian literature alludes to persecu-tion during Domitian's rule. Melito of Sardis says the 'only Emperors who were ever persuaded by malicious men to slander our teaching were Nero and Domitian',

comes almost entirely from writers of a subsequent generation who sought to flatter the present Emperor by making previous ones look bad.[38] Domitian may have committed cruel deeds in Rome, but many provincials held a favorable view of his reign.[39] The well-known claim of ancient writers that Domitian wanted subjects to address him as *dominus et deus noster* ('Our Lord and God') might tell more about Domitian's

Eusebius, *Hist. Eccl.* 4.26.9. Tertullian says 'Nero was the first to rage with the imperial sword' against Christians. Domitian, 'who was a good deal of a Nero in cruelty, attempted it; but…he soon stopped what he had begun, and restored those he had banished', *Apol.* 5.3-4. Based on such evidence, E. Stauffer postulates that Domitian executed a few Christians in Rome, which provoked persecution of Christians in Asia; Stauffer, *Christ and the Caesars* (London: SCM Press, 1955), pp. 163-66. C. Rowland points out that 'evidence from Roman historians gives us very little reason for supposing that Domitian moved in any systematic way against the Christians', *Open Heaven*, p. 407. Cf. Collins, *Crisis and Catharsis*, pp. 56, 69-73. Thompson challenges the portrait we find among Roman historians of Domitian as rabid tyrant. 'They present private information and psychological motivation about Domitian to which they could not possibly have access…their maligning of Domitian is contradicted in almost every instance by epigraphic and numismatic evidence as well as by prosopography…', *Revelation: Apocalypse and Empire*, p. 101. Fiorenza acknowledges that a later generation of Roman historians may have wanted to tarnish Domitian's image. The notion that Domitian was benign, however, 'is not borne out by the experience articulated in Revelation and other NT writings', *Revelation: Justice and Judgment*, p. 8. The following pages of my study offer evidence that at least *some* Christians were doing well in the Roman world. To the extent that persecution in Asia Minor did happen under Domitian, we must assume it was just starting up as John wrote Revelation. The earliest and best non-Christian corroboration of Christian martyrdom in Asia Minor remains the correspondence between Pliny the Younger and Emperor Trajan (c. 112 CE). Pliny, *Ep.* 10.96.

38. Tacitus, Pliny the Younger, Juvenal and Suetonius—standard sources for the bleak portrait of Domitian—all wrote during or shortly after the reign of Trajan. Thompson, *Revelation: Apocalypse and Empire*, p. 115; Collins, *Crisis and Catharsis*, p. 72.

39. Thompson notes there are two contrasting views of Domitian in ancient sources: the 'official' literary tradition that depicts him as evil, and the 'provincial tradition' (e.g., *Sib. Or.* 12) which praises him as a good Emperor, *Revelation: Apocalypse and Empire*, p. 137. Even Suetonius says of provincial officials and governors that 'at no time were they more honest or just' than under Domitian, *Dom.* 8. Cf. D. Magie, *Roman Rule in Asia Minor*, I (2 vols.; Princeton: Princeton University Press, 1950), p. 577. For a well-argued modern view that Domitian was a tyrant, see W.H.C. Frend, *Martyrdom and Persecution in the Early Church* (Oxford: Basil Blackwell, 1965), pp. 211-18.

flatterers than about the Emperor himself.[40] There is no doubt the title was in circulation during Domitian's reign, but little evidence that the Emperor encouraged its use. Domitian commissioned or requested literary works by Statius and Quintilian, for example, and neither author uses the extravagant title.[41]

Most literature from Domitian's reign does not reflect a situation of lethal persecution against Christians.[42] The author of Hebrews says readers suffer hostility and trials (Heb. 12.3, 7), but they 'have not yet resisted to the point of shedding...blood' (12.4).[43] The writer of 1 Clement (5, 6) mentions Christian martyrs only in connection with the deaths of Peter and Paul, implying a spate of persecution happened in

40. Suetonius, *Dom.* 13.2; cf. Dio Cassius, *Hist. Rom.* 67.4.7, 67.13.4. Martial refers to his 'master and god' without implying Domitian himself sought the title (5.8.1). Dio Chrysostom refers to Domitian as 'the most powerful, most stern man, who was called by all Greeks and barbarians both master and god', *Or.* 45.1.

41. These authors use titles such as *Caesar, Germanicus, Augustus, dux, maximus arbiter, parens* and *vates,* but never *dominus et deus;* see Thompson, *Apocalypse and Empire*, p. 105. However, the mere fact that anyone gave divine titles to Domitian would have been enough to alienate John of Patmos; he had no way of knowing whether the Emperor himself sought the honor.

42. Certainly Domitian killed many people in Rome, but there is scant evidence that Christians were singled out for abuse. Even Beckwith, certain there was harsh persecution of Christians under Domitian, grants that 'details of his measures are for the most part wanting', *Apocalypse*, p. 204. The best evidence for persecution of Christians Beckwith can muster is Dio Cassius' account of Domitian putting Flavius Clemens to death and banishing his wife Domitilla, both on charges of atheism (ἀθεότης). This episode scarcely documents widespread persecution, however, since it is not certain Clemens and his wife even were Christians. Dio says Domitian accused Clemens of following Jewish customs, *Hist. Rom.* 67.14. 'Following Jewish customs' here might actually mean conversion to Christianity, since merely becoming Jewish usually was not punishable by death or exile under Roman law. See M. Sordi, *The Christians and the Roman Empire* (London: Croom Helm, 1983), pp. 43-53. Suetonius, however, says nothing of Clemens or Domitilla being Christians, *Dom.* 15. Eusebius—writing centuries later—tells of a certain Christian woman named Domitilla whom Domitian exiled to Pontia in 96 CE. Whereas Suetonius says Domitilla was the wife of Flavius Clemens, Eusebius says she was his niece, *Hist. Eccl.* 3.18.4. It is possible Domitian exiled two Domitillas.

43. The author of Hebrews probably wrote between 60 and 95 CE. The book is late enough to address second-generation Christians (Heb. 2.3) and to have a well-developed Christology. That Hebrews predates *1 Clement* seems evident by the fact that the latter quotes Hebrews. See H.W. Attridge, 'Hebrews', in Mays (ed.), *Harper's Bible Commentary*, p. 1259.

Rome under Nero a generation earlier.[44] Preoccupied with internal church matters at Corinth, 1 Clement does not mention persecution in Rome or in the East.

Among late first-century Christian writings, 1 Peter alone gives evidence of a church in serious trouble. The author addresses believers in the whole of Asia Minor (1 Pet. 1.1), and joins John of Patmos in labelling Rome as 'Babylon' (1 Pet. 5.13). A 'fiery ordeal' afflicts the church (4.12), and believers suffer simply for being Christians (4.16). The church faces some form of hardship throughout the Mediterranean world (5.9).

The serenity reflected in 1 Clement either predates the persecution mentioned in Revelation and 1 Peter, or it reflects the optimistic view of a Christian who feels secure in his relationship with Rome.[45] John may have written Revelation in the mid-90s, just before the persecution portrayed in 1 Peter began in earnest.[46] Although the 'souls of those who had been slaughtered for the word of God' already appear in heaven (Rev. 6.9), these may be victims of Nero's persecution in Rome a generation earlier.[47] Christians throughout the Empire knew of Nero's cruelty, and it is not surprising John would say the harlot is 'drunk with the blood of the saints' (17.6; cf. 16.6, 18.24, 19.2). Beheading was (or will be) the fate of some Christians who 'had not worshiped the beast or its image and had not received its mark' (20.4).

Widespread suffering still lies in the future, however, as John writes.[48]

44. Internal evidence in *1 Clement* suggests a date between 75 and 110 CE, and most critics place it in the last decade of the first century. See introduction to *1 Clement* by Kirsopp Lake in *The Apostolic Fathers* (LCL; London: Heinemann, 1985), pp. 3-7.

45. The contrast between Revelation and *1 Clement* is most evident in the latter's use of (Roman) army discipline as a role model for Christian obedience and submission within the church (*1 Clem.* 37.1-4), and in the statement that God granted Roman rulers their authority and power (61.1-2). 'Clement's church was loyal to the Empire and expected to live in peace with it' concludes Frend, *The Rise of Christianity* (Philadelphia: Fortress Press, 1984), p. 146.

46. For recent presentations of the argument that John wrote just after the death of Nero in 68 CE, see Rowland, *Open Heaven,* pp. 403-13; Jenks, *Origins and Early Development,* pp. 228-56. I agree with Rowland's comment (p. 403) that in many respects 'the precise dating of Revelation does not radically affect the exegesis of the document, as the issues which appear to confront the writer can be understood in broadly similar terms whenever we date it'.

47. On Nero's persecution, see Tacitus, *Ann.* 15.44.

48. Christians at Smyrna, writing c. 155 CE, state that Polycarp 'was, together with those from Philadelphia, the twelfth martyr in Smyrna', *Mart. Pol.* 19.1. This

In the meantime, whole Christian communities are lulled by their comfort and apparent security. 'Wake up, and strengthen what remains', Christ exhorts the church at Sardis (3.2). At Laodicea there is so little conflict between church and society that Christians have the luxury of lukewarm conviction (3.15). These references to complacency make plausible the statement by Collins that John wrote to Christians in Asia Minor in order 'to point out a crisis that many of them did not perceive'.[49]

3. *Syncretism in Revelation and the Early Church*

The urgent message of Revelation is that idolatry not only pervades political and economic structures of the Empire, but has taken root within the churches of Asia Minor. In characterizing Christian proponents of idolatrous belief and practice, John uses names of notorious figures in Jewish history. At Pergamum some believers 'hold to the teaching of Balaam, who taught Balak to put a stumbling block before the people of Israel, so they would eat food sacrificed to idols' (2.14). At Thyatira a prophetess whom John calls 'Jezebel' is 'teaching and beguiling my servants to practice fornication and to eat food sacrificed to idols' (2.20).

After condemning the 'teaching of Balaam' at Pergamum (2.14), John adds, 'you also have some who hold to the teaching of the Nicolaitans' (2.15). Neither Revelation nor any other first-century literature gives a satisfactory description of the Nicolaitans; John simply condemns them in the same breath with other heretics. We cannot know in detail what these people believed, but they had insinuated themselves into the churches and apparently advocated accommodation to the pagan environment. Caird says 'the sum total of the Nicolaitans' offence...is that they took a laxer attitude than John to pagan society and religion'.[50]

John's use of Old Testament names to describe heretics in the church is more illuminating than the label 'Nicolaitans'. Both Balaam and Jezebel led Israel into idolatrous relationship with pagan gods. Numbers 31.16

---

seems to reflect selective prosecution, not wholesale slaughter of Christians.

49. Collins, *Crisis and Catharsis*, p. 77.

50. Caird, *Commentary*, p. 39. Thompson says the 'Nicolaitans seem to be outsiders seeking to establish themselves' in the Ephesus church; the adherents of Balaam *were* a part of the church at Pergamum (Rev. 2.14). They were among those who 'did not deny my faith even in the days of Antipas' (2.13). Thompson, *Revelation: Apocalypse and Empire*, p. 122.

(cf. 25.1-3) accuses Balaam of inciting Midianite women to lure Israelites into worship of Baal Peor. The people feasted, bowed, and sacrificed to gods—acts of obeisance John may have seen as analogous to pagan cult ceremonies of his own day.

Apparently John evokes the memory of Jezebel to underscore Rome's seductive influence on the Christian church. Jezebel, wife of wicked king Ahab, came from a Phoenician royal family (1 Kgs 16.31). Her influence resulted in Ahab worshipping Baal and building an altar in Israel to the foreign deity. A powerful priesthood of Baal emerged (1 Kgs 18.19). Prophets of Yahweh perished or had their lives threatened (1 Kgs 18.4). Elijah exhorted Israelites to make a decisive choice of loyalties: 'How long will you go limping with two different opinions? If Yahweh is God, follow him; but if Baal, then follow him' (1 Kgs 18.21).

Similarly, the prophet John now exhorts Christians to decide who is Lord. 'I wish you were either cold or hot', he writes to Laodicea (Rev. 3.15). Rome now holds military and economic hegemony in the Mediterranean basin, as did ancient Phoenicia. The 'harlotries and sorceries' of religious syncretism, once the bane of Jezebel's influence (2 Kgs 9.22), now beguile kings and peoples of Asia Minor (Rev. 17.1, 2; 18.9).[51] Asherah (1 Kgs 16.33) and homage to Baal have given way to an image of the 'beast' and the cult of Emperor worship (Rev. 13.14), complete with its own priesthood. Prison and death await true prophets of God.

John heaps these unsavory associations upon a certain leader in Thyatira whom he calls 'Jezebel'. Religious syncretism and idolatry not only tempt the church; they have taken root within the faith community itself.[52] As the church deals with this matter, there will be conflict both within the Christian community and from without. It may be, as some scholars suggest, that John wrote Revelation in opposition to an incipient Gnostic movement in Asia Minor.[53] Such a movement could have

51. Among Hebrew prophets sexual infidelity was a common image for religious syncretism. Jeremiah and Hosea describe worship of other deities as harlotry (Jer. 2.20, 3.2, 6-10; Hos. 4.12-14; cf. Isa. 57.5-10, Ezek. 16.15-52).

52. Fiorenza concludes there was rivalry within the seven churches between the prophetic 'schools' of John and Jezebel. It may overstate the case to speak of 'schools', but certainly among the churches there were conflicting viewpoints on the acceptable level of Christian involvement in Graeco-Roman society. Fiorenza, *Revelation: Justice and Judgment*, pp. 115-17.

53. W.H.C. Frend, 'The Gnostic Sects and the Roman Empire', *JEH* 5 (1954), pp. 25-37.

taught adherents to remain faithful to Christ on a spiritual level while their bodily selves engaged in sinful activity. Perhaps it is anachronistic to speak of 'Gnostics' already in the first century. A dualistic and libertine view of Christian involvement in pagan society, though, does appear to be an object of concern in Revelation.[54]

The urgency of John's message is apparent in his repeated use of the term 'conquer'.[55] A battle is brewing that will test the 'endurance and faith of the saints' (13.10). Since John's concern with idolatry seems closely related to economic matters, we must search for a setting where pagan worship had financial implications.

Jude, 2 Peter, and Balaam's Error
When John condemns people in the church at Pergamum who 'hold to the teaching of Balaam', he emphasizes the matter of eating food sacrificed to idols (2.14). The issue of food appears again in his censure of 'that woman Jezebel' at Thyatira (2.20).

Several New Testament authors shed light on the setting and motivation for the kind of heresy associated with the name Balaam in the early church. The letter of Jude[56] addresses the problem of 'intruders' in the church who 'pervert the grace of our God into licentiousness and deny[57] our only Master and Lord, Jesus Christ' (Jude 4). Here the exclusive claim of Jesus as the 'only Master and Lord'[58] comes through as clearly as in the book of Revelation,[59] and may refer to Christians who participate in pagan ceremonies or the imperial cult.[60]

---

54. Fiorenza says the Nicolaitans in the seven churches 'express their freedom in libertine behavior, which allows them to become part of their syncretistic pagan society and to participate in the Roman civil religion'. 'Apocalyptic and Gnosis', p. 570.

55. Some form of νικάω occurs seventeen times in Revelation, more than in the rest of the NT combined.

56. R.J. Bauckham says the message of Jude finds its most plausible context in a largely Jewish Christian community in a Gentile environment. 'Asia Minor, with its large Jewish communities...and antinomian movements attested by Revelation 2.14, 20, is a strong possibility...' *Jude, 2 Peter* (WBC, 50; Waco: Word, 1983), p. 16.

57. ἀρνούμενοι—the word John uses in letters to Pergamum and Philadelphia to describe what faithful Christians did *not* do (Rev. 2.13, 3.8).

58. τὸν μόνον δεσπότην καὶ κύριον.

59. Cf. Rev. 1.5.

60. Bauckham describes the intruders mentioned in Jude as 'itinerant charismatics' who purveyed antinomian teaching. In their sexual misconduct they 'may be deliberately flouting accepted standards of Jewish morality and conforming to the

Jude asserts that those who pervert the gospel 'abandon themselves to Balaam's error *for the sake of gain*'[61] (Jude 11). He says these people 'pour themselves out' to Balaam's sin, using a word (ἐξεχύθησαν) that sometimes refers to cultic libations (cf. Lev. 4.7, LXX). This may be a reference to pagan worship or even to the imperial cult, with its libations of wine and incense to the Emperor.[62] Some people in the church participate in pagan rituals for financial objectives. The author fears such individuals will corrupt the church's love-feasts (Jude 12).

The matter of heretical teachers surfaces again in 2 Peter, with significant parallels to the letter of Jude.[63] 'False prophets' have entered the church, who 'deny (ἀρνούμενοι) the Master who bought them' (2 Pet. 2.1).[64] These people abandon their Lord for the sake of gain, motivated by greed (2.3,14). They follow the way of Balaam, who 'loved the wages (μισθὸν) of doing wrong' (2.15). They 'revel in the daytime'—perhaps at ceremonies of other cults—then want to join the Christian feasts (2.13).[65]

Both Jude and 2 Peter address issues that could relate to the imperial

---

permissiveness of pagan society' (*Jude, 2 Peter*, p. 11). Perhaps Jude did not specifically have the imperial cult in mind. Nevertheless, antinomian teaching brought by 'intruders' in Jude illustrates a larger problem of compromise with society among some late first-century churches.

61. The word 'gain' is μισθοῦ, understood as a genitive of purpose. T. Fornberg notes that Balaam often was associated with greed, and at the end of the first century CE was regarded as the heretic *par excellence* in parts of Asia Minor, *An Early Church in a Pluralistic Society* (Lund: Gleerup, 1977), p. 40.

62. Pliny writes to Trajan that he released persons charged as Christians when they 'repeated after me an invocation to the Gods, and offered adoration, with wine and frankincense, to your image...together with those of the Gods, and who finally cursed Christ—none of which acts, it is said, those who are really Christians can be forced into performing', *Ep.* 10.94. Cf. *Sib. Or.* 8.487-95.

63. Delay of the *parousia* is among concerns of 2 Peter, suggesting a date toward the end of the first century, along with other works that touch on the same topic (Lk. 12.45, Mt. 24.48). Bauckham dates the letter about 80-90 CE. '2 Peter', in Mays (ed.), *Harper's Bible Commentary*, p. 1288; *Jude, 2 Peter*, pp. 157-58.

64. Note parallel to 'Jezebel' as false prophetess in Rev. 2.20.

65. Bauckham says the ethical practice of opponents in 2 Peter, in which sexual immorality seems prominent, 'is plausibly seen as accommodation to the permissiveness of pagan society, a perennial temptation in the early church, especially when Christian morality impeded participation in the social life of the cities'. *Jude, 2 Peter*, p. 156.

cult.[66] These include: (1) heretical teachers; (2) Christians denying the exclusive lordship of Christ; (3) believers engaged in idolatry 'for the sake of gain';[67] and (4) concerns about cultic feasting.

It would be difficult to argue that these two writers were concerned *primarily* with the imperial cult; the issue could have been a broader one of Christian involvement in any number of pagan ceremonies. Yet these letters reflect challenges facing the church at a time when participation in political, economic and social institutions often involved pagan cultic meals and food offered to the gods.[68]

Aliens and Exiles in 1 Peter

The letter of 1 Peter confirms that some Christians withdrew from pagan associations. This late first-century work addresses believers in five provinces of Asia Minor, including the area of the seven churches of Revelation (1 Pet. 1.1). The author reminds readers they once lived like Gentiles, in 'licentiousness, passions, drunkenness, revels, carousing and lawless idolatry' (4.3). Paul Achtemeier understands this as a reference to the fact that 'Christians no longer participated in the many religious festivals celebrated in the Hellenistic world'.[69] Confession of Jesus as Lord set believers apart from society so clearly they functioned as 'aliens and exiles' (2.11). Their distinctiveness came to the attention of neighbors and acquaintances, who were 'surprised' (ξενίζονται, 4.4) that Christians no longer joined the usual activities.

People in Asia Minor sometimes abused Christians, perhaps because of their separatist way of life. The author of 1 Peter gives counsel to Christians for '*when* you are maligned' (1 Pet. 3.16). Persecution is severe enough to rank as a 'fiery ordeal' (4.12), and other Christians throughout the world 'are undergoing the same kinds of suffering' (5.9).

---

66. There appears to be some literary relationship between Jude and 2 Peter. Either one text provided the original for the other, or they have a common prototype. On this, see Fornberg, *An Early Church*, p. 34.

67. Note the correlation of greed and idolatry in Col. 3.5. In language parallel to Revelation, the author of Ephesians says 'no fornicator or impure person, or one who is greedy (that is, an idolater), has any inheritance in the kingdom of Christ' (Eph. 5.5).

68. Fiorenza names settings in Graeco-Roman society where food offered to idols may have been served: family celebrations, gatherings of private associations and clubs, and public festivals. Fiorenza, '1 Corinthians', in Mays (ed.), *Harper's Bible Commentary*, p. 1180.

69. P. Achtemeier, '1 Peter', in Mays (ed.), *Harper's Bible Commentary*, p. 1279.

Tension is apparent in 1 Peter between loyalty to Christ and loyalty to institutions of human society. On the one hand, Christians constitute a 'chosen race, a royal priesthood, a holy nation' (2.9) set apart from the pagan world. On the other hand, believers still need to function under the structures of government (2.13-17), slavery (2.18-25) and marriage (3.1-7). Although the author counsels readers to accept these institutions, he plants the seeds of a radical transformation in attitudes. Christian slaves should quietly choose to obey their masters just as Christ suffered and went to the cross (2.21-24).[70] Such slaves can view their masters as part of the same sinful power structure that Christ overcame in death and resurrection. Some day the 'one who judges justly' (2.23) will call even abusive slave masters to give account. The day of reckoning cannot be far, since the 'end of all things in near' (4.7).

Seeds of transformation also appear when 1 Peter speaks of marriage. Women should lovingly accept their husbands' authority, even if the husband is not a believer. Pagan husbands 'may be won over without a word by their wives' conduct' (3.1-2). Christian men must show 'consideration' and 'honor' to their wives (3.7), expressions of mutuality not common in the ancient world.[71]

By his choice of addressees in the 'household code', the author of 1 Peter might give evidence of the roles in society that he feels are appropriate for Christian 'resident aliens' (παροίκους, 2.11) to take: subjects of Emperor and Governor (2.13, 14), slaves (2.18), wives and husbands (3.1-7). The author does not mention the possibility that faithful Christians might be in positions of power in the government (e.g. as

---

70. J.H. Yoder describes the *Haustafeln* in the New Testament (Col. 3.18–4.1; Eph. 5.21–6.9; 1 Pet. 2.13–3.7) as expressions of 'revolutionary subordination'. Rather than reinforcing the socio-political structures of society, these instructions elevate subordinate persons to the status of free moral agents who *choose* to accept the temporal authority of another. Jesus modeled and taught this approach. It 'enables the person in a subordinate position in society to accept and live within that status without resentment, at the same time that it calls upon the person in the superordinate position to forsake or renounce all domineering use of his status'. J.H. Yoder, *The Politics of Jesus* (Grand Rapids: Eerdmans, 1972), p. 190.

71. R. Scroggs says 'Contrary to the position of subordination in which women generally lived in first-century Mediterranean culture, the position they discovered in the early Christian communities was one of acceptance and, particularly in the earliest decades, equality'. R. Scroggs, 'Women in the NT', in *IDBSup*, p. 966. Scroggs (p. 968) notes that 1 Peter no longer advocates full equality. The epistle does, however, give women a greater role in Christian marriage than pagan society would have granted.

governors) or the economy (e.g. as slave owners). Here the 'household code' of 1 Peter differs from that of other New Testament authors, who assume Christians for the present will continue to be slave owners (Eph. 6.9, Col. 4.1).

In contrast to Ephesians and Colossians, the letter of 1 Peter implies Christians will make a costly withdrawal from roles of socio-economic power in society. It probably is more than coincidence that persecution of the church is prominent in 1 Peter, but scarcely evident in Ephesians or Colossians. This contrast may reflect the difference in practical experience between believers who took a radical stance against involvement in Graeco-Roman society, and those who held positions of power.

In comments about government, the author of 1 Peter says 'For the Lord's sake arrange yourself under (ὑποτάγητε) every *human* creation (ἀνθρωπίνῃ κτίσει), whether to the Emperor as supreme...' (1 Pet. 2.13, my translation). The critical point here is the *humanity* of earthly rulers, an emphasis that implicitly makes the imperial cult unacceptable.[72] The author tells readers to 'honor everyone' (πάντας τιμήσατε), then pointedly uses the same verb to say they shall 'honor the Emperor' (τὸν βασιλέα τιμᾶτε, 2.17). This suggests that Christians should view the Emperor as being on the same human level as any one else in society.

Word order here may be significant: exhortation to 'honor the Emperor' follows immediately *after* a reminder of the Christian's ultimate commitment to 'fear God'. Christians function within the structures of society 'for the Lord's sake', a motivation that points to God as supreme. Every earthly political power is a mere 'creation', disallowing the possibility that believers can properly worship anything less than the Creator of all.

Paul and Pagan Foods at Corinth
Already in Paul's day, Christians debated the matter of participation in pagan feasts. In 1 Corinthians Paul argues against a libertine ('strong') attitude typified by the expression 'all things are lawful for me' (1 Cor. 6.12). He recites an argument apparently advanced by believers who saw no problem with eating meat offered to idols: 'no idol in the world really exists' (8.4). Since 'there is no God but one', they reasoned, why worry about eating meat offered to a non-existent deity? By this logic Christians could participate in cultic meals honoring pagan gods. Theissen

---

72. I am indebted to P. Achtemeier for this insight. See his forthcoming commentary on 1 Peter in the Hermeneia series.

points out that people of low economic class could not afford luxury foods, and probably ate meat only at public religious festivals or at cultic meals in the guilds. For them there was a much closer correlation between meat and idol worship than there was for members of the higher social strata who routinely ate meat in their own homes.[73]

Paul moves the discussion to a practical level, making a statement that had implications for anyone tempted to participate in the imperial cult. He says there are many 'so-called gods in heaven or *on earth*' (8.5). Yet for Christians there is 'one God...and one Lord, Jesus Christ...'. (8.6). By the time Paul wrote these words in 54 CE, the imperial cult was well known.[74] His mention of 'so-called gods' on earth could have included any Emperor living or dead who was the object of worship. Christians acknowledged only one Lord; neither pagan gods nor Roman Emperor merited worship or primary loyalty.[75]

Paul takes a middle course in the dispute over meat offered to idols. Recognizing there is some validity to the libertine argument about non-existent gods, he nevertheless argues that certain believers lack this 'knowledge' (8.7). If less mature Christians see the libertine actually 'eating in the temple of an idol', they may be drawn back into idol worship (8.10). Paul sets forth his personal stance: for the sake of other believers, he will avoid pagan feasts (8.13). Later he agrees Christians may eat any meat sold in the market. They should not partake at a feast, however, if the hosts announce they are serving food offered in sacrifice (10.25-28). Paul's standard would rule out the possibility of Christians participating directly in pagan ceremonies at guild meetings or elsewhere.[76]

Several ancient writers testify that Corinth was a thriving center of commerce and banking.[77] Ceremonies of trade associations and guilds are a likely context for Paul's comments in 2 Cor. 6.14-17:

73. Theissen, *The Social Setting*, p. 128.

74. Most scholars date 1 Corinthians around 54 CE. Fiorenza, '1 Corinthians', in Mays (ed.), *Harper's Bible Commentary*, p. 1168.

75. Paul (or a disciple) believed an evil end-time ruler would claim divine status: 'He opposes and exalts himself above every so-called god or object of worship, so that he takes his seat in the temple of God, declaring himself to be God', 2 Thess. 2.4.

76. Paul's discussion in 1 Cor. 10.14-22 reflects the 'common belief of antiquity...that those who partake of the cultic meal become companions of the god'. F. Hauck, 'κοινός', in *TDNT*, III, p. 805. If Christians shared this view and came to believe the Emperor was evil, they would refuse food associated with the imperial cult.

77. Strabo says 'Corinth is called "wealthy" because of its commerce, since it is

> Do not be mismatched with unbelievers. For what partnership is there between righteousness and lawlessness? Or what fellowship is there between light and darkness? What agreement does Christ have with Beliar? Or what does a believer share with an unbeliever? What agreement has the temple of God with idols?...Therefore come out from them, and be separate from them, says the Lord, and touch nothing unclean...

This admonition 'breathes the same spirit as Revelation', especially the imperative to 'come out from them' (cf. Rev. 18.4).[78] Paul rejects 'partnership' (μετοχή) and 'association' (κοινωνία) with unbelievers, using words that in a legal context meant joint ownership.[79]

Guild members jointly owned temples or assembly halls of their associations, and committed themselves to mutual aid.[80] This is the kind of pagan entanglement Paul seems to reject. The apostle expresses an apocalyptic world view, in which people and institutions inevitably align themselves either with good or with evil. Both Paul's juxtaposition of 'light and darkness' and his reference to 'Beliar' are reminiscent of certain Qumran scrolls in which Rome is the chief ally of 'Beliar' and the powers of darkness.[81]

In contrast to John of Patmos and the community at Qumran, Paul did not view the Roman government as categorically evil (cf. Rom. 13.1-

---

situated on the Isthmus and is master of two harbours, of which the one leads straight to Asia, and the other to Italy; and it makes easy the exchange of merchandise from both countries...', *Geog.* 8.6.20. Plutarch, in his discussion of money-lending, mentions first the 'usurer or broker' of Corinth, followed by bankers from Patrae and Athens, *Moralia* 831a.

78. J.P.M. Sweet, *Revelation* (Philadelphia: Westminster Press, 1979), p. 268.

79. C.K. Barrett, *The First Epistle to the Corinthians* (New York: Harper & Row, 1968), p. 197. These terms describe a business partnership between fishermen in Lk. 5.7 (μέτοχος) and 5.10 (κοινωνός).

80. In his study of guilds at ancient Ostia, G. Hermansen says a guild 'was a closely knit group. It was a real brotherhood: some guild members called each other brother (*frater*)...All guild brothers owned all guild property in common, they shared a common cult, and they had a common burial place. They had many common meals'. G. Hermansen, *Ostia: Aspects of Roman City Life* (Edmonton: University of Alberta Press, 1981), p. 110.

81. In *1QM* and *1QpHab*, the chief worldly allies of Beliar are the 'Kittim'. It is generally accepted among scholars that this is a reference to the Romans; see G. Vermes, *The Dead Sea Scrolls in English* (London: Penguin Books, 3rd edn, 1987), p. 29. *1QpHab* 6.3-5 speaks of the greed and idolatry of the Kittim: 'they gather much booty and are cruel...They sacrifice to their *signa* [imperial military standards] and their weapons are their object of worship'.

7). He eagerly sought opportunity to visit Rome (Rom. 1.9-15), and viewed the imperial capital as an ideal springboard for his mission to Spain (Rom. 15.28). His repeated concerns about idolatry, and his statement that 'authorities are [merely] God's servants' (Rom. 13.6), make it virtually certain he would not have joined any cultic acts that treated the Emperor as divine.[82] Yet he fellowshipped with Erastus, a believer who served in the provincial hierarchy as treasurer for the city of Corinth (Rom. 16.23; perhaps the same person mentioned in Acts 19.22 and 2 Tim. 4.20). Theissen probably is correct in saying Erastus 'could have kissed his public office goodbye had he on principle rejected invitations to feasts at which pagan rites and meat sacrificed to idols were unavoidable'.[83]

Despite his exhortation to 'touch nothing unclean', Paul elsewhere indicates a believer's frame of mind is more important that the mere act of eating food dedicated at idolatrous rituals. 'Nothing is unclean in itself', he says, 'but it is unclean for anyone who thinks it unclean' (Rom. 14.14). The implication is that mature believers may be able to eat foods associated in some way with pagan cults, but 'those who have doubts are condemned if they eat, because they do not act from faith' (14.23).

Paul's treatment of this issue is less than definitive. Though eating food offered to idols is theoretically acceptable, Christians must be cautious in their actual practice. They cannot be so conscientious, however, that they withdraw completely from any contact with pagan society. Believers need to have some interaction with 'the immoral of this world' and with 'idolaters'—so long as the latter people do not also claim to be part of the Christian community (1 Cor. 5.9-13).

Paul's discussion typifies ambiguities that must have festered in the church at Corinth and elsewhere in the East. Apparently some Christians felt they had 'knowledge' (1 Cor. 8.1, 7) and could eat meat offered to idols even at feasts honoring pagan gods or the 'divine' Emperor.[84] This

82. In addition to passages already cited, see 1 Thess. 1.9, 1 Cor. 12.2, Gal. 5.20 and Rom. 1.21-23. Paul wrote to Christians in Rome at a time when Emperor worship was gathering momentum, and lamented that some persons 'worshiped and served the creature rather than the Creator' (Rom. 1.25). He could have meant to include imperial statues or figures of pagan gods when he wrote of those who 'exchanged the glory of the immortal God for images resembling a mortal human being' (Rom. 1.23).

83. Theissen, *The Social Setting of Pauline Christianity*, p. 98.

84. Fiorenza cites early Christian writings and says, 'the libertine direction of Gnosticism expressed its higher knowledge mainly in practicing immorality and in the eating of food sacrificed to idols'. This understanding of freedom 'allowed

left more conscientious believers with the burden of deciding at what point they must 'drive out the wicked person' (1 Cor. 5.13) from the church fellowship.

The author of 2 Peter, familiar with Paul's letters, notes 'there are some things in them hard to understand, which the ignorant and unstable twist to their own destruction' (2 Pet. 3.16). The book of Revelation illustrates that questions of Christian involvement in society still were hard to understand a generation after Paul's death. Collins summarizes the concern of John for the seven churches of Asia Minor: 'At stake here was the question of assimilation: what pagan customs could Christians adopt for the sake of economic survival, commercial gain, or simple sociability?'[85]

The Martyrdom and Ascension of Isaiah

A Christian interpolation in the *Martyrdom and Ascension of Isaiah* illustrates that John was not the only Christian late in the first century who believed the Church was in a crisis of idolatry.[86] In a clear reference to Nero, the author says 'Beliar...will descend from his firmament in the form of a man, a king of iniquity, a murderer of his mother—this is the king of this world—and will persecute the plant [the Church] which the twelve apostles of the Beloved [Jesus] will have planted.' People of the world will unquestioningly obey Nero. All people 'will sacrifice to him and will serve him, saying, "This is the Lord, and besides him there is no other"'. Most appallingly, '*the majority* of those who have associated together to receive the Beloved he will turn aside after him. And the power of his miracles will be in every city and district, and he will set up his image before him in every city' (*Mart. Isa.* 4.2-11).

This text reflects both the ubiquity of imperial cult ceremonies ('in every city') and the astonishing willingness of a 'majority' of Christians to demonstrate loyalty to an Emperor who claimed divine status. The author indicates that profit motivated a compromise of allegiance:

the Gnostic to live in peaceful co-existence with the pagan society'. Fiorenza, 'Apocalyptic and Gnosis', p. 570.

85. Collins, 'Persecution and Vengeance', pp. 740-41.

86. The *Martyrdom and Ascension of Isaiah* is a composite work written between the second century BCE and the fourth century CE. The Christian passage cited here probably dates from the end of the first century. See introduction to *Mart. Isa.* by M.A. Knibb, *OTP*, II, pp. 144-55.

> And many [Christians] will exchange the glory of the robes of saints for
> the robes of those who love money; and there will be much respect of
> persons in those days, and lovers of the glory of this world...And in those
> days there will not be many prophets...because of the spirit of error and
> of fornication, and of vainglory, and of the love of money...(3.25-28)

Here we see a potent combination of influences on the Christian church:
materialism ('love of money'), desire for social acceptance ('much
respect of persons') and syncretism ('fornication'). Reference to robes in
this passage may illuminate a similar allusion in Revelation, in which
John describes believers who remained faithful under persecution as
those 'who have washed their robes and made them white in the blood
of the Lamb' (Rev. 7.14). Later John contrasts these faithful Christians
to certain 'fornicators' and 'idolators', presumably people who found it
convenient to avoid persecution and preserve their social or financial
status by participating in pagan ceremonies. The latter remain outside
the New Jerusalem (Rev. 22.14-15).

The Apostolic Decree
Both fornication and idolatry figure in the Apostolic Decree written by
church leaders gathered at Jerusalem in the middle of the first century.
At issue was whether Gentiles needed to accept circumcision before
joining the Christian church, and the assembled body decided not to
'trouble' converts with that Jewish ritual. In the end, church leaders
simply required Gentile converts 'to abstain only from things polluted
by idols and from fornication and from whatever has been strangled and
from blood' (Acts 15.20, cf. 15.29).

Most modern scholars understand this fourfold directive as a concession to Jewish religious and cultic scruples.[87] A major textual variant,
however, suggests that some parts of the early church construed this
directive as a warning against participation in whole areas of pagan
society. Irenaeus[88] and the so-called 'Western' textual tradition[89] delete
the phrase 'whatever has been strangled', leaving prohibitions against

---

87. For concern about idols in the Hebrew scriptures, see Exod. 34.13-17 and
Lev. 26.1; about forbidden sexual relations see Lev. 18.6-30; about strangled animals
see Gen. 9.4; Lev. 19.26; Deut. 12.16, 23-27 and 15.23; and about eating blood see
Lev. 3.17; 17.10-14.

88. *Adv. Haer.* 12.14. Irenaeus, however, cites Acts 15 during a discussion of the
doctrine of God, not in the context ethics or the relationship of Christians to society.

89. Notably Codex Bezae (*Cantabrigiensis*).

only three things: idolatry, fornication and blood. The same tradition adds a negative form of the Golden Rule immediately after the prohibitions: Gentile converts are 'not to do whatever they do not want others to do to them'. This addition makes rejection of 'blood' a prohibition against murder.

The Apostolic decision of Acts 15.20 (29), as rendered in the Western text, makes sense in the light of the figurative categories of Revelation. 'Idolatry' could refer to imperial cult (or other pagan) ceremonies that were ubiquitous in trade guilds and political associations. 'Fornication' may be a figure for any type of promiscuous economic or political ties with Rome. Prohibition against 'blood' could be an implicit call for Christians to avoid the Roman military that gave provincials an attractive avenue for upward mobility.

It is unlikely that the *original* Apostolic Decree used these terms in the figurative sense we find in Revelation. However, the Western textual tradition suggests that some early believers found it helpful or necessary to interpret Acts 15.20 (29) in this way, proscribing Christian participation in certain cultic, political and military aspects of Roman imperial society. Leaders at Jerusalem had sent their directive to Antioch, a major trade center that blended cult and commerce as thoroughly as any city in Asia Minor. As a busy port and political forum, Antioch presented conscientious Christians with the same possibilities for compromise that John of Patmos calls 'idolatry' and 'fornication'.

Hegesippus and the 'Angelic' Kingdom

The second-century Christian writer Hegesippus tells of a time when Emperor Domitian struck against the Jews and 'gave orders for the execution of those of the family of David'.[90] The narrative reveals that certain 'heretics' in Palestine accused grandchildren of Jesus' brother Judas of being Jewish, and an officer brought Jesus' relatives before the Emperor to answer charges. We owe preservation of this story to the dubious fourth-century historiography of Eusebius, and should not unduly press the account for accuracy.[91] Nevertheless, the eschatology of the courtroom defense is striking, and may reflect a political stance

90. Eusebius, *Hist. Eccl.* 3.20.1-7.

91. M. Sordi reviews historical problems of this account and summarizes how some modern commentators evaluate its accuracy. She credits the basic veracity of the story, but thinks Hegesippus erred in dating it to Domitian's reign rather than that of Vespasian or Titus. Sordi, *Christians and the Roman Empire*, pp. 38-43.

that enabled some Christians of the era to survive under jealous Roman rule.

The Emperor opened the hearing by extracting admission from the accused that they in fact were 'of the house of David'. He then moved directly to economic matters: How much property did the accused have? How much money did they control? In this case the defendants were impoverished, owning between them a mere nine thousand denarii worth of property. They paid taxes on this land and tilled it by their own calloused hands. With their economic status established, the Emperor turned to political matters and 'asked concerning Christ and his kingdom, its nature, origin, and the time of appearance'. The Christians explained that the kingdom of Christ

> was neither of the world nor earthly, but heavenly and angelic, and it would be at the end of the world, when he would come in glory to judge the living and the dead and reward every man according to his deeds. At this Domitian did not condemn them at all, but despised them as simple folk, released them, and decreed an end to the persecution against the church. But when they were released they were the leaders of the churches...and remained alive in the peace which ensued until Trajan.[92]

Far removed as they were from the urban commercial settings of Asian Christianity, these small landholders from Palestine nevertheless represent a spiritualized view of Christian faith that others in the East may have shared. This story apparently originated (and perhaps already circulated) late in the first century. It told of Christians who saved their lives in a Roman court by convincing the Emperor that Christian faith had no political implications that meaningfully threatened or challenged imperial sovereignty. Loyalty to a 'heavenly and angelic' kingdom at the 'end of the world' was an arrangement that could have allowed undiscerning believers to adopt a libertine stance toward participation in pagan society.

By spiritualizing their concept of Jesus' kingdom, and consigning its realization to an indefinite future, suffering Christians reportedly brought an end to persecution and were able to live in peace. This eschatology stands in stark contrast to that of John on Patmos. He wrote, 'The kingdom of the world has become the kingdom of our Lord and of his Messiah, and he will reign forever and ever' (Rev. 11.15). John himself may have seen full expression of the kingdom as a future event, but it was an event so near in the future that it made all other loyalties relative.

92. Eusebius, *Hist. Eccl.* 3.20.3-6.

Pliny and the Nature of Pressure on Christians

I have noted there is little evidence of orchestrated, Empire-wide persecution of Christians in the first century. There is reason to believe, however, that late in the first century Christians experienced social and political pressure to join the imperial cult or other pagan rituals. Refusal to worship either the Emperor or traditional Roman gods made Christians (and Jews) look ungrateful, disloyal and dangerously impious.

When Pliny—an experienced lawyer from Rome—described trials of Christians in Bithynia (c. 112 CE), he said he never previously attended such trials.[93] This suggests Roman authorities did not often take Christians of Rome to court during Pliny's years in the capital city. Even in Asia Minor, Roman authorities were not aggressive in their prosecution of believers. Pliny did not initiate prosecution of Christians in Bithynia, but acted only when they were 'denounced' to him. 'A placard was set up', he reports, 'without any signature, accusing a large number of persons by name'. Pressure on Christians originated from fellow provincials, not from Roman officials.[94] This peer pressure (with legal ramifications) weighed on the church already during the last decade of the first century. Pliny reports Christians abandoned their faith, 'some three years, others many years, and a few as much as twenty-five years ago'.

It is not completely clear from Pliny's correspondence why provincials put such pressure on their Christian neighbors. There may have been an economic motive for limiting Christian influence. After a few executions of obstinate Christians, Pliny says,

> ...the temples, which had been almost deserted, begin now to be frequented; and the sacred festivals, after a long intermission, are again revived; while there is a general demand for sacrificial animals, which for some time past have met with but a few purchasers.[95]

93. Pliny, *Ep.* 10.96.
94. In his counsel to Pliny on the handling of Christians, Trajan says, 'no search should be made for these people'. However, 'when they are denounced and found guilty they must be punished', *Ep.* 10.97. Throughout the second century trials against Christians typically stemmed from accusations by a private *delator*, and authorities could drop charges if the accuser did not carry through. Tertullian, late in the second century, tells of a Roman judge who dismissed charges against a Christian when the accuser failed to materialize in court, *Ad Scap.* 4.4. See Frend, *Martyrdom and Persecution*, 167.
95. Pliny, *Ep.* 10.96.

At least in this circumstance, Christian belief and practice had a noticeable impact on the local economy. Temples to many gods formed a significant part of urban finance and employment.[96] The 'sacred festivals'—perhaps including those related to the imperial cult—suffered as well. Many cities in the East held several imperial festivals each year: on the Emperor's birthday, on the anniversary of his accession, after success in war or in honor of other members of the imperial family. Such festivals included feasts, distributions, games, processions and cultic observances.[97] Large crowds representing all levels of society gathered for these occasions and provided a ready market for the wares of craftsmen and merchants.[98] If a large number of Christians avoided the festivals, local entrepreneurs suffered.

When Christians withdrew from the imperial cult, they also diminished an expression of loyalty to Rome that many provincials were eager to promote. Refusal to honor the Emperor at temples and festivals brought suspicion 'not only from the imperial government itself but from these conquered peoples who recognized Rome as a source of their prosperity'.[99] The recent Jewish revolt (66–70 CE) accented the

96. This was true in any Hellenistic city. Pausanias makes a passing reference to the marketplace of Corinth, 'where most of the sanctuaries are', Pausanias, *Description of Greece* 2.4.6.

97. It was difficult for residents of eastern cities to avoid such festivals. When processions passed through city streets, for example, convention required house-holders to sacrifice on small altars outside their homes. Neighbors may have noticed if a householder did not sacrifice. See Price, *Rituals and Power*, pp. 108, 123; Thompson, *Revelation: Apocalypse and Empire*, p. 162. Tertullian, a century after Revelation, laments that on imperial festival days in Africa one could 'find more doors of heathens without lamps and laurel-wreaths than of Christians'. The lamps, he says, are not 'an honour to God, but to him who is honoured in God's stead by ceremonial observances of that kind...', Tertullian, *De Idol.* 15.

98. Dio Chrysostom mentions governors, orators, prostitutes and craftsmen, *Or.* 35.15. Cited by Thompson, *Revelation: Apocalypse and Empire*, p. 161.

99. T.A. Robinson, *The Bauer Thesis Examined* (Lewiston: Edwin Mellen, 1988), p. 112. When the Stoic Thrasea Paetus received the death sentence at Rome in 66 CE, charges included the fact that 'At the beginning of the year, Thrasea evaded the customary oath' and 'took no part in the national vows'. He 'never offered a sacrifice for the welfare of the Emperor'. Tacitus, *Ann.* 16.22. Celsus, in his knowledgeable critique of Christian faith and practice (written ca. 177–180 CE), underscored the political implications of Christian refusal to pay divine honors to the Emperor: 'If everyone were to do the same as you, there would be nothing to prevent him [the Emperor] from being abandoned, alone and deserted, while earthly things would come

political significance of cultic acts involving imperial interests: insurrectionists marked the start of their war against Rome by discontinuing daily sacrifices for the Emperor's welfare in the temple at Jerusalem.[100]

The refusal of any group to participate in traditional Graeco-Roman religion appeared to threaten the stability of the Empire, since impiety could provoke disfavor from the gods.[101] Cicero praised the religious devotion of Romans, and said the Empire itself 'was won by those commanders who obeyed the dictates of [traditional Roman] religion'.[102] The very fabric of society depended on continued devotion to the traditional gods. Cicero believed 'the disappearance of piety towards the gods will entail the disappearance of loyalty and social union among men as well, and of justice itself...'[103] In his popular history of the Roman people, Livy has one character caution that 'all things turned out well when we obeyed the gods, and ill when we spurned them'.[104]

In the eyes of conscientious pagans, Christians appeared to spurn the gods. Although charges of atheism did not surface until the second century,[105] during Paul's ministry residents of Ephesus feared traditional worship practice would suffer from the spread of Christian faith. More than mere piety was at issue, since idol worship (and eventually Emperor worship) generated substantial income at several levels of imperial society. A silversmith at Ephesus recognized the economic implications of Christianity when he addressed his fellow artisans.

> Men, you know that we get our wealth from this business. You also see and hear that not only in Ephesus but in almost the whole of Asia this Paul has persuaded and drawn away a considerable number of people by saying that gods made with hands are not gods. And there is danger not only that

into the power of the most lawless and savage barbarians', *Contra Celsum* 8.68.

100. Josephus says cessation of sacrifice on behalf of Caesar 'laid the foundation of the war with the Romans', *War* 2.17.2 (409).

101. I am indebted to Frend for directing me to the classical references in this paragraph, *Martyrdom and Persecution*, pp. 105-6.

102. Cicero, *De Natura Deorum* 2.3.8.

103. Cicero, *De Natura Deorum* 1.2.4. In the third century CE, Dio Cassius voiced similar concerns: 'Those who attempt to distort our religion with strange rites you should abhor and punish, not merely for the sake of the gods (since if a man despise these he will not pay honour to any other being)... Do not, therefore, permit anybody to be an atheist or a sorcerer', *Hist. Rom.* 52.36.1-2.

104. Livy, 5.51.5. Cf. Horace, *Odes* 3.6.

105. For example, Athenagoras, *Legatio* 3. If Flavius Clemens and his wife were Christians, then atheism charges surfaced as early as 95 CE.

this trade of ours may come into disrepute but also that the temple of the
great goddess Artemis will be scorned…(Acts 19.25-27)[106]

Ordinary residents of Ephesus—not government officials—put heat on
the Christians (Acts 19.28-41).[107] This pattern of popular (rather than
official) harassment was typical of Christian experience in society
throughout the first and second centuries.[108] Believers who wished to
participate in social or commercial institutions would have felt pressure
from neighbors and peers to conform to religious conventions of the
groups they sought to penetrate.

We know from a letter by Emperor Hadrian in about 124 CE that
some residents of Asia Minor continued to put heat on fellow provincials
who were Christian. Hadrian instructed Minucius Fundanus, governor of
Asia, to prevent people from being 'harassed' and to guard against 'the
rascality of informers'. The Emperor's reply suggests that mere profession of Christianity was not enough to alarm the Roman rulers. Hadrian
says,

> If then anyone accuses them, and shows that they are acting illegally,
> decide the point according to the nature of the offence, but by Hercules, if
> anyone brings the matter forward for the purpose of blackmail, investigate
> strenuously and be careful to inflict penalties adequate to the crime.[109]

106. Cf. Wis. 15.8-12.

107. Scholars debate the historical accuracy of Luke's account. It is possible Acts
19 tells more about Christian relations with provincial rulers when Luke wrote (late
first century?) than about circumstances in Paul's day. If that is true, then Luke's
work, if anything, shows an increasing tendency of Christians in Asia Minor to make
friends with government officials. This would be precisely the sort of development
John rejects in Revelation.

108. Frend, summarizing the period of 70–135 CE, says 'the authorities, after careful consideration, treated the Christians with indulgence'. Yet, 'almost as if in defiance
of the indulgence of the Roman authorities, the sub-apostolic age marks the long
climax of the first wave of Christian apocalyptic, and in these yearnings Rome was
cast in the role of the Second Babylon…' (Frend, *Martyrdom and Persecution*,
pp. 181-82). Frend's analysis supports the argument that most Christians found it
possible to get along with Rome.

109. Eusebius, *Hist. Eccl.* 4.9; Justin, *1 Apol.* 68. For discussion of this rescript
and Hadrian's policy toward Christians, see Sordi, *Christians and the Roman
Empire*, pp. 66-67; M. Hengel, 'Hadrians Politik gegenüber Juden und Christen',
JANESCU 16/17 (1984–85), pp. 153-82 (161-70). Hengel (p. 166) points out that
Hadrian had just returned from a trip through Asia Minor, and likely was better
informed than his predecessors about circumstances in that region, including the
status of Christians.

Mention of 'informers' and 'blackmail' suggests the nature of hostility against Christians of Asia Minor a generation after John wrote the Apocalypse. Impetus for harassment sprang from local sources, not primarily from Rome. Just as Trajan seemed less than enthused about prosecuting believers a decade earlier, Hadrian showed little interest in bringing Christians to court simply because they carried the name of a religious sect. We must assume that certain provincials felt threatened by Christians, perhaps for economic reasons or because Christian ideology presented a dissonant chord in an otherwise unanimous chorus of fidelity to a government most provincials wished to honor.

Continuing Struggle over Christian Involvement in Society
Our interpretation of Revelation proceeds with the notion that most Christians in Asia were functioning well in society. John and a few others eventually came into conflict with fellow provincials and Roman authorities; but other believers enjoyed comfortable status. Members of the seven churches struggled to decide how involved Christians could be in the affairs of pagan society around them.[110] This debate over the Christian role in society began a generation earlier during the ministry of Paul. By the time John wrote Revelation, residents of Asia Minor noticed that some Christians drew back from the imperial cult. The refusal of some believers to make *any* concessions to the cult limited their participation in social and economic life of the region. Suspicious of the motives for such withdrawal from society, some provincials harassed believers or hounded them into court on various charges.

Apparently John was the victim of such harassment, and expected other believers soon to experience the same. At the root of this persecution he saw Rome and the values it instilled. To understand how Rome was involved in Asian society, and how provincials responded, I turn next to a study of imperial relations with the region of the seven churches.

110. I agree with Collins, who says Revelation 'cannot be understood as a response to a new initiative against the Christians taken by Roman authorities'. Rather, 'it was written to awaken and intensify Christian exclusiveness, particularly vis-à-vis the imperial cult'. Collins even suggests the imperial cult 'was not an objectively significant problem for the congregations in Asia Minor'. That is, many believers in the region did not feel any tension over the issue. Collins, *Crisis and Catharsis*, pp. 73-74.

Chapter 2

NATIONS HAVE DRUNK HER WINE

...all the nations have drunk of the wine of the wrath of her fornication, and
the kings of the earth have committed fornication with her... (Rev. 18.3)

Ruins of an elegant house at the site of ancient Ephesus produced the following graffito: 'Rome, queen over all, your power will never end.'[1] Whether the anonymous author wrote these words in hope or despair we cannot know. The idea of Rome being eternal, however, was not rare among residents of the ancient Mediterranean world. Even Josephus (admittedly not the average Jew!) observed Rome's clean sweep of power and concluded its Empire was invincible. 'God', he said, 'who went the round of the nations, bringing to each in turn the rod of Empire, now rested over Italy'.[2]

For several centuries, Rome was so powerful it seemed to control the destinies of individuals and nations. By dint of treaty and conquest, Rome gradually extended its domains to include all the Mediterranean basin. Nations foolish enough to resist the Roman yoke met a terrible fate. When the Jews revolted in 66–70 CE, Rome brought Jerusalem to its knees with a ruthless siege and gruesome slaughter.[3] Yet most provincials did not resist Roman rule, and many were pleased to be part of the Empire. Every province had native groups eager to show loyalty to the Emperor, since Rome provided security and prosperity for its friends.

John of Patmos not only condemned the imperial cult, but also the social, commercial and political institutions that fostered adoration of the Emperor. Provincials who allied themselves with Rome, he said, were intoxicated with 'the wine of the wrath of her fornication' (Rev. 18.3).

1.   'Ρώμα ἡ παμβασίλεια, τὸ σὸν κράτος οὔποτ' ὀλεῖται. *I. Eph.* 599.
2.   Josephus, *War* 5.9.3 (367).
3.   This event influenced Christian and Jewish attitudes toward Rome for decades, and it provides the historical backdrop for visions of a New Jerusalem in Revelation 21–22.

'Fornication', as John uses the term, refers to the reciprocal exchange of benefits and loyalties that bonded provincials to the imperial rulers. While most people of the East viewed this network of reciprocal relationships as positive and useful, John condemns it as immoral, self-serving and idolatrous.

1. *Background to Roman Rule in Asia Minor*

By the time John put his vision into writing, people of Asia had experienced more than two centuries of Roman rule. Italians first got a foothold there in 133 BCE, when King Attalus III of Pergamum died and willed his rich domain to Rome.[4] The early years of Italian rule impoverished the region, as Rome demanded repayment of debts and plundered wealth accumulated by the Attalids. The area became a Roman province, ruled at the caprice of a governor sent annually from Italy.

During this era groups of Italian businessmen settled permanently in many cities, including Pergamum and Ephesus.[5] These entrepreneurs exploited the province, and Roman tax-farming syndicates drained the region of further revenues. The harsh nature of early Roman presence in Asia Minor was partly responsible for the bloody revolt of Mithridates that began in 88 BCE, during which rebels massacred some eighty thousand Italians.[6]

The revolt lasted for two decades, but some provincials remained loyal, and Rome found ways to reward them. In 78 BCE the Roman Senate granted privileges to three ship's captains, calling them 'Friends of Rome' for their loyalty and assistance.[7] These men and their heirs enjoyed permanent exemption from all local and imperial taxes.

4. Attalus III was unmarried and without heir. Internal strife threatened his kingdom, and he may have felt only the strong arm of Rome could maintain order. Magie, *Roman Rule*, I, pp. 29-33.

5. In each city such resident Romans formed an organization called a *conventus Civium Romanorum*, often called simply 'the Romans engaged in business', Magie, *Roman Rule*, I, p. 162.

6. Magie, *Roman Rule*, I, pp. 216-17.

7. The ship captains were from Miletus and Clazomenae in Asia, and from Carystus on the island of Euboea. Magie, *Roman Rule*, I, p. 236. Clazomenae is twenty miles west of Smyrna, Miletus thirty miles south of Ephesus. In the decades before 78 BCE, an organization formed in Asia Minor of persons 'individually received in friendship with Rome'. Magie, *Roman Rule*, I, p. 174. A resident of Pergamum belonged to this group. *IGR*, IV, 291, cited in *Roman Rule*, II, p. 1064 n. 48.

Privileged Provincials Loyal to Rome
The ship's captains were part of an emerging class of 'highly-privileged provincials', people who saw their own best interests served in cooperating with Rome.[8] When it became clear Italy would maintain its grip on Asia, even cities that recently had fought against Rome sought to become allies. Ephesus was among the cities that rebelled during Mithridates' uprising, and it paid a considerable price when Rome reasserted control. Imperial officials tried and executed local leaders of the rebellion, and the province of Asia had to pay a fine of twenty thousand talents.[9]

When Octavian (Caesar Augustus) emerged as undisputed ruler of the East in 31 BCE, Asians understood the importance of demonstrating their loyalty. Many provincials also appreciated the value of having the whole of the Mediterranean peacefully united into one economic and political system. The several centuries since Alexander the Great had brought countless wars and enormous human suffering. When Augustus ushered in the era of *pax Romana,* it was the greatest benefit many of his subjects could imagine.

Gratitude among provincials only increased as the years passed and the benefits of Roman rule became more obvious. Piracy, long a plague on the seas, virtually ceased. Brigandage on the highways diminished, and trade flourished.[10] Wars continued to fester on distant frontiers of the Empire, but the Mediterranean basin itself got a respite from battle. Roman rule brought physical and economic security to many people in Asia Minor.

---

8.   Magie, *Roman Rule*, I, p. 236. Of this era Rostovtzeff says, 'There was an *élite,* the rich and influential magnates of the cities, who by servility and bribes, and a judicious choice of friends and protectors, succeeded in retaining and increasing their fortunes…', M. Rostovtzeff, *The Social and Economic History of the Hellenistic World*, II (Oxford: Clarendon Press, 1941), p. 1018.

9.   Magie, *Roman Rule*, I, p. 238.

10.   Epictetus, the freedman from Asia Minor who became a leading Stoic philosopher at Rome during the reign of Domitian, rejoiced that 'Caesar has obtained for us a profound peace. There are neither wars nor battles, nor great robberies nor piracies, but we may travel at all hours, and sail from east to west'. Dio Chrysostom, *Or.* 3.13.9. Strabo (*Geog.* 3.2.5) expressed gratitude for the 'present peace, because all piracy has been broken up, and hence the sailors feel wholly at ease'. Rostovtzeff speaks of 'the new opportunities for economic expansion' which Rome offered the East already in the second century BCE, 'by throwing open Italy as a market for its products and by the rapid increase in the buying capacity of its Italian customers'. Rostovtzeff, *Hellenistic World*, II, p. 1019.

Imperial Cult as Expression of Gratitude

Some Easterners responded with expressions of loyalty that raised their new rulers to near-divine status. The provincial council (*koinon*) of Asia established a cult of Roma and Augustus at Pergamum in 29 BCE, and promised toaward a crown to the person who devised the greatest honors for 'the god' who now ruled the world. In 9 BCE, lavish praise of Augustus appeared on a stele at Pergamum: 'Greeks in the province of Asia' expressed gratitude for the 'savior who put an end to war and established peace'. Caesar 'exceeded the hopes of all who had anticipated good tidings', and Asians honored him by arranging their calendar to start with his birthday.[11]

The cult of Emperor worship emerged spontaneously among peoples of Asia Minor, and Rome did not impose it 'from above'.[12] It had long been customary for Hellenistic peoples of Asia to accord divine honors to native kings, but it was new for them to apply the practice to a foreign ruler.[13] Easterners were so eager to pay homage to Augustus that intense rivalry erupted between cities over the privilege of building imperial

11. N. Lewis and M. Reinhold (eds.), *Roman Civilization*, II, (Harper Torchbooks; New York: Harper & Row, 1966), p. 64. A Roman coin (Augustus tetradrachm, *BMC*, I, p. 112 nos 691-93 [plate 17, no. 4]) struck at Ephesus in 28 BCE reads: *IMP(erator) CAESAR DIVI F(ilius) CO(n)S(ul) VI LIBERTATIS P(opuli) R(omani) VINDEX* ('Emperor Caesar, son of the divine Julius, consul for the sixth time, defender of the liberty of the Roman people'). The reverse of the coin depicts the female figure of Pax holding a *caduceus*—a herald staff typically associated with the god Mercury. Niels Hannestad notes that Mercury is the god of trade, and sees the coin as propaganda celebrating the commercial benefits of the Roman peace under Octavian. N. Hannestad, *Roman Art and Imperial Policy* (Aarhus: Aarhus University Press, 1988), p. 62.

12. Dio Cassius says Augustus gave permission for the imperial cult in Ephesus, Pergamum, Nicaea and Nicomedia. However, 'in the capital [Rome] itself and in Italy generally no Emperor, however worthy of renown he has been, has dared to do this', *Hist. Rom.* 51.20.6-8. Tacitus corroborates other evidence that initiative for the new cult came from Asia Minor, not from Rome, *Ann.* 4.37. Friesen says aspects of the provincial cult that were directly under Rome's control were more restrained in their use of divine titles for the Emperor than locally inspired expressions: 'It cannot be argued that the Cult of the Sebastoi was a foreign import, foisted upon the province of Asia by a tyrant seeking divine glory'. Friesen, *Twice Neokoros*, p. 166.

13. Price says the imposition of foreign rule created a political and religious crisis for the Hellenistic peoples of Asia Minor, who responded by categorizing the seemingly omnipotent Roman *imperator* among the familiar Greek gods they had always worshipped. Price, *Rituals and Power*, pp. 29-30.

temples. In 23 CE Smyrna became the second city in Asia to win the right to establish a provincial center of the imperial cult, this one dedicated to Tiberius, his mother Livia and the Senate.[14] Miletus established a third provincial cult during the reign of Caligula.[15]

Imperial cult temples at Pergamum, Smyrna and Miletus served the entire province of Asia. In addition to these provincial sites there were numerous municipal temples to the Emperors. By the time John wrote Revelation at least thirty-five cities in Asia Minor carried the title of 'temple warden' (νεωκόρος) for the divine Caesars.[16] Usually Easterners who participated in the imperial cult made sacrifices to the gods on the Emperor's behalf, not to the Emperor himself.[17] But that technicality must have made little difference to someone like John, since imperial images often stood in pagan temples that he deemed idolatrous in any case.[18]

Money for construction of imperial temples usually came from wealthy provincial families, and priests came from the local elite.[19] Rome took seriously the pledge of provincials to build an imperial temple. When citizens of Cyzicus failed to complete a temple dedicated to Augustus, the insult contributed to Tiberius' decision to remove the city's 'freedom'.[20] Willingness to help finance the cult distinguished a family as people of local standing, and could enhance their relationship with Rome.

Pergamum organized a choral association to 'sing hymns to the god

14. Tacitus, *Ann.* 4.15.

15. Friesen, *Twice Neokoros*, pp. 21-26.

16. Price, *Rituals and Power*, pp. 66-67. A late first-century Christian passage in *Mart. Isa.* 4.1-3 portrays Nero as the incarnation of Beliar, a king who persecutes the apostles of Jesus. Alluding to the imperial cult, the author says people of the earth 'will sacrifice to him and will serve him…and he will set up his image before him in every city'. Such veneration sprang from gratitude, as indicated by the honors conferred on Vespasian in several parts of Asia naming him 'Benefactor' or even 'Benefactor of the World and Saviour and Benefactor of all [Human]kind'. Magie, *Roman Rule*, I, p. 572

17. *IGR*, IV, 1398 from Smyrna, for example, reads 'the whole world sacrifices and prays on behalf of the Emperor's eternal duration and unconquered rule'. Cited by Price, *Rituals and Power*, p. 210. Cf. Philo, *Leg. Gai.* 349-67.

18. Thompson says 'the imperial cult was rejected [by Christians] as a correlate to the rejection of traditional cults. The forms of traditional Greek religion were central, the imperial cult was secondary to that'. *Revelation: Apocalypse and Empire*, p. 164.

19. Price, *Rituals and Power*, pp. 62-63.

20. Price, *Rituals and Power*, p. 66.

Augustus in the temple precinct dedicated by Asia'.[21] Early in the second century CE all but four of its thirty-six members held Roman citizenship, illustrating how those who enjoyed benefits from Rome showed gratitude by offering praise. People who joined the choral association were from the wealthy elite; its entry fee was seven times higher than that known for any other guild.[22]

If some Roman subjects venerated the Emperor out of gratitude, others did so for less noble reasons. I noted earlier that Domitian himself probably did not require subjects to address him as *dominus et deus noster.* Collins says the title

> seems to have been used by those, such as Martial, who were not in the inner circle and wished to gain access by it. It was used, apparently, in blatant attempts to flatter and thus gain influence.[23]

While Domitian himself may not have wanted to receive divine titles, state propaganda pointed in that direction. After he sponsored the Secular Games in 88 CE, Domitian struck a series of coins celebrating both the games and the advent of a new golden century, the Flavian era.[24] The coins depict a larger-than-life Domitian standing beside (or in) a temple (see Figure 1). Three figures with outstretched arms kneel in supplication before the Emperor. Below the scene appears the standard legend *S[enatus] C[onsulto]* ('by authorization of the Senate'). It is likely that the Emperor in this image is dictating prayers rather than receiving veneration himself, but such a distinction may have been lost on people who knew the Emperor sometimes was worshipped.[25]

While several first-century Emperors enjoyed divine status in the Roman Empire after their death, Domitian apparently sought elevation of himself and his family before the end of his earthly reign. Coins struck

21. *I. Eph.* 18d.11-14.

22. Price, *Rituals and Power*, p. 90.

23. *Crisis and Catharsis*, p. 72. Thompson notes that Martial 'sought, but never gained, entrance into Domitian's inner court... As a potential beneficiary, Martial probably uses extravagant titles to show his devotion to Domitian'. Thompson speculates that 'Other potential beneficiaries approaching power from below also probably used titles such as *dominus* and *deus* and were eager to display their zeal for Domitian'. *Revelation: Apocalypse and Empire*, p. 106.

24. Domitian sestertii, *BMC*, II, pp. 392-98, nos. 419-38 (plates 78, nos. 3, 5-11, and plate 79, nos. 1-4). See Hannestad, *Roman Art*, p. 141.

25. H. Mattingly and E. Syndenham, *Roman Imperial Coinage*. II. *Vespasian to Hadrian* (London: Spink & Son, 1926), p. 201 n. 377.

Figure 1. Reverse of a sestertius of Domitian. Three figures with outstretched arms kneel in supplication before the Emperor. The inscription reads *LVD[i] SAEC[ulares] FEC[it] CO[n]S[ulatus] XIII S[enatus] C[onsulto].* ('He conducted the Secular Games, 14th consulship, by authorization of the Senate'). Probably the Emperor in this image is dictating prayers rather than serving as the object of devotion. Such a distinction, however, may have been lost on people who objected to Emperor worship. The obverse of the coin gives Domitian the titles of *P[ontifex] M[aximus] TR[ibunicia] P[otestate] VIII CENS[or] PER[petuus] P[ater] P[atriae].* Domitian Sestertius, *BMC*, II, p. 393, no. 424 [plate 78, no. 5]. Copyright British Museum.

under Domitian emphasize the *present* nature of divinity in the imperial family. Several coins allude to the Emperor's beloved son, who died in infancy. Some feature his wife Domitia, with inscriptions reading 'mother of the divine Caesar'–indicating that the dead child now was a god.[26] One coin depicts the deceased infant as the naked god Jupiter, seated on a globe with his hands outstretched; above and around him are seven stars, and the inscription reads 'the divine Caesar, son of the Emperor

26. *DIVI CAESAR MATRI* (Domitian sestertius, *BMC*, II, p. 413, no. 501 (plate 82, no. 3) and *DIVI CAESARIS MATER* (Domitian sestertius, *BMC*, II, p. 413 no. 502). See E.P. Janzen, 'The Jesus of the Apocalypse Wears the Emperor's Clothes', in E.H. Lovering, Jr (ed.), SBLSP, 1994 (Atlanta: Scholars Press, 1994), pp. 637-61 (p. 644, and p. 644 n. 38).

Domitian'.[27] The appearance of seven stars on some Domitian coins could have motivated John to answer with his own image of Jesus, world conqueror, holding seven stars in his right hand (Rev. 1.16).[28]

Roman coins circulated in all the provinces, where further signs of excessive veneration appeared. The *dominus et deus* practice apparently began when Domitian issued a circular letter, in the name of his procurators, that bore the lofty title.[29] Cities in Asia Minor sought ways to venerate the Emperor, and it is possible the huge statue of Domitian found at Ephesus is the very 'image of the beast' condemned by John of Patmos (Rev. 13.13-15).[30] In such a climate, the danger of persecution against Christians came 'not with imperial policy but with popular opportunism among those seeking benefits from Domitian'.[31]

Pliny illustrates how a government official could use the imperial cult to personal advantage. In about 98 CE he wrote to Emperor Trajan, requesting a one-month leave of absence from his responsibilities as prefect of the treasury.[32] Pliny needed to travel to Tifernum to make rental arrangements for his farms in that district, properties that could earn 'more than 400,000' sestertii. Before stating the real reason for his trip, however, he displays his enthusiasm for the imperial cult in three ways: (1) Pliny refers to Trajan's father Nerva as the 'deified Emperor;' (2) he

27. *DIVVS CAESAR IMP DOMITIANI F.* Domitian aureus, *BMC*, II, p. 311, no. 62 (plate 61, no. 6); Domitian denarius, *BMC*, II, p. 311, no. 63 (plate 61, no. 7). See Janzen, 'Jesus of the Apocalypse', pp. 644-45.

28. Janzen, 'Jesus of the Apocalypse', p. 653. Janzen (pp. 656-57) presents a plausible argument that the 'seemingly endless and ever-escalating numismatic propaganda of the *imperium*' was a direct factor in shaping the message of John and other preachers and prophets of the early church.

29. Suetonius says, 'With no less arrogance he [Domitian] began as follows in dictating a circular letter in the name of his procurators, "Our Master and our God bids that this be done". And so the custom arose of henceforth addressing him in no other way even in writing or in conversation', *Dom.* 13. Suetonius thus blames Domitian for the pompous title. The fact that the circular letter went out in the name of his procurators, though, suggests they may have generated the title themselves.

30. See Price, *Rituals and Power*, p. 97. Alternatively, John could have had in mind the 120-foot high statue *(colossus)* of Nero that once stood in the vestibule of the Domus Aurea (Nero's 'Golden House') in Rome. The huge statue portrayed Nero as the Sun, complete with the familiar *corona radiata* (radiated crown) that Nero wears on some coin portraits issued during his reign. Flavian Emperors later altered the statue and placed it beside the Colosseum. See Hannestad, *Roman Art*, p. 113.

31. Thompson, *Apocalypse and Empire*, p. 106.

32. Pliny, *Ep.* 10.8.

tells how he built—at his own expense—a temple in Tifernum for statues of former Emperors; and (3) he asks permission to add Trajan's statue to others in the temple. Together with the latter petition—in the same sentence!—Pliny inserts his request for a leave of absence from official duties. He promises speedy accomplishment of his 'act of loyalty' *(pietas)*, clearly expecting Trajan to give a favorable reply.

2. *Asia, the Richest of Provinces*

It is not surprising Rome placed loyal subordinates in Asia Minor, since the province had natural and human resources that would be the envy of any Empire.[33] Inland mountains produced a bounty of minerals and timber; fertile valleys and coastal plains gave a rich harvest of grains and fruit. A network of rivers and tributaries covered the whole region, supplying water and forming valleys ideal for ground transportation.

The most important source of wealth for the seven cities mentioned in Revelation was the manufacture of textiles. At Ephesus there were prosperous guilds of wool-workers and cloak dealers. Smyrna was famous for its purple garments, and Sardis was a leader in the manufacture of carpets and dyes. Philadelphia, Thyatira and Laodicea each produced tapestries, garments and textile luxuries that went to cities throughout the Roman world.[34] In addition to textiles, Asia produced and exported pottery on a large scale.[35] A leather industry thrived, and Pergamum manufactured world-famous parchment. Ephesus, Sardis and Smyrna all made perfumes for the world market, and several cities of the region were noted for their metal-working in gold or silver (cf. Acts 19.23-27).

In addition to producing its own products for the Empire, Asia played a vital role in collecting trade taxes for Rome. A long first-century inscription from Ephesus records the 'customs law of Asia, for import and export over land and by sea' for products coming from Cappadocia, Galatia and Bithynia. The document, endorsed by the Roman Senate,

33. For a general overview of resources and industry in Asia, see Magie, *Roman Rule*, I, pp. 34-52, and M.P. Charlesworth, *Trade Routes and Commerce of the Roman Empire* (Cambridge: Cambridge University Press, 1926; repr. Chicago: Ares Publishers, 1974), pp. 76-96.

34. Great weaving centers, such as Laodicea, Tarsus and Alexandria produced luxury garments for export that cost up to twenty times as much as those made for the poorest classes. Jones, *The Roman Economy*, pp. 352-53.

35. On pottery, leather, perfume and metal-working industries, see Magie, *Roman Rule*, I, pp. 49-50.

authorizes Asian tax farmers to collect revenues of two and a half percent on all products exported from the region. Smyrna and Ephesus are among ports where ships from Asia Minor could stop to pay the tax. The privileged relationship merchants had with Rome, particularly in cultic matters, is evident in the provision that 'no one is liable to pay tax for whatever he carries on behalf of the people of Rome; nor for whatever he transports or conveys for religious purposes'.[36]

3. *The Spoils of Conquered Nations*

Rome consumed more than its share of resources from the Empire, and entrepreneurs from the East often helped produce the goods and ferry them to Italy.[37] The appetite of Rome for certain agricultural products oriented the provinces toward an export market rather than internal needs. Asia Minor, for example, produced great quantities of olive oil[38] and wine for export to Rome and other cities throughout the world.[39]

Export crops employed so much local land in Asia Minor that cities of the region regularly had to import grain from Egypt or the Black Sea region.[40] Provincials who did not own financial interest in shipping or agriculture paid for this arrangement in the form of higher prices for

36. H. Engelmann and D. Knibbe, 'Das Zollgesetz der Provinz Asia: Eine neue Inschrift aus Ephesos', *Epigraphica Anatolica* 14 (1989), par. 1-9, 25. Cited in F. Meijer and O.V. Nijf, *Trade, Transport and Society in the Ancient World: A Sourcebook* (London: Routledge, 1992), pp. 80-81.

37. Rostovtzeff notes that even after Rome asserted control over the East, merchants from Asia Minor, Syria and Egypt dominated affairs of trade. 'They retained their position as countries of transit, and their role as carriers, for the trade with Iran, India, and China', Hellenistic World, II, p. 1021.

38. T.R.S. Broughton, 'Asia Minor under the Empire, 27 BC–337 AD', in T. Frank (ed.), *An Economic Survey of Ancient Rome*, IV (4 vols.; Baltimore: Johns Hopkins, 1938), pp. 593-902 (611).

39. Broughton cites dozens of ancient references to the quality of Asian wines and their importance as an export, 'Asia Minor', pp. 609-11. *Periplus Maris Erythraei*, a first-century guide for pilots and merchants traveling to the Far East, reports Mediterranean wines went to Africa and India. See L. Casson, *The Ancient Mariners* (Princeton: Princeton University Press, 2nd edn, 1991), pp. 203-205.

40. Tralles, Samos, Priene and Miletus were among places that had to import grain. Broughton, 'Asia Minor', p. 607. Magie says 'the produce of a city's territory barely sufficed for the needs of its inhabitants, and in the event of the failure of a harvest it became necessary to import grain from elsewhere. This process was not only expensive but often difficult'. Magie, *Roman Rule*, I, p. 580.

food staples.[41] When residents of Prusa threatened to riot because grain prices were so high, Dio Chrysostom insisted he had no grain to put on the market. 'I rarely, if ever, have sold grain', he said, 'even when the harvest is unusually productive'. He claimed he never even had enough grain for his own needs, since 'the income from my land is derived exclusively from wine and cattle'.[42]

The primary destination of provincial exports was Rome,[43] the city that 'lived luxuriously' (Rev. 18.7).[44] Seneca, Nero's court philosopher, was appalled by Roman consumption run riot. He called down curses 'upon the wretches whose luxury overleaps the bounds of an Empire that already stirstoo much envy'.[45] He decried the Roman penchant for expensive delicacies that generated much of the international trade. 'What need of commerce *(Quid mercaturis)?*' he demanded. 'Why do you launch your ships?... Why do you pile riches on riches?'[46] Even the grain traffic disturbed Seneca.

41. Broughton says the 'inclusion of Asia in Domitian's edict forbidding the planting of vines indicates...that it was still producing wine at the expense of other food supplies for an export market...', 'Asia Minor', p. 877. Pliny, reflecting an aristocratic viewpoint, asserts the grain traffic was benign. He cites 'prices agreed between buyer and seller; hence, without causing starvation elsewhere, we have plenty here in Rome', *Pan.* 29.5. Of this statement Wengst says Pliny 'deceives himself: "abundance here and lack nowhere" applied at any time only to the upper classes', *Pax Romana*, 185.

42. Dio Cassius, *Hist. Rom.* 46.8.

43. The *Monte Testaccio* ('Mount Potsherd') near the docks at Rome, formed by millions of broken oil and wine jars from the provinces, suggests the size of the city's appetite for imports. The mound is about 850 meters in circumference and 35 meters high. While many of the jars date from the second and third centuries CE, they confirm that Rome became increasingly dependent on provincial imports. See L. Richardson, Jr, *A New Topographical Dictionary of Ancient Rome* (Baltimore: Johns Hopkins University Press, 1992), p. 380, and T. Frank, 'Notes on Roman Commerce', *JRS* 27 (1937), pp. 72-79. For a general discussion of Rome's lavish consumption, see Wengst, *Pax Romana*, pp. 31-35.

44. The word ἐστρηνίσεν ('live in luxury' or 'live sensually') is a verbal form of στρῆνος ('sensuality, luxury'), which in Rev. 18.3 is what generates wealth for the merchants, BAGD, p. 771; cf. 2 Kgs 19.28 (LXX). Sweet says the word στρῆνος is 'closer to hubris than lewdness'; it is 'arrogant power which enabled the merchants of Rome and Asia Minor to grow fat at the expense of peasant and townsman'. Sweet, *Revelation*, p. 268.

45. Seneca, *Epist. Mor.* 10.2.

46. Seneca, *De Consolatione ad Helviam* 10.5-7. Seneca makes these comments in a caustic passage lambasting Romans for wasting huge resources to

> How long shall we continue to fill with grain the market-places of our great
> [Italian] cities? How long must the people gather it in for us? How long
> shall many ships convey the requisites for a single meal, bring them from
> no single sea?[47]

He wondered if nature gave Romans such insatiable bellies that they
should 'outdo the hugest and most voracious animals in greed'.[48] He
condemned the sumptuous lifestyle of people in Rome, lamenting that
'an exhibition all too lavish is made of the spoils of conquered nations'.[49]

4. *The Rise of Provincials*

Rome may have devoured much of what it controlled, but it also gave
opportunity for accommodating provincials to improve their economic
or political status.[50] Claudius provided high-profile examples of this by
entrusting key imperial offices to freedmen from the East.[51] Nero continued the trend, consolidating his power by courting provincial elites.

bring exotic foods from the ends of the Empire.

47. Seneca, *Epist. Mor.* 60.2-3.

48. Seneca, *Epist. Mor.* 60.3.

49. Seneca, *Epist. Mor.* 87.41. Pliny the Elder says Roman opulence derived
directly from subjugated nations: 'It was the conquest of Asia that first introduced
luxury into Italy'. Pliny, *Nat. Hist.* 33.148. In a stratified imperial society, however,
only a small part of the population ever lived in luxury. K. Hopkins concludes that,
even in Rome, the 'poor were miserably poor... Many, perhaps even most, people
lived near the level of minimum subsistence'. 'Roman Trade, Industry, and Labor', in
Grant and Kitzinger (eds.), *Civilization of the Ancient Mediteranean*, I, p. 771.

50. Most visibly this was true of political leaders who cooperated with Rome. Dio
Cassius tells how Claudius 'restored Commagene to Antiochus', sent Mithridates the
Iberian 'home again to resume his throne', and granted to another Mithridates the
kingdom of Bosporus. Claudius 'enlarged the domain of Agrippa of Palestine...and
to his brother Herod he gave the rank of praetor and a principality'. *Hist. Rom.*
60.8.1-3.

51. Magie, *Roman Rule*, I, p. 540. M. Rostovtzeff, *The Social and Economic
History of the Roman Empire*, I (Oxford: Clarendon Press, 2nd edn, 1957), pp. 82-
83. Suetonius ridiculed the way Claudius depended on his freedmen: 'Wholly under
the control of these [freedmen] and of his wives...he played the part, not of a prince,
but of a servant, lavishing honours, the command of armies, pardons or punishments,
according to the interests of each of them, or even their wish or whim...', *Claud.* 29.
Tacitus despised the way persons of low estate could rise to power: 'in evil times even
freedmen take part in government', he lamented, *Hist.* 1.76. Such freedmen, in some
level of the imperial bureaucracy, might be among those Paul referred to as 'saints...
of the Emperor's household' (Phil. 4.22).

Usually these were equestrians who filled imperial and provincial offices recently vacated by the shrinking senatorial class. (Under Nero families of the senatorial order had fewer children, and their numbers dropped precipitously because of the Emperor's mistreatment).[52]

During the entire Flavian period (69–96 CE), an increasing number of Easterners held imperial offices. Under Titus and Domitian the first Easterners served as Roman proconsuls,[53] and in 92 CE a man from Asia became the first citizen from an eastern province and not of Italian descent to serve as consul.[54] Beginning in 98 CE with Trajan (born in Spain), provincials sometimes even replaced Italians as Emperor. Wealth and power remained in the hands of a small group, but the composition of that group changed radically as provincials of modest background moved into social and political positions once reserved for Roman aristocrats.[55] Provincials ambitious for power or wealth in the imperial society looked to their successful and well-placed countrymen for friendship and assistance.[56]

At Rome the rise of provincials embittered Juvenal, who satirized people of humble origin in positions of power.

> ...let the Tribunes wait their turn; let money carry the day; let the sacred office give way to one who came but yesterday with whitened feet into our city.[57]

The latter phrase is a sarcastic reference to chalk marks on the feet of imported slaves. So many Easterners flooded Rome that Juvenal declared, 'For years now the Syrian Orontes has poured its sewerage into our native Tiber'.[58]

52. Rostovtzeff, *Roman Empire*, I, pp. 101-103.

53. B. Levick, 'Domitian and the Provinces', *Latomus* 41 (1982), p. 62. B.W. Jones, *Domitian and the Senatorial Order* (Philadelphia: American Philosophical Society, 1979), pp. 28-29.

54. The man was Tiberius Julius Celsus Polemaianos. Friesen, *Twice Neokoros*, p. 159.

55. By the early third century Italians had lost their absolute majority in both the senatorial and equestrian orders. P. Garnsey and R. Saller, *The Roman Empire: Economy, Society and Culture* (Berkeley: University of California Press, 1987), p. 9. For further discussion of upward mobility in the first century, see Broughton, 'Asia Minor', p. 745; Meeks, *First Urban Christians*, p. 14; and F. Millar, *The Emperor in the Roman World* (London: Gerald Duckworth, 1977), pp. 290-91.

56. R.P. Saller, *Personal Patronage Under the Early Empire* (Cambridge: Cambridge University Press, 1982), p. 187.

57. Juvenal, *Sat.* 1.109-111.

58. Juvenal, *Sat.* 3.62.

Juvenal ridiculed immigrants from Asia Minor, including those from the island of Samos and the cities of Tralles and Alabanda near Ephesus. Newcomers from these backwaters were disgustingly ambitious, 'all ready to worm their way into the houses of the great and become their masters'.[59] Easterners threatened the social status of well-bred Romans: 'Is a man to sign his name before me', Juvenal asked, 'and recline upon a couch above mine, who has been wafted to Rome by the wind which brings us our [plums] and our figs?'[60]

Similarly, Plutarch sarcastically speaks of ambitious provincials from Chios, Galatia or Bithynia

> ...who are not content with whatever portion of either repute or power among their own fellow-countrymen has fallen to their lot, but weep because they do not wear the patrician shoe; yet if they do wear it, they weep because they are not yet Roman praetors; if they are praetors, because they are not consuls; and if consuls, because they were proclaimed, not first, but later.[61]

Participation in the imperial cult seems to have eased the advancement of ambitious provincials at Ephesus, as illustrated by the career of a certain Tiberius Claudius Aristio. We first know of this man's rise to provincial office from inscriptions related to inauguration of the new imperial cult temple in 89/90 CE. After this, Aristio's name appears in many other Ephesian inscriptions. He apparently held nearly every major civic office in the city,[62] and Pliny referred to him as 'the leading citizen of Ephesus [*princeps Ephesiorum*], popular for his generosity and politically harmless'.[63]

5. *Principal Routes of Upward Mobility*

As opportunities for advancement of elites appeared at the top of the imperial structure, doors opened for ordinary provincials as well. A

---

59. Juvenal, *Sat.* 3.69-72.

60. Juvenal, *Sat.* 3.81-83.

61. Plutarch, *Mor.* 470c.

62. Friesen, *Twice Neokoros*, p. 162.

63. Pliny, *Ep.* 6.31.3. The description of Aristio as 'politically harmless' (*innoxie*) probably means he presented absolutely no challenge or threat to the prevailing imperial ideology. As *princeps* of Ephesus, Aristio was at the pinnacle of a local power structure just like the Emperor was *princeps* at the pinnacle an Empire.

humble provincial could ascend the social and political pyramid by two main avenues.[64]

(1) Freeborn men could enter the Roman military service, acquire citizenship[65] or even equestrian status, and use that as a springboard to higher office.[66]

(2) Anyone—including freedmen—could amass enough wealth through business to gain status by purchase of municipal office and a generous display of donations (λειτουργοί) to the city.[67]

Either strategy enhanced socio-economic standing and increased opportunities for a provincial's children. By the time of Nero, many equestrians and even senators were descendants of slaves.[68] These people did not rise to privilege unassisted; they had learned how to access a vast network of reciprocal relationships that pervaded Roman society throughout the Mediterranean. They also were savvy enough to participate

64. P. Petit, *Pax Romana* (Berkeley: University of California Press, 1967), p. 175. Garnsey and Saller, *The Roman Empire*, p. 124.

65. A.N. Sherwin-White describes the 'over-rapid extension of Roman privileges in the provinces' beginning with the reign of Claudius and continuing throughout the first century. *Roman Society and Roman Law in the New Testament* (Oxford: Oxford University Press, 1963), p. 173. Luke illustrates how a military man, amassing enough finances, could gain citizenship (Acts 22.28).

66. See Garnsey and Saller, *Roman Empire*, pp. 23, 124, and G. La Piana, 'Foreign Groups in Rome during the First Centuries of the Empire', *HTR* 20 (1927), p. 222.

67. Dio Cassius, writing about the reign of Claudius, says many people applied to the Emperor for citizenship or bought it from the imperial freedmen. Citizenship had many benefits, and 'the privilege was at first sold only for large sums'. Soon, however, it became 'cheapened by the facility with which it could be obtained'. Dio Cassius, *Hist. Rom.* 60.17.5-6. Garnsey and Saller note the irony that freedmen often had better prospects for social advancement than did the humble freeborn. 'Insofar as profits could be made in commerce and manufacture, the more enterprising members of this group were well placed to make them, their masters having given them the incentive, the degree of independence, the initial capital and frequently the training that was required', Garnsey and Saller, *Roman Empire*, 124. Thompson says the system of λειτουργοί (public service) helped provincial cities, since 'opportunities in the imperial service stimulated wealthy provincials to serve their cities in order to gain recognition by the Emperor and to be promoted into the imperial ranks', *Revelation: Apocalypse and Empire*, p. 157.

68. Tacitus, *Ann.* 13.27. See J.H. D'Arms, *Commerce and Social Standing in Ancient Rome* (Cambridge, MA: Harvard University Press, 1981), pp. 139-40; Lewis and Reinhold, *Roman Civilization*, II, p. 125; and R. Meiggs, *Roman Ostia* (Oxford: Oxford University Press, 1973), p. 222.

enthusiastically in the new religious expression of loyalty to the Empire. Paul Zanker says,

> As in Rome, wealthy freedmen in the provinces used the imperial cult to win for themselves public recognition and honors... For such 'social climbers', the need for recognition in society was of course especially great, and they were among the first to seize upon the new opportunities.[69]

6. *Vestiges of the Patronage System*

The genius of Roman rule was an ability to make more friends than enemies, even among subject peoples. Some Jews recognized the value of friendship with Rome as early as the second century BCE. Judas Maccabeus 'heard of the fame of the Romans, that they were very strong and were well-disposed toward all who made alliance with them, that they pledged friendship to those who came to them' (1 Macc. 8.1). Augustus raised to an art this pattern of building Empire through reciprocal relationship.

> [Augustus] united the kings with whom he was in alliance by mutual ties, and was very ready to propose or favour intermarriages or friendships among them. He never failed to treat them all with consideration as integral parts of the Empire... and he brought up the children of many of them and educated them with his own.[70]

Not all subsequent Emperors were as skillful at such diplomacy as Augustus, but the same general strategy prevailed.

Roman culture of the first century was class-conscious, with well-defined strata of wealth and social status. Three aristocratic orders held preeminence, and their members filled imperial offices across the Empire.[71] These were:

> SENATORS: An elite order, several hundred families of prestigious birth who had a census (net worth) of at least one million sestertii. Their legal mark of privilege was the toga with a broad purple stripe.

> EQUESTRIANS: A few thousand freeborn men with a census of at least 400,000 sestertii. Members of this order held important military and

---

69. P. Zanker, *The Power of Images in the Age of Augustus* (Ann Arbor: University of Michigan Press, 1988), p. 316.

70. Suetonius, *Aug.* 48.

71. The following summary is adapted from Garnsey and Saller, *Roman Empire*, pp. 112-18.

administrative positions throughout the Empire. Most were local notables, permitted by law to wear a golden ring and a narrow purple stripe on the toga.

DECURIONS: Thousands of local aristocrats who served as town councillors or as minor officials in the imperial administration. Their census requirement was about 100,000 sestertii. Sons of freedmen could aspire to enter this order.

The Emperor and the Roman Senate retained authority to admit candidates to any of these three orders.

An elaborate pyramid of patron-client relations was the 'glue' that enabled these orders to relate to each other and to govern the rest of the Empire. At the top, the Emperor presided alone as *princeps*, or 'first citizen'.[72] Below him were the Roman Senate and the senatorial order, members of which often served as provincial governors or other high officials. Provincial rulers ('kings of the earth' in Revelation) were at the pinnacle of regional social pyramids.[73] Under their authority were regional and municipal assemblies, comprised of equestrians and decurions. These provincial elites, in turn, entered into reciprocal relationship with people of lower status: the freeborn, freedmen and slaves.

John of Patmos was aware of class stratification, and in one sentence

72. A letter of Claudius to the Alexandrians (c. 41 CE) illustrates the role of the Emperor as prime patron. Claudius names and acknowledges a list of local elites who formed an embassy to him. Addressing residents of Alexandria, Claudius says these men came to Rome 'directing my attention to your good will toward us'. In particular, Claudius says 'you are by nature reverent toward the Emperors' and 'have taken a warm interest—*warmly reciprocated* [my emphasis]—in my house... Wherefore I gladly accepted the honors given to me by you' and 'I agree to the erection by you...in their several places of the statues of myself and my family'. Claudius then denies permission for residents of Alexandria to appoint a high priest and build a temple in his honor. (Subsequent Emperors were not so modest!) It is significant for this study that people of Alexandria *wanted* to establish an imperial cult of the living Emperor. (There already was a cult in Egypt for deceased Emperors.) In response, Claudius confirms various privileges granted by previous Emperors, and adds new ones—including citizenship for select groups. See, British Museum Papyrus No. 1,912; translation adapted from LCL by Lewis and Reinhold, *Roman Civilization*, II, p. 366.

73. 'In their official capacities governors could help provincials secure citizenship, offices and honours from Rome, and they could also make administrative and legal decisions in their favour.' Governors received gifts (bribes?) from wealthy provincials, as well as support in the event of prosecution for maladministration while in office. Garnsey and Saller, *Roman Empire*, pp. 151-52.

actually names four recognizable categories of the imperial social order.[74] The diagram in Figure 2 names principal social groups of the Empire, with corresponding Greek words John uses in Rev. 6.15. Power, legal status, social status and (usually) wealth increased with each step up the pyramid. Society functioned smoothly, so long as every participant entered into reciprocal relationship with the more powerful above and the less powerful below.[75]

Pliny understood how the pyramid worked, with the Emperor providing benefits for the whole world. On the anniversary of Trajan's accession to power, Pliny wrote to the Emperor,

> We have celebrated with due solemnity the day on which the security of the human race was happily transferred to your care, commending our public vows and thanksgiving to the gods to whom we owe your authority.[76]

While Pliny ascribes the Emperor's ultimate source of authority (*imperium*) to 'the gods', John of Patmos says Roman imperial authority (ἐξουσία) came from Satan (Rev. 13.2).

'Friendship' in the Social Pyramid

The Roman patronage system, which reached classic form during the Republic, was 'an exchange relationship between [people] of unequal status'.[77] Such reciprocity was common in the first-century Roman world, even though the actual terms 'patron' and 'client' gradually diminish in literature and inscriptions of the era.[78] Social convention

74. The presence of the Emperor was ubiquitous in John's thought and social world, even though John does not actually name him in Rev. 6.15. The Emperor appears variously as a head of the beast (Rev. 13.3), the beast itself (17.8) or a king (17.9-11).

75. Pliny was ready to help friends climb the social pyramid, but had no patience for egalitarian ideas. In writing to Tiro, an administrator in the province of Baetica, Pliny affirms the man's tact in 'making every honest man your friend, and winning the affection of the humble without losing the regard of their superiors'. Pliny adds, 'I meant to congratulate you on the way in which you preserve the distinctions of class and rank; once these are thrown into confusion and destroyed, nothing is more unequal than the resultant "equality".' *Ep.* 9.5.

76. Pliny, *Ep.* 10.102.

77. Saller, *Personal Patronage,* p. 8. Cf. Garnsey and Saller, *Roman Empire,* pp. 152-53.

78. As late as 190 CE, however, an inscription put up by the Association of Laborers and Rag Dealers at Regium, Italy, named a certain Tutilius Julianus as patron of the organization. *CIL,* XI, 970. Cf. Lewis and Reinhold, *Roman Civilization,* II, p. 276.

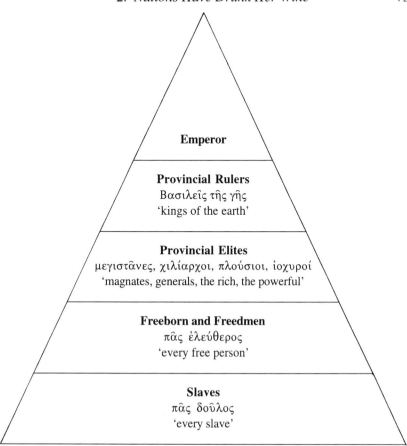

Figure 2. Diagram of principal social classes in the Roman Empire, showing the hierarchy of power from Emperor to slave. Corresponding Greek terms (here with English translation) appear in Rev. 6.15. Some freedmen and freeborn advanced upward, either through the military or through commerce. Former slaves, because their masters may have provided training and financial backing, sometimes enjoyed greater advancement than freeborn individuals who lacked such a background.

during the Principate preferred the language of 'friendship', perhaps as a way to protect the dignity of a client.[79]

79. Saller says 'in none of the major prose writers of the post-Augustan Principate (Seneca, Tacitus, Pliny the Younger and Suetonius) is *patronus* used in the general sense of an "influential protector"'. However, the term *patronus* appears frequently among inscriptions from North Africa, meaning 'protector' or 'benefactor'. *Personal Patronage*, pp. 9-10. Several references in the New Testament seem to present patron-client relations in the language of friendship. Jesus tells of a host honoring his 'friend' by seating him in the place of honor at a banquet (Lk. 14.7-11).

Benefits proffered by prominent people to their 'friends' might include business contracts, appointment to political office, legal services, employment, money gifts or dinner invitations.[80] In return, recipients extended political support, gathered at their patron's door for the daily greeting *(salutatio)*,[81] applauded his speeches in court or otherwise made public display of gratitude.[82] Gratitude apparently motivated numerous inscriptions found at Ephesus and elsewhere, in which individuals honor their benefactors.[83]

Seneca wrote several works on how patron and client should exchange 'benefits'.[84] The philosopher himself came from a provincial family in Spain that knew how to advance in the social pyramid: his brother Gallio became proconsul of Achaia (Acts 18.12), and his aunt married the governor of Egypt. While Emperor Nero was still a child, Seneca was his tutor and later served as co-regent of the Empire.

Jesus instructed his followers to disregard the normal pattern of reciprocity by inviting dinner guests who 'cannot repay you' rather than 'friends', relatives, or rich neighbors (Lk. 14.12-14). When Jesus was on trial before Pilate, the Jews used Pilate's client relationship with Rome to press for a guilty verdict: 'If you release this man, you are no friend of the Emperor' (Jn 19.12). Luke reports that Paul had 'friends' among high officials at Ephesus (Acts 19.31). James labels some of his readers 'adulterers' since they do not realize that 'whoever wishes to be a friend of the world becomes an enemy of God' (Jas 4.4). Such 'friendship' may have included entanglements of the patronage system.

80. Pliny, for example, writes, 'it was I who persuaded the Emperor to raise Sextus to senatorial rank and grant him a quaestorship, and it is on my nomination that he is now standing for the office of tribune', *Ep.* 2.9; cf. 1 Kgs 4.5, and Bel 2.

81. The *salutatio* was a time when 'clients and lesser friends of the great and powerful congregated at the doors of their patrons in the early morning to pay their respects in return for food, money, clothing and other favours'. Garnsey and Saller, *Roman Empire*, p. 122.

82. Saller, *Personal Patronage*, p. 29.

83. At Comum, Italy, the city itself apparently put up the (now fragmentary) inscription that survives honoring Pliny the Younger. The inscription probably stood over public baths in the city, since it acknowledges that Pliny in his will gave money to build the baths, along with 300,000 sestertii for furnishing them and 200,000 for their upkeep. He also gave huge sums of money to support a hundred of his freedmen, to provide an annual dinner for people of the city, and to support the library. *Pliny: Letters and Panegyricus*, II (LCL; London: Heinemann, 1969), appendix A.1, pp. 549-51.

84. He summarizes the patronage code by quoting a popular phrase, *'ille illi gratiam rettulit'* (Seneca, *Ep. Mor.* 81.9). R.M. Gummere (LCL) translates this as 'A. has made a return for the favour bestowed by B'.

Seneca makes it clear there is an implicit contract between patron and client. It is disgraceful for recipients of favors to imagine such benefits 'are currency which they can use without interest'.[85] Strictly speaking, the benefactor should give with no thought of a return. In practice, though, the self-respecting recipient will go to almost any length to show appreciation and loyalty: 'you must be willing to go into exile, or to pour forth your blood, or to undergo poverty'.[86]

Shortly after the death of Domitian, Plutarch advanced the same idea in an essay called 'Precepts of Statecraft'.[87] He directed this work to a man from Sardis, illustrating how a man of power and influence in the Empire expected his fellow Easterners to pay attention to intricacies of the classic patronage system.[88] A native of Greece, Plutarch himself was a provincial who ascended through the patronage system. Diplomatic assignments took him to Rome, where he made friends among prominent politicians. He acquired Roman citizenship and perhaps consular rank under Trajan.[89]

Plutarch says an aspiring municipal statesman who attaches himself to a good patron will rise to power 'just as ivy rises by twining itself about a strong tree'.[90] Once in power, the statesman must reward clients in many areas of society:

> Hand over to one friend a case at law which will bring in a good fee…to another introduce a rich man who needs legal oversight and protection, and help another to get some profitable contract or lease.[91]

Similarly, Pliny illustrates how the spoils of power produced privilege for well-connected Roman subjects. He writes to Priscus, a legate of the Roman military:

85. Seneca, *Ep. Mor.* 81.18.

86. Seneca, *Ep. Mor.* 81.27. Seneca paid a high price for his loyalty to the demented Nero. In 65 CE Seneca committed suicide, anticipating violence from the young Emperor. Tacitus, *Ann.* 14.52-56, 15.63; Suetonius, *Nero* 35.5.

87. Plutarch, *Praecepta Gerendae Republicae*. Plutarch (815 D) refers to events that took place 'recently under Domitian'.

88. The man was Menemachus, whose 'countryman' was Pardalas of Sardis. Plutarch, *Praecepta*, 813 F, 825 D. If Menemachus was not from Sardis itself, he certainly was from the province of Asia.

89. The Suda lexicon, a Greek dictionary from c. 1000 CE states Trajan bestowed upon Plutarch the high rank of ex-consul. F.W. Walbank, 'Plutarch', *Encyclopædia Britannica*, XIV (15th edn, 1978), pp. 578-80.

90. Plutarch, *Praecepta* 805 F.

91. Plutarch, *Praecepta* 809 A.

> Your command of a large army gives you a plentiful source of benefits to
> confer, and...your tenure has been long enough for you to have provided
> for your own friends. Turn to mine—they are not many.[92]

Pliny then describes a dear friend and requests that Priscus 'grant him
the highest office in your power'. A combination of factors makes the
friend worthy for such advancement. His father was a distinguished
equestrian, and recently he held a priesthood (of the imperial cult) in
Spain. For this friend, Pliny already has obtained from Emperor Nerva
the privileges granted to parents of three children. Adulation of the
Emperor was part of Pliny's own rise to influence: he was a priest of
the imperial cult at the Italian city of Comum.[93]

Emperor as Prime Benefactor

A vast network of relationships, emanating from the person of the
Emperor, distributed benefits *(beneficia)* 'downward' all the way to the
most humble freedman or slave. Likewise a steady flow of gratitude
(gratia) welled 'upward' from the lower social classes, bestowing loyalty
and honor upon benefactors. A sense of loyalty to the Emperor ran
deep in Asia Minor, as illustrated by this oath taken in 3 BCE in northern
Asia Minor.

> In the third year from the twelfth consulship of the Emperor Caesar
> Augustus, son of a god...the following oath was taken by the inhabitants
> of Paphlagonia and the Roman businessmen dwelling among them: 'I
> swear by Jupiter, Earth, Sun, by all the gods and goddesses, and by
> Augustus himself, that I will be loyal to Caesar Augustus and to his children
> and descendants all my life in word, in deed, and in thought, regarding as
> friends whomever they so regard...that in defense of their interests I will
> spare neither body, soul, life, nor children...'[94]

---

92. Pliny, *Ep.* 2.13.

93. An inscription from Comum honoring Pliny the Younger lists among his
offices and accomplishments *FL DIVI T AUG,* meaning *'flamen divi Titi'* or
'[imperial cult] priest of the deified Emperor Titus', *Pliny: Letters and Panegyricus,*
II (LCL), p. 553, appendix A.3.

94. *OGIS,* 532; *ILS,* 8781. Cited by Lewis and Reinhold, *Roman Civilization,* II,
p. 34. Augustus himself introduced this oath, and it 'became a standard ritual of the
Principate', *Roman Civilization,* II, p. 34. A similar inscription from 11 CE at
Narbonne reads: 'Vow taken to the divine spirit of Augustus by the populace of the
Narbonensians in perpetuity: "May it be good, favorable and auspicious to the
Emperor Caesar Augustus, son of a god, father of his country, *pontifex maximus...*
and to the colonists and residents of [this colony]...who have bound themselves to
worship his divine spirit in perpetuity!"' *CIL,* XII, 4333; *Roman Civilization,* II, p. 62.

Nearly a century before John wrote Revelation, Roman businessmen and other provincials in Asia Minor pledged comprehensive loyalty to their foremost patron.[95]

Augustus and subsequent Emperors usually were not slow to shower benefits upon loyal clients in Asia Minor. Augustus restored financial privileges to the temple of Artemis at Ephesus.[96] Tiberius gave financial assistance to Sardis, Philadelphia and Ephesus after the earthquake of 17 CE.[97] Claudius constructed an aqueduct at Sardis,[98] and exempted Cos from taxation in honor of his personal physician (a native of the island).[99] Nero dredged the harbor at Ephesus,[100] and Flavian Emperors significantly improved roads in Asia Minor.[101] Domitian sponsored numerous public works, including a stadium at Laodicea, an aqueduct at Smyrna and a rebuilt wall around the imperial temple precinct at Ephesus.[102] Countless provincial freedmen received Roman citizenship in the first century. If they were former slaves of the Emperor's household, they often adopted the family name of the Emperor who made their new status possible. Hence inscriptions and literature of the era reveal a large number of people named Claudius and Flavius.[103]

Aristocratic Romans expected these and other signs of gratitude or loyalty from provincials for benefits provided by Rome. In a speech recorded by Tacitus, a Roman officer tells the people of Gaul: 'If the Romans are driven out—which Heaven forbid—what will follow except universal war among all peoples?' Provincials would be wise 'not to

---

95. A similar oath taken in 37 CE 'by the council and the Roman businessmen among us and the people of Assus' in Asia Minor reads: 'We swear by Zeus the Savior and by the deified Caesar Augustus…to be loyal to Gaius Caesar Augustus…' The authors unapologetically solicit the new Emperor's patronage, stating their intention to send an embassy to Rome 'to seek an audience and congratulate him, and beg him to remember the city [of Assus] with solicitude, as he personally promised…', Lewis and Reinhold, *Roman Civilization*, II, p. 87.

96. Broughton, 'Asia Minor', p. 679.

97. Broughton, 'Asia Minor', p. 712.

98. Broughton, 'Asia Minor', p. 723.

99. The Coans responded by giving Claudius the names 'Zeus' and 'Saviour', and by establishing a festival in his honor. Magie, *Roman Rule*, I, p. 542.

100. Tacitus, *Ann.* 16.23.

101. Charlesworth, *Trade Routes*, pp. 81, 257; Magie, *Roman Rule*, I, p. 570; Petit, *Pax Romana*, p. 182.

102. Magie, *Roman Rule*, I, p. 578.

103. Lewis and Reinhold, *Roman Civilization*, II, p. 130.

prefer defiance and ruin to obedience and security'.[104]

There are indications that Roman rule in fact was quite popular even among impoverished provincials. Rome stabilized provincial society, and benefited lower classes by requiring wealthy elites (including Roman citizens) to take responsibility for local municipal services ('liturgies') in their cities of residence. Occasionally disenfranchised people—such as John of Patmos—cried out against the masters of the Mediterranean. But such protests came from a small minority, and stand over against 'a mountain of indirect proof of the popularity of the Empire among the lower classes'.[105]

Jesus knew that patronage relationships pervaded the Roman world, and served notice that the kingdom of God would not conform to such a status-based system. 'The kings of the Gentiles lord it over them,' he told his followers, 'and those in authority over them are called benefactors. But not so with you; rather the greatest among you must become like the youngest, and the leader like one who serves' (Lk. 22.25-26).[106]

7. Economic Opportunity for Provincials

For many provincials, the greatest benefit provided by Rome was an opportunity for prosperity in a stable society. Asia Minor in the first century CE had a flourishing economy,[107] part of a commercial boom

104. Tacitus, *Hist.* 4.74.

105. R. MacMullen, *Enemies of the Roman Order* (Cambridge, MA: Harvard University Press, 1966), p. 166. Thompson rejects the argument of Rostovtzeff (*Roman Empire*, I, p. 117) that class conflict between rich and poor reached crisis proportions in first-century Asia Minor. Thompson probably is correct that class conflict was not the primary factor motivating John of Patmos to condemn Rome. He overstates the case, however, in saying 'serious social distinctions and class conflicts emerged after the end of the first century CE', *Revelation: Apocalypse and Empire*, p. 155. Revelation reflects keen perception of 'serious social distinctions' before the end of the first century.

106. Luke's Gospel immediately follows this rejection of the patronage system with Jesus' statement to his followers that 'I confer on you, just as my Father has conferred on me, a kingdom...' (Lk. 22.29). This sounds exactly like the pyramid of patronage so familiar in the Roman world—except for the critical factor that the pyramid in the kingdom of God is *upside-down:* Jesus is among his followers 'as one who serves' (22.27).

107. Rostovtzeff, *Roman Empire*, I, pp. 91-93. Collins summarizes the arguments of S. Walton, R. MacMullen and F.E. Peters, to the effect that the new wealth in Asia Minor was poorly distributed. As a result, 'the poor were more discontented rather

that covered much of the Empire.[108] Evidence for this expanding economy includes a large number of shipwrecks dating from 200 BCE to 200 CE found by underwater archaeologists. During that era there was more seaborne trade in the Mediterranean than ever before, and more than there would be again for the next thousand years.[109]

Dio Chrysostom of Bithynia summarizes the economic and political fortunes of his grandfather, who prospered in the middle of the first century CE. 'He spent on public benefactions all that he had from his father', Dio says, 'and then he acquired a second fortune by his learning and from imperial favour'. Dio never explains what his grandfather's 'learning' was, but is quick to emphasize that imperial connections were helpful in amassing a fortune. Dio's grandfather dutifully played his part in the social and political hierarchy of the Empire: he 'guarded and husbanded' for the people of Prusa 'the goodwill of the Emperor [Claudius?]'.[110]

When John wrote Revelation late in the first century, the economy had accelerated to a new level. The number of Roman merchants in the East began to diminish late in the first century BCE, and provincial entrepreneurs more than filled the void.[111] Commercial magnates from Italy still made enormous profits, but such wealth now spread more widely across the Empire.[112] People from virtually all levels of imperial society crowded into commerce: manufacturers' stamps on clay artifacts bear the names of everybody 'from the Emperor down to obscure people of uncertain status and slaves'.[113] In response to growing commercial demands, there was a 'huge rise' in the volume of silver coins minted under Emperors Vespasian and Titus.[114] Provincial merchants

---

than less'. She says the regional conflict over wealth was a contributing factor to the polemic against Rome in Revelation, especially in ch. 18. Collins, *Crisis and Catharsis*, pp. 88-89, 94.

108. Charlesworth, *Trade Routes*, p. 224.

109. Hopkins, 'Roman Trade, Industry, and Labor', p. 766.

110. Dio Chrysostom, *Or.* 46.4.

111. La Piana, 'Foreign Groups', p. 53. Rostovtzeff, *Roman Empire*, I, p. 169.

112. Petit, *Pax Romana*, p. 85.

113. J. Aubert, *Business Managers in Ancient Rome: A Social and Economic Study of Institores, 200 BC–AD 250* (Leiden: E.J. Brill, 1994), p. 275.

114. K. Hopkins, 'Taxes and Trade in the Roman Empire (200 B.C.–A.D. 400)', *JRS* 70 (1980), p. 115. Production of silver came at enormous human cost in Roman times. Each metric ton probably required five hundred to one thousand man work-years. Hopkins, 'Roman Trade, Industry, and Labor', p. 758.

and middlemen apparently did so well during this era that Emperor Hadrian later felt compelled to rein in their profits.[115]

Christians in the province of Asia found themselves in urban areas that thrived in the imperial economy. Pliny the Elder listed Ephesus, Smyrna, Pergamum, Sardis and Laodicea among the ten leading cities of the province.[116] We get some measure of the wealth of these cities from inscriptions on many buildings constructed or repaired in them during the late first and early second centuries.[117] Ephesus and Smyrna were busy port cities; Laodicea was wealthy enough to rebuild itself without imperial aid after the earthquake of 60 CE.[118]

Ephesus was the official residence of the proconsul, and site of the world-renowned temple of Artemis.[119] Early in the first century CE Strabo already could say Ephesus 'grows daily, and is the largest emporium in Asia this side of the Taurus'.[120] In the mid-second century, Aelius Aristides described Ephesus as 'the common treasury of Asia and her recourse in need'. The city had adequate resources 'to satisfy every mode of life that men can adopt or prefer'.[121]

8. *Role Models of Success*

Inscriptions at Ephesus[122] and Acmonia[123] honoring a certain T. Flavius Montanus illustrate how the climate of economic expansion enabled provincials to enjoy economic as well as social and political advancement. Montanus was not from an old noble family, but apparently became wealthy through trade.[124] He amassed enough fortune to qualify for the

115. At Athens, for example, Hadrian restricted olive oil exports. These had enriched producers and merchants but raised the cost of living for the rest of the populace. At Pergamum he restricted big banks in favor of small traders. Petit, *Pax Romana*, pp. 9, 86.

116. See summary of Pliny's account in Broughton, 'Asia Minor', p. 708.

117. Broughton, 'Asia Minor', 746-57. Magie, *Roman Rule*, I, pp. 582-83.

118. Tacitus, *Ann.* 14.27.

119. The temple of the goddess Artemis had a 'majesty that brought all Asia and the world to worship her', Acts 19.27.

120. Strabo, *Geog.* 14.1.24.

121. Aristides, *To Rome* 23.24.

122. *I. Eph.* 2061.

123. *CIG*, III, 3858e. Cited by W.M. Ramsay, *The Social Basis of Roman Power in Asia Minor* (Aberdeen: Aberdeen University Press, 1941), p. 33.

124. Ramsay, *The Social Basis*, p. 162.

equestrian order, and Domitian made him a Roman citizen in 96 CE. Montanus adopted a Roman surname (Flavius) and crowned his career by serving as high priest of Asia for the imperial cult.

For every provincial who achieved such spectacular success there were many who made only modest gains. Yet enough former merchants had joined the provincial elites to serve as influential role models for their less fortunate countrymen. Aristocratic Greeks and Romans held commerce itself in low esteem,[125] and Roman law restricted the involvement of senators in maritime trade.[126] For non-aristocratic people, however, wealth derived from such trade could provide the leverage necessary to obtain social status.[127]

Lucian and the Lure of Commerce
Lucian's second-century satire *The Ship* outlines a dream of commercial success that must have been shared by thousands of provincials.[128] A Greek named Adimantus imagines the gods bless him with enough

125. Juvenal ridicules the man who spends his 'whole life' on a ship from Asia Minor, 'a poor contemptible trafficker of stinking wares, finding your joy in importing sweet wine from the shores of ancient Crete...', *Sat.* 14.266-71. Philostratus tells how Apollonius chided a youth of noble descent for engaging in trade: '...is there any shame worse than this, for a man who is a citizen of Sparta...to secrete himself in the hold of a ship...thinking of nought but of cargoes and petty bills of lading?', *Life Apoll.* 4.32. Cf. Dio Chrysostom, *Or.* 36.25. These typical aristocratic attitudes were well-entrenched in classical thought long before the Roman Empire. See D'Arms, *Commerce and Social Standing,* pp. 2-7.

126. The *Lex Claudia* of 219–218 BCE 'was designed to render illegal the possession by a senator, or the son of a senator, of any sea-going vessel *(maritimam navem)* of more than 300 amphoras' capacity, the size which was deemed sufficient for carrying the produce of an estate, any form of trade being considered beneath a senator's dignity', Livy 21.63.3-4. This law was still in effect in the third century CE, as attested by the jurist Paulus: 'Senators or their parents, if they are under their authority, are not allowed to collect taxes or to own ships for making profits', *Opinions* 5.28a3. Cited by Meijer and Nijf, *Trade, Transport and Society,* pp. 15-16.

127. People of limited means probably took out loans to get started in the shipping business. K. Hopkins estimates a fully laden grain ship was worth at least 500,000 sestertii—more than the minimum census of an equestrian. Investors probably split risks of such a venture by taking shares in several ships—as in Plutarch, *Parallel Lives,* 'Cato the Elder' 21. 'Roman Trade, Industry, and Labor', p. 758. People who could finance maritime commerce were the rich and the powerful, who benefited from Roman rule and were most likely to be associated with the imperial cult.

128. Lucian, *The Ship*, 11-25.

resources to purchase a large merchant ship. Profits from the vessel, combined with discovery of hidden treasure, allow him to purchase slaves, clothes, carriages, horses, and a fine house in Athens.[129] Financial success brings the marks of social status: 'my dress will be of purple and my life the height of luxury', he chortles. Imaginary wealth boosts him high on a fantasy social ladder: 'Friends will come and ask for favours and they'll all bow down and grovel... Some of them I shall not even look at, but if there is a poor man there, as I was before my treasure, I shall show him favour... But the others, the rich, will choke with envy...'[130]

Adimantus imagines he will serve banquets on golden utensils, since 'silver is cheap and unworthy of me'. The menu will feature pickled fish from Spain, wine from Italy, and peacock from India. Adimantus will enhance his prestige by generous gifts to the people of Athens. These will include a hundred drachmas to every citizen per month, along with 'public theatres and baths to beautify the city'.[131]

Lucian's caricature of the provincial merchant traces general outlines of upward mobility attained through commerce. Merchants such as Adimantus hoped to attain wealth from trade, invest in land, quit commerce, and raise their children as aristocrats.[132] Already in the first century BCE, Cicero spelled out how a person of modest means might use commerce as a springboard to more genteel status.

> Commerce should be considered vulgar if it is a rather small affair. If it is extensive and well-financed, importing many products from all over the world and distributing them to many customers honestly, one should not criticize it severely. In fact, it even seems to deserve the highest respect if a merchant who has had his fill of trade, or I should say is satisfied with his profit, retires from the quayside to his farmhouse and estates, just as he sailed so many times from the sea to a harbour.[133]

129. A sailor on a large merchant vessel tells Adimantus the ship earns its owner 'A minimum of twelve Attic talents' per year. Lucian, *The Ship*, 13.

130. Lucian, *The Ship*, 22.

131. Lucian, *The Ship*, 23-24.

132. T. Frank speaks of freedmen who grew wealthy in commerce, and found 'they must wash their hands of the taints of business in order to acquire any social standing. They changed their names, sold their business, moved out to country villas, bought some books and pictures and passed as gentleman farmers'. T. Frank, *A History of Rome* (New York: Henry Holt, 1923), p. 402.

133. Cicero, *De Officiis* 1.150-52. Cited by Meijer and Nijf, pp. 16-17.

Seneca said a man aspiring to wealth thinks first of trying maritime trade.[134] There is evidence that the strategy worked: in Egypt[135] and Asia Minor[136] shippers became the richest people of the population. By the second century CE these successful provincial entrepreneurs 'very often dominated the social life of their cities and were known to every one not only in the city, but...even throughout the whole province'.[137] Few merchants ever achieved the fabulous wealth of these tycoons.[138] Enough provincials gained status and respectability through trade,[139] however, to provide a role model that others sought to emulate.

Commerce provided one means by which people from lower levels of society—even former slaves—could hope to improve their standing. The bulk of traders during the first century were in fact freedmen, 'or at any rate very small fry'.[140] Plutarch says people commonly appointed their trustworthy slaves as farmers, shippers (ναυκλήρους), merchants (ἐμπόρους), house-stewards and bankers.[141] If such capable slaves attained freedom, they were in a good position to become independent merchants.

Plutarch's comment points to the variety of investments that attracted wealthy aristocrats: farming, shipping, commerce and banking. Even Cato (234–149 BCE), champion of traditional Roman values, found maritime investment an irresistible temptation.

---

134. 'I was already looking about to see some stretch of water on which I might embark for purposes of trade...and some merchandise that I might acquire', Seneca, *Ep. Mor.* 119.5.

135. P. Lampe, *Die stadrömischen Christen in den ersten beiden Jahrhunderten* (Tübingen: Mohr [Siebeck], 1989), p. 205.

136. In analyzing the emerging wealthy class in Lycia, for example, Magie concludes that 'trade by sea appears to have been a principal means of building up such fortunes', Magie, *Roman Rule*, I, p. 538.

137. Rostovtzeff, *Roman Empire*, I, 153.

138. H.W. Pleket, 'Urban Elites and Business in the Greek Part of the Roman Empire', in P. Garnsey, K. Hopkins and C.R. Whittaker (eds.), *Trade in the Ancient Economy* (London: Chatto & Windus, 1983), p. 139.

139. Inscriptions record numerous merchants who achieved social status along with fortune. The sarcophagus of a certain M. Aurelius Alexander Moschianus from Hierapolis (a few miles from Laodicea), e.g., identifies him as a 'purple-seller' and 'town-councillor'. Pleket, 'Urban Elites', p. 141.

140. D'Arms, *Commerce and Social Standing*, p. 15. Ironically, even a large portion of slave traders were themselves freedmen. Pleket, 'Urban Elites', p. 139.

141. Plutarch, *Mor., De Liberis Educandis* 7.

He also used to lend money in what is surely the most disreputable form of speculation, that is the underwriting of ships. Those who wished to borrow money from him were obliged to form a large association, and when this reached the number fifty, representing as many ships, he would take one share in the company. His interests were looked after by Quintio, one of his freedmen, who used to accompany Cato's clients on their voyages and transact their business. In this way he drew a handsome profit, while at the same time spreading his risk and never venturing more than a fraction of his capital.[142]

Because commerce carried a stigma, it was common for aristocrats to follow Cato's example of using agents—slaves or freedmen—to manage business for them.[143]

People of modest means who wanted to operate a major commercial venture needed the support of a wealthy financier. Philostratus (early third century CE) provides a glimpse of the loan arrangements necessary for shippers with limited financial resources:

> ...can you mention any rabble of people more wretched and ill-starred than merchants (ἐμπόρων) and skippers (ναυκλήρων)? In the first place they roam from sea to sea, looking for some market that is badly stocked; and then they sell and buy, associating with factors and brokers, and they put out their own capital at the most unholy rate of interest in their hurry to get back the principal;...but if their gains do not balance their debts they...dash their ships on to the rocks, and make no bones as sailors of robbing others of their substance.[144]

Dio Chrysostom of Bithynia says the estate he inherited from his father included various foreign business ventures, with significant loans outstanding.[145] Commercial financiers such as Dio's family were people who had prospered in the imperial economy; they were part of an elite that usually favored Rome. From that same elite came individuals who could afford to purchase government office or a priesthood in the imperial cult.

9. *Upward Mobility among Jews and Christians*

Although some Jews and Christians resented Roman rule, many others prospered during the first century and made no complaint. Theoretically,

---

142. *Cato the Elder* 21.5-6. Meijer and Nijf, *Trade, Transport and Society*, p. 69.
143. See Aubert, *Business Managers in Ancient Rome*, pp. 1-39.
144. Philostratus, *Life Apoll.* 4.32.
145. Dio Chrysostom, *Or.* 46.6.

the two main avenues of upward mobility—the military and commerce—
were open to them. Members of both religious communities, though,
showed a distinct preference for the latter.

Military Route to Upward Mobility
A dramatic increase in the number of Easterners serving in the Roman
army during the late first and early second centuries suggests the
military was a popular route to upward mobility. Some twenty-three
legions came from eastern provinces in the era of Claudius and Nero.
Within a generation the number had risen to 110, and Easterners were
the largest sector of the military population.[146] There was no conscription; these were volunteers.[147] Some scholars argue that Christians had
little opportunity to join the army, since recruits for the legions had to be
Roman citizens, and few Christians held citizenship. Even if we assume
few Christians were citizens, however, we still must reckon with that fact
that auxiliary troops frequently were slaves and other non-citizens.[148]
   Christians usually avoided military service during this era,[149] in part

146. During the period of Vespasian through Trajan, eastern provinces supplied
110 legions, Italy seventy-three, western provinces ninety, and the Rhine-Danube area
sixty-one. Petit, *Pax Romana*, p. 22. See Rostovtzeff, *Roman Empire*, I, p. 89, and II,
pp. 573-74 n. 8.

147. L.J. Swift says 'involuntary conscription is not attested in the sources before
the fourth century, and anyone who had scruples about a military career could easily
avoid getting involved'. L.J. Swift, *The Early Fathers on War and Military Service*
(Wilmington: Michael Glazier, 1983), p. 27. Domitian made the military more attractive by significantly raising soldiers' pay for the first time since the days of Julius
Caesar. Hannestad, *Roman Art*, p. 136.

148. Evidence of this appears in an edict of Domitian (88–89 CE), which states that
'veteran soldiers among you are to be freed and exempt from all state taxes...that
they, their wives, children and parents...are to be Roman citizens with fullest legal
right'. *ILS*, 9059. Lewis and Reinhold, *Roman Civilization*, II, p. 527. This edict
essentially restates privileges granted to veterans by Octavian in 31 BCE. Cf. Berlin
Papyrus No. 628, in Lewis and Reinhold, *Roman Civilization*, I, p. 392.

149. Aside from Acts 10, there is no evidence of Christian involvement in the
Roman military before the legendary 'Thundering Legion' episode (ca. 173 CE).
Tertullian, *Apol.* 5.6; *Ad Scap.* 4.6; Eusebius, *Hist. Eccl.* 5.4.3-5.5.7; Dio Cassius,
Hist. Rom. 72.8-10; R.H. Bainton, 'The Early Church and War', *HTR* 39 (1946),
pp. 189-212; H.F. von Campenhausen, *Tradition und Leben Kräfte der Kirchenge-
schichte* (Tübingen: J.C.B. Mohr, 1960), pp. 203-15; J.-M. Hornus, *It Is Not Lawful
For Me to Fight* (Scottdale: Herald Press, 1980), p. 129. The Roman centurion
Cornelius became a Christian (Acts 10.1-48), but Luke does not indicate whether

because Jesus instructed his followers to love enemies (Mt. 5.43-46; cf. Rom. 12.20-21) and 'put back' the sword (Mt. 26.52, Jn 18.11).[150] However, an issue other than love of enemies also kept early Christians out of the armed service: the imperial cult and other pagan ceremonies had a prominent role in military life.[151] Officers had to sacrifice and privates had to participate.[152] Tertullian says, 'Roman religion, every bit of it a religion of [military] camps, venerates the standards, swears by the standards, sets the standards before all the gods'.[153] Cults entrenched in the army included those dedicated to the Roman eagle, to images of the Emperor, and to personified virtues such as *Disciplina* and *Virtus*.[154] Already in John's day imperial propaganda elevated loyalty of the troops to high visibility: Roman coins frequently commemorated the

Cornelius stayed in the army. Luke portrays the centurion as a man disposed to worship another human: Cornelius fell at Peter's feet and worshiped him. Peter objected, 'Stand up; I am only a mortal' (Acts 10.26; cf. Add. Est. 13.14, Ep. Jer. 6.7 and Rev. 19.10, 22.8-9). These words had particular meaning for a military man accustomed to worshiping the Emperor.

150. Early church writers who address questions of warfare tend to echo Jesus' teaching on love of enemies. Justin Martyr says 'we who delighted in war, in the slaughter of one another...have in every part of the world converted our weapons of war into implements of peace', *Tryph.* 110.3; cf. *1 Apol.* 39; Irenaeus says Christians are unaccustomed to fighting, and when struck, offer the other cheek (Mt. 5.39), *Adv. Haer.* 4.34.4. Tertullian asks 'how will [a Christian man] war, nay, how will he serve even in peace, without a sword, which the Lord has taken away?' *De Idol.* 19; cf. *De Cor.* 11. See Athenagoras, *Legatio pro Christianis* 1.4; Origen, *Contra Celsum* 7.25; Hippolytus, *Apostolic Tradition* 17-19.

151. Full development of the military religious calendar is evident in the 'Feriale Duranum' document found at Dura-Europos on the Euphrates. Probably from the early third century, the document names over forty annual army festivals, many of them related to the Emperor cult. J. Helgeland, who gives the text in full, says it 'is the conclusion of most scholars that a copy of this document was sent to every unit of the army at least down to the cohort level...', 'Roman Army Religion', *ANRW*, II, 16.2 (1978), p. 1481.

152. Bainton, 'The Early Church and War', pp. 200-201. G.R. Watson states flatly, 'The army religion and the state religion were identical', *The Roman Soldier* (Ithaca: Cornell University Press, 1969), p. 128.

153. Tertullian, *Apol.* 16.8.

154. Watson, *The Roman Soldier*, pp. 127-33. Helgeland says a sacred shrine (*aedes*) stood at the center of every army camp. The shrine housed the legion standards, the regimental savings bank, the eagle, a bust of the Emperor and his image. Helgeland, 'Roman Army Religion', p. 1476, cf. p. 1491.

FIDES EXERCITVVM ('loyalty of the armies').[155]

In the eyes of many Jews[156] and Christians, the imperial army was a bastion of idolatry. A scroll from Qumran declares that Romans ('Kittim') 'sacrifice to their standards and worship their weapons of war'.[157] Such a view was not farfetched: Josephus reports Roman troops, after storming the temple at Jerusalem in 70 CE 'carried their standards (σημαίας) into the temple court and, setting them up opposite the eastern gate, there sacrificed to them'.[158] Tertullian illustrates how Christians resonated with Jewish concern about idolatry. He viewed Roman military standards *(signa)* as pagan idols, and declared the unconditional oath of loyalty to the Emperor unacceptable for Christians.[159]

Representations of the Emperor in the form of medallions often appeared on military standards, along with the Roman eagle or other heraldic animals.[160] Josephus tells how Pontius Pilate once brought 'busts of the Emperor that were attached to military standards' into the city of Jerusalem.[161] Jewish law forbade the making of images,[162] and Josephus

155. Hannestad, *Roman Art*, p. 118.

156. When Tiberius repressed the Jews in Rome and tried to force them into the army as punishment, many 'refused to serve for fear of breaking the Jewish law'. Josephus, *Ant.* 18.3.5 (84). Specifically, Jewish 'superstition' included concern for Sabbath and dietary laws (*Ant.* 14.10.12 [225], 14.10.13 [228], 14.10.14 [231], 14.10.18 [237]).

157. *1QpHab* 6.3-5.

158. Josephus, *War* 6.6.1 (316).

159. Concerning military service, Tertullian wrote 'There is no agreement between the divine and human sacrament, the standard *(signo)* of Christ and the standard *(signo)* of the devil... One soul cannot be due to two masters—God and Caesar', *De Idol.* 19. Elsewhere Tertullian says 'I will not call the Emperor God, either because I do not know how to lie, or because I dare not make fun of him, or because even he himself does not want to be called God', *Apol.* 33.3. An author of the pastoral epistles was aware of the unswerving loyalty demanded in the [Roman] army: 'No one serving in the army gets entangled in everyday affairs; the soldier's aim is to please the enlisting officer', 2 Tim. 2.4. Even though some Christians appeared in the Roman army in the second and third centuries, Emperor worship continued to be a concern. Eusebius tells of a soldier named Marinus, who was denied advancement to the rank of centurion and subsequently executed at Caesarea in Palestine in c. 260 CE because 'he was a Christian and did not sacrifice to the Emperors', *Hist. Eccl.* 7.15.1-3.

160. M. Radin, *The Jews Among the Greeks and Romans* (Philadelphia: Jewish Publication Society, 1915), pp. 280-81. C.H. Kraeling says all Roman military standards 'were in some sense sacred'. C.H. Kraeling, 'The Episode of the Roman Standards at Jerusalem', *HTR* 35 (1942), p. 265.

161. *Ant.* 18.3.1 (55). Cf. *War* 2.9.2-3 (169-74). Josephus also records an incident

interprets Pilate's action as a deliberate effort to subvert Jewish religion. When Jews from Jerusalem and the countryside flocked to Caesarea and pleaded with Pilate to remove the images, the governor threatened them with death. The protesters 'laid their necks bare, and said they would take their death very willingly' rather than accept desecration of the temple. Pilate changed his mind and took the 'images' (εἰκόνας, cf. Rev. 13.14) out of Jerusalem.

Commerce as a Preferable Route

Because aversion to idolatry (or violence) kept most Jews[163] and Christians out of the Roman military,[164] those who wanted to improve their status were likely to do so through business and commerce. Jews and Christians were similar to each other in their range of attitudes toward trade, perhaps because early Christianity emerged from Jewish communities of the diaspora. While neither tradition was anti-business, both recognized spiritual and moral hazards associated with pursuit of wealth.

In language that anticipates concerns of the book of Revelation, a Jewish author in the second century BCE wrote,

---

of Jews tearing down and destroying the 'great golden eagle' Herod placed over the temple gate in Jerusalem. The Jews involved said they would suffer death 'with pleasure' rather than see the temple desecrated, *Ant.* 17.6.2-3 (152-63).

162. The LXX uses the word εἴδωλον in Exod. 20.4 and Deut. 5.8, but Josephus speaks of an εἰκών when he alludes to the second commandment—perhaps reflecting a Jewish heritage in which the imperial image (εἰκών) was idolatrous. John repeatedly refers to the image (εἰκών) of the beast (Rev. 13.14, 15; 14.9, 11; 15.2; 16.2; 19.20; 20.4). The synoptic Gospels translate Jesus' reference to the imperial image on coins as an εἰκών (Mt. 22.20, Mk 12.16, Lk. 20.24). Paul uses εἰκών to describe idols as 'images' resembling a mortal human being (Rom. 1.23). Εἰκών sometimes had a positive meaning in the early church, referring to humans shaped in the divine image (Rom. 8.29; 1 Cor. 11.7; 15.49; 2 Cor. 3.18; Col. 3.10) or to Christ as the image of God (2 Cor. 4.4; Col. 1.15).

163. Josephus records that as early as the mid-first century BCE Jews of Asia enjoyed official exemption from military service. *Ant.* 14.10.13 (228). Another document of the same era exempts from military service 'those Jews who are Roman citizens and are accustomed to practise Jewish rites'. This privilege was 'in consideration of their religious scruples', *Ant.* 14.10.18 (236-37).

164. Apparently concern about idolatry also kept Christians out of prominent political office. Aelius Aristides, writing in the second century, notes that Christians 'neither worship the gods, nor sit on city councils' (*Orationes* 46.2.404).

My children, love of money leads to idolatry, because once [people] are led astray by money, they designate as gods those who are not gods. It makes anyone who has it go out of his mind (*T. Jud.* 19.1).[165]

In similar tones, Jesus ben Sirach warns: 'One who loves gold will not be justified; one who pursues money will be led astray by it' (Sir. 31.5). The same author, however, acknowledges that some members of his community are rich, and makes allowance for them:

Blessed is the rich person who is found blameless, and who does not go after gold. Who is he, that we may praise him? For he has done wonders among his people' (Sir. 31.9).[166]

This sentiment resonates with the familiar notion from Jewish Wisdom literature that hard work and righteous living will lead to legitimate wealth: 'Treasures gained by wickedness do not profit...but the hand of the diligent makes rich' (Prov. 10.2-4). In contrast to such a positive view of wealth in Wisdom literature, however, the attitude of Jewish apocalyptic writers usually was harsh: 'Woe unto you, O rich people! For you have put your trust in your wealth... In the days of your affluence, you committed oppression' (*1 En.* 94.8-9).[167]

While the New Testament sometimes reflects the positive attitude toward wealth that we find in Wisdom literature, a negative view characteristic of apocalyptic thought is more prominent. The parable of the talents in Matthew and Luke (Mt. 25.14-30 = Lk. 19.12-27) implicitly accepts the profit motive, yet both evangelists weave a harsh critique of wealth into their books. 'No one can serve two masters', Jesus warns in Matthew, 'You cannot serve God and wealth (μαμωνᾶς)' (Mt. 6.24 = Lk. 16.13). In Luke's Gospel Jesus proclaims 'woe' to the rich (Lk. 6.24) and tells of a wealthy man who suffered torment in Hades after callously ignoring the poverty of Lazarus (16.19-31). 'It is easier for a camel to go through the eye of a needle than for someone who is rich to enter the kingdom of God', Jesus says elsewhere (Mk 10.25 par.). The author of Hebrews states directly, 'Keep your lives free from the love of

165. For discussion of authorship and date, see introduction to *Testaments of the Twelve Patriarchs* by H.C. Kee, *OTP*, I, pp. 775-81.

166. Hengel says the scholar will 'look in vain for direct praise of the poor or of poverty in Jewish literature: it is first to be found in the gospel'. Hengel, *Property and Riches*, p. 16.

167. Cf. *1 En.* 97.8-10. *Sib. Or.* 2.132-34 says 'Abundant profit is not a good thing for mortals. Much luxury draws toward inordinate desires. Great wealth is proud, and it fosters arrogance'.

money, and be content with what you have' (Heb. 13.5).

If negative comments about wealth were all the New Testament had to say on the subject, we might conclude that the early church was largely ascetic or uniformly poor. Surely some members of the first congregations were poor either by choice or by circumstance (e.g. 2 Cor. 8.2). Yet evidence from the New Testament indicates the early church spanned virtually all social and economic levels of society, including the moderately wealthy and the merchant class. Despite his biting words about wealth, even Jesus fraternized with successful elites in the Jewish community (Lk. 14.1-14). He associated with tax collectors (notably Zaccheus, Lk. 19.1-10).[168] Tax collectors in Palestine were Jews who gained wealth by cooperating with the Roman power structures. If Jesus' followers continued this pattern of relating to all levels of society, it is likely some people of considerable social or economic status regularly came into the church.[169] New Testament authors repeatedly found it necessary to warn against accumulation of wealth,[170] an indication that accumulation of capital remained a live issue for the early church.[171]

The letter of James highlights tensions between rich and poor that emerged within one early congregation. The author suggests that 'the believer who is lowly boast in being raised up, and the rich in being brought low' (Jas 1.9). Gradually the letter becomes more pointed as James criticizes the church for showing favoritism to people who attend meetings wearing gold rings and fine clothes (2.2-3). Without accusing wealthy Christians of abuse, James portrays the monied class in general as predators: 'Is it not the rich who oppress you? Is it not they who drag you into court? Is it not they who blaspheme the excellent name that was invoked over you?' (2.6-7). Reference to rich people who 'blaspheme

168. Other references to tax collectors in the synoptic Gospels include Mt. 9.9-13; 11.19; 21.31; Mk 2.13-17; Lk. 3.12-13; 5.27-32; 7.34; 15.1-2.

169. Hengel says 'more and more members of the upper classes came into contact with the church, and Christians neither could nor wanted to exclude them'. Hengel points to Luke for examples from the New Testament: 'most excellent' Theophilus (Lk. 1.1-3, Acts 1.1); Joanna, whose husband Chusa was a financial administrator for Herod Antipas (Lk. 8.3); the centurion Cornelius (Acts 10.1-48); the Athenian assessor Dionysius (Acts 17.34); and Sergius Paulus, governor of Cyprus (Acts 13.4-12). Hengel, *Property and Riches*, p. 64.

170. Mt. 6.19-21, 24; 13.22; 19.16-30 and par.; Lk. 1.53; 12.13-21; Jas 1.11; 2.6; 5.1-6;

171. Paul's instructions about celebration of the Lord's supper (1 Cor. 11.17-34) reflect a congregation that included people of diverse economic circumstances.

the excellent name' is consistent with Jude, 2 Peter and other early
Christian writings that associate pursuit of wealth with blasphemous
compromise (see pp. 40-42).

James has particular concern about the spiritual hazards of commerce.
By repeating the phrase 'Come now...', the author weaves trade, avarice,
injustice and violence into one unholy fabric.

> Come now, you who say, 'Today or tomorrow we will go to such and such
> a town and spend a year there, doing business and making money'...
> Come now, you rich people, weep and wail for the miseries that are coming
> to you... Your gold and silver have rusted, and their rust will be evidence
> against you... Listen! The wages of the laborers who mowed your fields,
> which you kept back by fraud, cry out... You have lived on the earth in
> luxury and in pleasure... You have condemned and murdered the righteous
> one, who does not resist you. (Jas 4.13-5.6)[172]

The sequence of thought in James' argument moves from talk about
commerce (4.13) to management of an estate (5.1-6). This may reflect
James' judgment upon the familiar strategy of ambitious provincials who
used trade as a financial springboard into the more dignified propertied
class.[173]

172. See M. Hengel, 'Der Jakobusbrief als antipaulinische Polemik', in G.F.
Hawthorne and O. Betz (eds.), *Tradition and Interpretation in the New Testament*
(Grand Rapids: Eerdmans, 1987), pp. 248-65. Hengel sets forth the hypothesis that
the book of James is a polemic against the theology and missionary style of Paul.
Hence, we should read references to business travel in Jas 4.13-16 as *metaphorical*
language referring to the missionary travels of Paul and his associates rather than as
commentary on ordinary business dealings (pp. 255-59). Hengel says there is virtually no evidence of big business people (*Großkaufleute*) among the late first-century
Christians, so it is unlikely James is addressing them. Furthermore, elsewhere in the
NT the verb translated in the NRSV as 'make money' (κερδαίνειν, Jas 4.13) sometimes has the sense of 'winning' people to the gospel. Hengel may be correct in
reading parts of James as an answer to Paul, but internal evidence still requires us to
understand 4.13-16 as a reference to literal commercial transactions. James has keen
interest in economic issues (2.1-7), and the reference to business travel in 4.13-16
falls immediately before another passage that only makes sense as a discussion of
material wealth (5.1-6). The author links the latter two passages by repeating the
phrase 'Come now...' Regardless of whether or not any Christians actually were big
business people (*Großkaufleute*) late in the first century, certainly Christians in the
port cities of Asia Minor would have had opportunity for some kind of financial or
social dealings with large-scale entrepreneurs. This may have been enough for John
of Patmos to be concerned about 'fornication' with the imperial economic system.

173. See discussion of Lucian on pp. 83-86.

10. *Christian Missions among Merchants and Tradesmen*

Repeated warnings about wealth in the New Testament could be related
to the fact that the gospel seemed to have special appeal to merchants
and tradesmen.[174] During Paul's first missionary foray into Europe,
a merchant named Lydia became the first believer on that continent.
She was 'from the city of Thyatira and a dealer in purple cloth'
(πορφυρόπωλις, Acts 16.14).[175] She was wealthy enough to own
property and accommodate guests (16.15). She probably advanced her
economic and social status through commerce,[176] and may have
had professional ties with imperial Rome.[177] We do not know whether
Lydia continued in commerce after she became a Christian. Her story,
though, adds to the impression that merchants joined the early Christian
movement.[178]

174. Meeks, *First Urban Christians*, pp. 18, 44.

175. Luke calls Lydia a πορφυρόπωλις, one who deals in the same 'purple'
(πορφύρα) mentioned in Rev. 18.12. The word πορφύρα originally meant a
particular shell fish, then came to mean a dye derived from it. By the New Testament
era it denoted only purple cloth made with the dye, BAGD, p. 694. In Lk. 16.19, the
callous rich man who ignored the suffering of Lazarus was 'dressed in purple and
fine linen'. The soldiers who mocked Jesus as 'King of the Jews' dressed him in
purple (Mk 15.16-20). Josephus describes the royal garment placed on Mordecai in
the story of Esther as purple, *Ant.* 11.6.10 (256).

176. Ernst Haenchen says 'purple materials were a markedly luxury item for rich
people; Lydia will have been wealthy herself'. E. Haenchen, *The Acts of the Apostles:
A Commentary* (Philadelphia: Westminster Press, 1971), p. 494. G.H.R. Horsley
says 'A number of Latin inscriptions from Rome mention people who pursued this
[purple] business... One feature of these texts is that several people involved in this
business are explicitly designated as ex-slaves. This may well be the most appropriate
category in which to locate Lydia; that she is of freed status would be consonant not
only with her occupation, but also with her name. For "Lydia" suggests a servile
status, many slaves being accorded a name which reflected their geographical origin'.
G.H.R. Horsley, *New Documents Illustrating Early Christianity*, II (North Ryde:
Macquarie University, 1982), p. 27.

177. A fragmentary inscription from Miletus indicates that an imperial monopoly
on purple goes back at least as far as Nero, and suggests further that people active in
the purple trade were members of the *familia Caesaris*. See *AE* 800, cited by Horsley,
New Documents, II, p. 28. Cf. Bauckham, 'Economic Critique', p. 63.

178. A Christian tomb inscription from Tyre, from later than the first century,
marks the grave of 'John the purple-dyer and banker'. *I. Tyre* I.137, cited by
Horsley, *New Documents*, II, p. 26.

Luke reports that Paul, during his preaching mission at Athens, argued in the synagogue with the Jews and also 'in the marketplace every day with those who happened to be there' (Acts 17.17). Paul himself was a tentmaker, and stayed with Priscilla and Aquila at Corinth because they were of the same trade. Aquila was a Jewish native of Pontus who settled in Rome and later moved to Corinth (Acts 18.1-3). He and Priscilla had sufficient means to travel (Acts 18.18-19) and to host a house church in their own home (1 Cor. 16.19). Later they apparently returned to Rome and owned property there (Rom. 16.3-5). Priscilla and Aquila were prominent church leaders and missionary/trades-people who had a high level of mobility in Rome and the East. Their most natural sphere of influence would have been among customers and other merchants.

Paul indicates there was a Christian church at Cenchreae, the Aegean seaport for the city of Corinth and a busy commercial center (Rom. 16.1).[179] A woman named Phoebe was deacon of that congregation, and the apostle says she 'has been the benefactor (προστάτις) of many and of myself as well' (Rom. 16.2).[180] We do not know that Phoebe was active in commerce, but she was surrounded by trade and was wealthy enough to serve as patroness to Paul and many others. Paul urges his readers to help her 'in whatever she may require from you' (ἐν ᾧ ἂν ὑμῶν χρῄζῃ πράγματι). Theissen notes that πράγμα frequently means 'business' in the economic sense, and Paul's statement 'could be understood as a recommendation to support Phoebe in her "worldly" business'.[181]

Despite his apocalyptic outlook, Paul recognized the importance of earning a living. In a letter to Corinth the apostle puts commercial activity into an apocalyptic context.

> ...the appointed time has grown short; from now on, let...those who buy
> [be] as though they had no possessions, and those who deal with the world
> as though they had no dealings with it. For the present form of this world
> is passing away. (1 Cor. 7.29-31)

---

179. Like most harbors in the Mediterranean, Cenchreae was full of pagan religious symbols. See p. 125.

180. BAGD, p. 718, lists 'protectress, patroness, helper' as possible meanings.

181. Theissen says 'the generalizing relative clause all the more hints that something more than just congregational matters are involved'. Support of Phoebe's business 'would reciprocate Phoebe's service to Paul and others'. Theissen, *The Social Setting of Pauline Christianity*, p. 88.

Rather than prohibiting commerce, these instructions assume Christians will continue to engage in trade and 'deal with the world'. Paul's concern is that believers not become so captivated by materialism that they lose sight of the imminent reign of God at the end of the age.

These allusions to commerce and trade make sense in light of what we know about the diverse social and economic levels of first-century Christians in Greece and Asia Minor. While Meeks and others have pointed to evidence that Christians came from many levels of society, archaeological evidence suggests the same was true for members of trade guilds and associations.[182] The inscription from a customs house erected at Ephesus during the reign of Nero by an association of 'fishermen and fishmongers' bears the names of one hundred members.[183] Horsley analyzed the names and apparent status of those members. That group, he concludes, 'provides the first really illustrative indication that the composition of the Pauline churches reflects closely the same spread in civic rank [from slave to Roman citizen] found in a contemporary association at the metropolis of Asia'.[184] Such a parallel does not prove that Christians were members of the commercial associations, but it strengthens the argument that some Christians were in a social or political position to join.

Commerce and Compromise in Hermas

John of Patmos was not the only early churchman to write about Christians in the imperial marketplace. While John wrote in Asia to fellow provincials, Hermas was at the other end of the Asia–Italy trade artery. Like John, Hermas questioned whether Christians could participate in commercial pursuits that involved making concessions to idolatrous practice.[185]

A slave set free by his master in Rome, Hermas is a classic example of the freedman who achieved success through commerce.[186] On more than one occasion he visited Cumae, just a few miles from the port of

182. Meeks, *First Urban Christians,* pp. 51-73.
183. *I. Eph.* 20. See below, pp. 112-13.
184. Horsley, *New Documents,* V, p. 113; cf. p. 110.
185. For a full investigation of economic themes in Hermas, see C. Osiek, *Rich and Poor in the Shepherd of Hermas* (Washington: Catholic Biblical Association, 1983).
186. Freedmen may have been common among the Christian churches in Italy. Frend says the most important members of Clement's congregation at Rome 'seemed to have been freedmen in the houses of Roman aristocracy such as Clement and his friends Claudius Ephebus and Valerius Vito (1 *Clem.* 65.1)'. Frend, *The Rise of Christianity,* p. 132.

Puteoli.[187] Shippers and merchants from the East frequented that area, and Hermas may have achieved his own wealth through some aspect of maritime trade. He (or his fellow Christians) became rich enough to obtain 'lands and costly establishments and buildings and vain dwellings'.[188] The final composition of his work probably dates from the middle of the second century,[189] but he may have written the earliest stratum late in the first century.[190] If in fact he wrote some of his work as an old man, he must have been a young adult when John was on Patmos.[191]

Hermas comments on both the detrimental influence of wealth and the compromises necessary to obtain it. He speaks of successful Christian entrepreneurs, people 'which have faith, but have also the riches of this world'.[192] He seems to sanction limited involvement in business,[193] but fears the commercial environment may pressure believers to abandon their loyalty to Jesus Christ: 'When persecution comes, because of their wealth and because of their business (πραγματείας) they deny the Lord'.[194]

In what may be a reference to guild ceremonies or even the imperial cult, Hermas condemns 'double-minded' Christians who 'when they hear of affliction, become idolators through their cowardice' and are 'ashamed of the name of the Lord'.[195] Believers are brought 'under authority' (ἐπ' ἐξουσίαν), questioned and given opportunity to deny their faith.[196] Hermas does not specify whether these authorities represent Rome, the provincial government or the guilds. In any case, the profit motive drove some Christian business people to blasphemy; for the 'lust of gain, they played the hypocrite'.[197]

187. Hermas, *Vis.* 2.1.1.
188. Hermas, *Sim.* 1.1.
189. If the Clement mentioned in *Sim.* 2.4.3 is the bishop of Rome, then Hermas actually wrote late in the first century. Many scholars today accept the view of the Muratorian Canon that Hermas was a brother of Pope Pius, which suggests a date between 140 and 155. 'Hermas', *ODCC*, pp. 640-41.
190. D.E. Aune, 'Hermas', in *Encyclopedia of Early Christianity*, pp. 421-22.
191. Hermas, *Sim.* 9.11.5.
192. Hermas, *Vis.* 3.6.5.
193. 'But if anyone be occupied with but one business, he can serve the Lord also', Hermas, *Sim.* 4.7.
194. Hermas, *Vis.* 3.6.5. Cf. *Man.* 10.1.4-5.
195. Hermas, *Sim.* 9.21.2-3.
196. Hermas, *Sim.* 9.28.4.
197. Hermas, *Sim.* 9.19.3.

Hermas speaks of believers who 'because of their business blasphemed (ἐβλασφήμησαν) the Lord'—language reminiscent of the 'blasphemous names' (ὀνόματα Βλασφημίας) for idolatrous Rome (Rev. 17.3; cf. 13.1, 5).[198] While blasphemy may have been a common theme in early Christian literature, Hermas and John give it special meaning by emphasizing the danger of blasphemy or idolatry in the context of commerce. Both writers speak of conflict with authorities, imminent persecution and the spiritual hazards of wealth. Both lament the fact that many Christians are comfortable and secure, lulled into compromise with a pagan society.

Concern about profit and idolatry appears again in a letter of Polycarp (d. 155 CE). The person who 'does not abstain from avarice', he warns, 'will be defiled by idolatry, and shall be judged as if he were among the Gentiles...' (*Pol. Phil.* 11.2). This word of caution follows after a statement of woe upon any individual 'through whom the name of the Lord is blasphemed' (10.3), and mention of a former church member named Valens. Polycarp expresses deep sorrow that Valens 'so little understands' the office he held as elder in the congregation at Philippi (11.1). Apparently the church expelled Valens and his wife from the church (11.4) because pursuit of financial gain took them across the line into idolatry.

The concern of Hermas and Polycarp about profit and idolatry might shed light on a cryptic comment attributed to Paul. The author of 1 Timothy laments that a desire for economic gain drove some Christians to compromise or even abandon their faith:

> But those who want to be rich fall into temptation and are trapped by many senseless and harmful desires that plunge people into ruin and destruction. For the love of money is a root of all evil, and in their eagerness to be rich some have wandered away from the faith and pierced themselves with many pains. (1 Tim. 6.9-10)

Justin, late in the second century, indicates the problem of Christians involved in pagan cults did not go away. Trypho[199] pointed out to Justin that 'there are many who profess their faith in Jesus and are considered to be Christians, yet they claim there is no harm in their eating meats sacrificed to idols'.[200]

---

198. Hermas, *Sim.* 8.8.2-3.

199. Eusebius places the discussion between Trypho and Justin in Ephesus, *Hist. Eccl.* 4.18.6. Justin says Trypho lived in Corinth, *Tryph.* 1.

200. Justin, *Tryph.* 35.1. For similar citations see Irenaeus, *Adv. Haer.* 1.6.3,

Marcion, Wealthy Christian Shipper

In about the year 139 CE, a wealthy Christian shipper from Asia Minor donated two hundred thousand sestertii to the church at Rome and requested membership.[201] The man was Marcion, native of Sinope and successful merchant who traveled to Rome on his own ship. We know of his maritime trade background from comments made by opponents. Late in the second century Rhodo sarcastically referred to Marcion as 'the [ship] captain himself' (αὐτὸς ὁ ναύτης).[202] Likewise Tertullian dubbed him the 'shipmaster of Pontus',[203] and rhetorically asked whether Marcion was as conscientious with spiritual matters as he was with ship cargo.[204]

Marcion was born about 85 CE or soon thereafter, which means he probably was a boy when John wrote Revelation.[205] According to one ancient tradition, Marcion was a son of the bishop of Sinope.[206] If in fact his father was a prominent churchman, Marcion's involvement in shipping suggests maritime trade was an acceptable career for Christians of Asia Minor. Several church fathers mention shipping as Marcion's profession, but say nothing to indicate this line of work was unusual or inappropriate for believers. His very existence as a wealthy shipper heading to Italy strengthens the argument that John of Patmos had actual Christian entrepreneurs in mind when he wrote of 'shipmasters and seafarers' (Rev. 18.17) who traded with Rome.[207]

We do not have to imagine that such Christian shipmasters would

1.24.5, 1.26.3, 1.28.2 and Eusebius, *Hist. Eccl.* 4.7.7. Cited by Theissen, *The Social Setting of Pauline Christianity*, pp. 132-33.

201. Tertullian, *De Praesc.* 30.2; *Adv. Marc.* 4.4. For interpretation of the financial sums in these texts, see Lampe, *Die stadtrömischen Christen*, pp. 207-208 n. 295.

202. Eusebius, *Hist. Eccl.* 5.13.3.

203. *'Ponticus nauclerus'*. Tertullian, *De Praesc.* 30.1.

204. 'Wherefore…if you have never taken on board your small craft any contraband goods or smuggler's cargo, if you have never thrown overboard or tampered with freight, you are still more careful and conscientious…in divine things…', Tertullian, *Adv. Marc.* 5.1.

205. A. von Harnack, *Marcion: Das Evangelium vom Fremden Gott* (Darmstadt: Wissenschaftliche Buchgesellschaft, 1960), p. 21.

206. Epiphanius, *Panarion* 42.1. See Frend, *The Rise of Christianity*, p. 127.

207. Since Marcion rejected most apostolic writings and centered his theology on Paul, it is not surprising that he dismissed the book of Revelation as well. Tertullian, *Adv. Marc.* 4.3, 5. We can only imagine what his response was to John's polemic against shippers who traded with Rome.

have needed to be aristocratic or wealthy. While Marcion apparently sailed his own ships, it was possible for a shipmaster (*magister navis*) of modest means to secure financial backing from a shipper or principal (*exercitor*) of greater means. By the time Roman law was codified in the third century, it was possible for both shipper and shipmaster to be dependent or independent, free or slave.[208] Celsus, the great second-century opponent of Christianity, may have reflected a sociological reality of his own generation in his contemptuous remark that Jesus was able to attract disciples only among 'tax-gatherers and sailors', people 'who had not acquired even the merest elements of learning'.[209]

Christians Not Immune to Allurements of Rome
Roman rule in Asia Minor provides a backdrop for the image of Babylon and her allies in Revelation 18. In the light of historical context, we recognize the profile John draws of kings, merchants and shippers. These were cooperative provincials who used the Roman system of patronage to advance themselves socially and economically. No wonder they 'weep and wail' (Rev. 18.9; 11, 15) over Rome's collapse; they entrusted their lives, honor, loyalty and fortune to the success of the imperial city. In one hour it is all laid waste (18.17).

Christians and Jews were not immune to the allurements of Rome. Because the Roman army promoted pagan rituals offensive to Jews and Christians, people from both faith communities usually avoided the military as a route for upward mobility. Now John of Patmos identifies commerce—the second main route for advancement—as equally infested with idolatrous influence.

Many scholars see the merchants and shippers mentioned in Revelation 18 as people *outside* the Christian community.[210] Collins says

208. Aubert, *Business Managers*, pp. 58-64.
209. Origen, *Contra Celsum* 1.62.
210. M.E. Boring says the phrase 'Come out of her, my people' (18.4) could refer to Christians actually living in Rome. 'Yet the major thrust of this command cannot be literal—it is heard by John's hearer-readers in the churches of Asia, not by Roman Christians. The call to 'come out' is not a matter of geographical relocation but of inner reorientation...', M.E. Boring, *Revelation* (Louisville: John Knox, 1989), p. 189. Caird says John probably did not have believers in mind when he issued the call to 'come out', since the church 'has long since been carried on eagle's wings to the security of the desert [Rev 12.14]...', *Commentary*, p. 23. Ford, who reads 'Babylon' in Revelation as a reference to Jerusalem, assumes the merchants, traders and seafarers of ch. 18 included Jewish entrepreneurs. Ford, *Revelation*, pp. 304-306.

'John probably had in mind here citizens of the cities of western Asia Minor who had amassed great wealth from commerce'. She says the call to rejoice over Rome's fall (18.20) probably stemmed from the

> ...feeling of being an outsider, the lack of any feeling of identification with or sympathy for the provincial elite or even the cities that they led. The combination of hostility toward the local elite and toward the Roman authorities is not surprising, since they cooperated with and supported one another...[211]

John may have felt like an 'outsider', but there is reason to believe some Christians in the seven churches were trying their best to become 'insiders'. Far from lacking 'any feeling of identification with or sympathy for' the elites, some believers eagerly courted social and economic ties with people of prominence.

In summary, several factors lead us to conclude John was speaking to (or about) Christians actually engaged in shipping and international trade: (1) there is evidence of significant Jewish involvement in commerce (see chapter 5), and the early Christian church emerged from Jewish diaspora communities; (2) clues from the New Testament and other early Christian literature indicate there were Christians among the merchant class; and (3) the book of Revelation not only alludes to economic matters throughout, but specifically mentions merchants, shipmasters and sailors.

The next chapter examines activities and institutions in which these international entrepreneurs participated.

211. Collins, *Crisis and Catharsis*, p. 123.

Chapter 3

THE MERCHANTS HAVE GROWN RICH

> The merchants...who gained wealth from her will stand far off, in fear of
> her torment, weeping and mourning aloud, 'Alas, alas, the great city,
> clothed in fine linen, in purple and scarlet, adorned with gold, with jewels,
> and with pearls! For in one hour all this wealth has been laid waste!' (Rev.
> 18.15-17)

John was certain the imminent collapse of Rome would mean disaster
for more than just the imperial capital itself. Throughout the known
world a vast network of trade arteries supplied economic life blood upon
which the imperial beast depended. John believed people on many levels
of society would see their wealth or political status go up in smoke along
with Rome.

A symbiotic relationship bound Rome to thousands of provincial
merchants. First-century Italy increasingly depended on provincials to
obtain and transport food, raw materials and a wide range of consumer
goods. Conversely, a growing sector of the provincial population
depended on Rome as a profitable market for export products. People
who worked in the supply network and earned their living from it
included farmers, miners, manufacturers, bankers, dockworkers,
merchants, sailors and those from other subsidiary occupations.

This chapter examines the settings and institutions of international
commerce in the first century. Here in the realm of harbors, guild halls,
trade offices and banks we find mundane expression of what John saw
as Roman arrogance, greed and idolatry. In the sphere of economic
activity John found a virulent hybrid of materialism, social pressure and
imperial cult that threatened the very essence of Christian faith.

1. *The Object and Nature of Maritime Trade*

To a marginalized provincial, who did not profit from Rome's vast
commercial network, international trade looked like an orgy of

extravagance.[1] John says Rome, final destination of countless trade routes, lived in 'luxury' (18.3, 7) and consumed 'dainties' (18.14). She was clothed 'in fine linen, in purple and scarlet, adorned with gold, with jewels, and with pearls' (18.16).[2] These are bitter words from a man who neither shared in such riches nor approved of those who did.

John provides a bill of lading that brings into clear focus the nature of the trade he scorned. Ships plying the seas toward Rome carried

> ...gold, silver, jewels and pearls, fine linen, purple, silk and scarlet, all kinds of scented wood, all articles of ivory, all articles of costly wood, bronze, iron, and marble, cinnamon, spice, incense, myrrh, frankincense, wine, olive oil, choice flour and wheat, cattle and sheep, horses and chariots, slaves— and human lives (18.12-13).

John says merchants of these wares 'gained wealth' from Rome. Though they lament destruction of a great and beautiful city, their real concern is themselves: 'no one buys their cargo anymore' (18.11).

Ordinary and Luxury Cargo
A good portion of first-century maritime cargo consisted of ordinary products such as olive oil (18.13, cf. 6.6).[3] Yet elites in Rome and the provinces also spent large sums on exotic products from far reaches of

---

1.   A Jewish author in *Sifre* 354. e.g., speaks of what happens 'whenever a ship is lost in the Great [Mediterranean] Sea with a treasure of silver, gold, precious stones, pearls, glassware, and all other kinds of precious cargo'.

2.   The author of 1 Macc. 8.14 disparages the wearing of purple as a sign of pride. A first-century inscription from Ephesus reveals that purple shells, which produced the regal dye, were taxed at twice the rate of normal trade items (unless the purple was going to Rome!). Engelmann and Knibbe, 'Das Zollgesetz der Provinz Asia', par. 1-9, 25.

3.   Spanish oil amphorae from the era of the principate are ubiquitous throughout the western provinces. A.J. Parker, 'Trade Within the Empire and Beyond the Frontiers', in *The Roman World*, II (New York: Routledge & Kegan Paul, 1987), p. 640. G. Pucci says 'the statement that ancient long distance trade concerned only luxury goods is quite simply untrue'. He cites archaeological evidence from ancient shipwrecks that indicates some ships carried 'common ware' such as simple pottery. 'Pottery and Trade in the Roman Period', Garnsey *et al.*, *Trade in the Ancient Economy*, p. 111. Bauckham notes that the oil and wheat mentioned in John's bill of lading 'were not expensive as such, but were imported in such vast quantities that in total they must have cost a very great deal. Thus the list is very representative of Rome's more expensive imports'. 'Economic Critique', p. 75.

the Empire and beyond.[4] Pliny the Elder, perhaps with some exaggeration, says fifty million sestertii drained from the Empire each year in trade with India alone.[5] Many ships, some carrying as much as one thousand tons, plied waters of the Mediterranean Sea and Indian Ocean.[6]

The spices, ivory and silk mentioned in Rev. 18.11-13 came largely from India or China. These products made a long and difficult ocean journey to Egyptian ports on the Red Sea.[7] From there camels and donkeys carried them across desert to the Nile river in upper Egypt. Boats then moved the precious goods down to Alexandria where larger ships received them for delivery to ports around the Mediterranean. Ships trading with the east coast of continental Africa also came to Egypt, after a two year round trip as far south as Zanzibar. Along the way they purchased ivory, tortoise shell, myrrh and incense.

The extraordinary efforts required to obtain these imports made them expensive for Roman subjects.[8] Pliny says the least expensive cinnamon

4.   Parker says wealthy provincials, in their desire to be 'stylish', adopted expensive Roman habits and tastes. 'Trade Within the Empire', p. 642. Pliny the Elder names the 'most costly' products of the earth, a list remarkably parallel to Rev. 18.11-13, 16. These include pearls, diamonds, emeralds, gemstones, silk, citrus wood, cinnamon, cassia, amber, balsam, myrrh, frankincense, ivory, tortoise shell and purple dyes. Gold, he says, comes 'scarcely tenth' in the list of valuables and silver 'almost as low as twentieth'. Pliny, *Nat. Hist.* 36.204.

5.   '…in no year does India absorb less than 50,000,000 sesterces of our Empire's wealth, sending back merchandise to be sold with us at a hundred times its original cost', *Nat. Hist.* 6.26 (101-2). Pliny puts the combined drain to India, China and the Arabian peninsula at 100,000,000 sestertii each year: 'that is the sum which our luxuries and our women cost us', *Nat. Hist.* 12.41 (84). M.G. Raschke challenges Pliny's credibility and knowledge of trade with the Far East. M.G. Raschke, 'New Studies in Roman Commerce with the East', *ANRW*, II, 9.2 (1978), p. 634. Regardless of Pliny's statistical reliability, he reflects the *perception* of Roman subjects that trade with the East was massive. John of Patmos shared that perception.

6.   L. Casson, *Ancient Trade and Society* (Detroit: Wayne State University Press, 1984), p. 18.

7.   A round trip by boat from Egypt to India covered more than five thousand miles and took a year. Casson, *Ancient Trade*, pp. 182-98. *Periplus Maris Erythraei* (second century CE) provides remarkable insight into this trade. Without sophisticated navigation equipment, ancient pilots usually preferred to sail close to shore rather than take a more direct route across open seas. For Jewish citation of Egyptian trade with India, see *Sib. Or.* 11.298-99.

8.   Broughton says Asia Minor produced virtually all the products it needed for internal consumption, except wheat. 'Imports therefore tended to be restricted to

cost five denarii per pound,[9] about the price of fifty pounds of wheat.[10] In times of shortage, the price of cinnamon rose as high as fifteen hundred denarii.[11] Though we have no reliable evidence on the price of silk in the Roman Empire, one ancient source says it was worth its weight in gold.[12]

The imperial court itself consumed vast quantities of silk[13] and spice,[14] either purchased or collected as a levy on merchants who traded in them.[15] In addition to receiving products from the Far East, the Roman government took in substantial revenues from import duties. Merchants trading with the East paid taxes as high as twenty-five percent on imports at customs stations along the eastern frontier.[16] A considerable quantity of exports passed through the same stations on their way to the Far East, probably generating more revenue for the state.[17]

special articles of luxury or to rare objects at the caprice of connoisseurs.' Broughton, 'Asia Minor', p. 878.

9. Pliny, *Nat. Hist.* 12.97.

10. Casson, *Ancient Trade*, pp. 225-46.

11. Pliny, *Nat. Hist.* 12.93. Regarding the use of cinnamon in religious ceremony, Pliny the Younger says, 'His Majesty the Emperor Vespasian was the first person to dedicate in the Temples of the Capitol and of Peace chaplets of cinnamon surrounded with embossed gold. We once saw in the Temple of the Palatine erected in honour of his late Majesty Augustus…a very heavy cinnamon-root placed in a golden bowl…', *Ep.* 12.94.

12. 'Vita Aureliani' in *Historia Augusta*. Raschke marshals evidence to demonstrate that silk was indeed expensive, but not exorbitantly so ('New Studies', p. 624). Whether a price is 'exorbitant' depends, of course, on the perspective and resources of the buyer.

13. John may have known that Roman soldiers wore silk robes in the triumph celebrated at Rome for Vespasian and Titus in 71 CE, after the Jewish War. Josephus, *War* 7.5.4 (126).

14. Pliny the Elder says 'good authorities declare that Arabia does not produce so large a quantity of perfume in a year's output as was burned by the Emperor Nero in a day at the obsequies of his consort Poppaea'. He also mentions the extravagant use of perfumes 'given up to the gods' at funerals 'throughout the entire world'. Pliny, *Nat. Hist.* 12.83. Spices such as cinnamon were used as perfumes rather than as flavorings for food.

15. Raschke, 'New Studies', p. 650.

16. Raschke, 'New Studies', p. 636.

17. Exports from the Roman Empire to the Far East included wine, pottery, glass, sculpture, alabaster, and bronze. Raschke says cities in China and India 'with their wealth and high level of culture provided excellent markets for imported Roman manufactured items, particularly luxury goods'. Raschke, 'New Studies', p. 632. Archaeologists have found large numbers of Roman coins in the Far East.

Deserts east of the Empire provided many of the jewels and precious stones[18] that John names in Revelation (18.12, 21.19-21). Some stones, such as beryl (21.20), came from Asia Minor[19] or elsewhere within the Empire. Marble (18.12) came largely from state-owned quarries, especially those of Asia Minor.[20] The Emperor acquired the quarries by 'conquest, legacy or confiscation', and put slaves or condemned criminals to work in them.[21] Marble took pride of place in state buildings of imperial Rome, and served for thousands of monuments public and private. Monolithic columns weighing over one hundred tons each commonly went from Asia Minor to Rome.[22]

John recognizes that Rome's appetite for this array of exotic goods goes beyond ordinary use. Consumption has become a warped spiritual obsession, a fetish[23] that rots Rome to the core: 'The fruit for which your soul longed has gone from you, and all your dainties and your splendor are lost to you, never to be found again!' Like an addict deprived of a demon drug, Rome soon will reel in the agony of withdrawal. Merchants, complicit because they made their wealth supplying the addict, 'will stand far off, in fear of her torment...' (Rev. 18.15).

18. Parker, 'Trade Within the Empire', p. 651.
19. Pliny, *Nat. Hist.* 37.79.
20. Broughton, 'Asia Minor', pp. 624, 653.
21. Parker, 'Trade Within the Empire', p. 647.
22. Parker, 'Trade Within the Empire', p. 650. Cf. Strabo, *Geog.* 12.8.14.
23. Using the phrase 'fetishism of commodities', Karl Marx gives full treatment to the spiritual dimension of commercial consumption. Because humans assign value to a given commodity, it becomes 'a very queer thing, abounding in metaphysical subtleties and theological niceties'. Commodities take on an apparent value that may be little more than a mental construction in the mind of seller and buyer. To find an analogy to this, Marx says 'we must have recourse to the mist-enveloped regions of the religious world. In that world the productions of the human brain appear as independent beings [i.e., gods] endowed with life, and entering into relation both with one another and the human race. So it is in the world of commodities with the products of human hands'. F. Engels (ed.), *Capital: A Critique of Political Economy*, I (London: Lawrence & Wishart, 1954), pp. 76-77. Being an atheist, Marx neither believed God was real nor that commodities actually acquire the inflated values often attached to them. John of Patmos, in contrast, was certain God existed. John discerned a real (demonic) spiritual presence lurking within the Roman imperial drive to consume commodities.

Grain the Mainstay of Maritime Trade
Though ships carried large quantities of luxury items, the main product shippers and merchants carried to Rome was grain. From Egypt, North Africa and the Black Sea region they ferried some 400,000 tons of grain annually for the capital city.[24] While provincials paid high prices for grain and sometimes had none, 200,000 families in Rome received from the government a regular 'dole' of free grain.[25]

There was never any doubt that imperial policy favored the food supply of Rome over that of any province. An inscription found at Ephesus addresses grain dealers and records how a second-century[26] Emperor put needs of the capital first:

> ...you will act prudently regarding this concession [to supply Ephesus with grain from Egypt], taking into account that the first necessity is that there be a plentiful supply for the ruling city (τῇ βασιλευούσῃ πόλει)[27] of the wheat held ready for market and collected from everywhere; after this, in the same way the other cities are to supply their necessities.[28]

The privilege of carrying grain to hungry provinces was a 'concession' (συνχωρήσις) granted by the Emperor. He assumed grain shippers would be cooperative enough to supply Rome first, even at the expense of provincial cities.

Some people who owned ships or helped to manage maritime commerce came from Rome, but many were provincials. John distinguishes between provincial kings who 'committed fornication' with Rome (Rev. 18.3, 9) and the merchants who have 'grown rich' from the imperial city (18.3).[29] Some maritime merchants active in Mediterranean trade came

---

24. Casson calculates this quantity using statements made by Aurelius Victor and Josephus (*Ancient Trade*, pp. 96-97). Garnsey gives a more modest estimate of 150,000 tons, *Roman Empire*, p. 119; 'Grain for Rome', *Trade in the Ancient Economy*, pp. 118-130. Meijer and Nijf (in *Trade, Transport and Society*, p. 98) suggest 200,000 tons.

25. Augustus cites the number 200,000 in *Res Gestae* 15. The dole at Rome began during the Republic, and for political reasons Emperors would not end the practice.

26. Casson suggests this date in *Ancient Trade*, p. 100.

27. Cf. Rev. 17.18, where John calls Rome ἡ πόλις...ἔχουσα Βασιλείαν.

28. *I. Eph.* 211.

29. John may have in mind provincial rulers who acquiesced to Roman power and did obeisance before the Emperor. Augustus boasted of kings who fled to him as 'suppliants', *Res Gestae* 32. Armenia, territory long disputed between Rome and Parthia, came under Roman sovereignty when its ruler Tiridates journeyed through Asia Minor by horseback to meet Nero at Rome. Nero sat enthroned before a huge

from Asia Minor, as illustrated by the account of Paul's last voyage to Rome. The centurion holding Paul prisoner placed him 'on a ship of Adramyttium that was about to set sail to the ports along the coast of Asia' (Acts 27.2). Adramyttium is a short distance north of Pergamum. The vessel that carried Paul may have been a merchant ship, since it planned to put in at a series of harbors. Its owner, captain and crew probably were the kind of individuals John and others in the seven churches knew in their local communities. When the vessel carrying Paul anchored at Myra in southwest Asia Minor, the centurion transferred his Christian prisoner to 'an Alexandrian ship bound for Italy' (Acts 27.6). The latter may have been one of countless freighters carrying grain from Egypt to Rome,[30] and its presence at a city in Asia Minor illustrates how people of that region came into regular contact even with the imperial grain trade.

Inscriptions from Asia Minor and across the Empire indicate it was common for provincials to travel widely for commerce. With characteristic sarcasm, Juvenal laments that in his day there were more people at sea in search of wealth than on land.[31] The tombstone of a merchant from Hierapolis in Phrygia says he traveled to Rome from Asia Minor seventy-two times.[32] Citizens from the inland town of Tralles travelled to Cos, Rhodes, Athens, Rome and Vienna, where they left inscriptions.[33]

crowd in the Forum, where Tiridates declared, 'Master, I am...thy slave. And I have come to thee, my god, to worship thee as I do Mithras'. Nero proclaimed him 'King of Armenia', and 'when Tiridates had been made to sit beneath his feet, he placed the diadem upon his head'. Dio Cassius, *Hist. Rom.* 63.1.2-5.4; adapted by Lewis and Reinhold, *Roman Civilization*, II, p. 111. It is reasonable to postulate that John of Patmos heard about the visit of Tiridates to Rome: the Armenian capital Artaxata was temporarily renamed Neroneia to commemorate the occasion.

30. Myra was 'a principal port for the Alexandrian corn-ships, and precisely the place where [the centurion] Julius would expect to find a ship sailing to Italy in the imperial service'. C.J. Hemer, *The Book of Acts in the Setting of Hellenistic History* (ed. C.H. Gempf; Winona Lake, Indiana: Eisenbrauns, 1990), p. 134.

31. 'Look at our ports, our seas, crowded with big ships! The men at sea now outnumber those on shore. Whithersoever hope of gain shall call, thither fleets will come...', Juvenal, *Sat.* 14.275-78.

32. 'Flavius Zeuxis, merchant, who sailed seventy-two trips around Cape Malea to Italy, built this tomb for himself and his children...', *IGR*, IV, 841. Translation by Lewis and Reinhold, *Roman Civilization*, II, p. 196, who tentatively date it to the second century. The name 'Flavius' may indicate the merchant or his father once was a slave of the Flavian imperial family.

33. Broughton, 'Asia Minor', p. 875. Pleket cites recent studies illustrating that Nicomedian shippers travelled all over the world. 'Urban Elites', p. 134.

At Rome and Puteoli numerous monuments name people from places in Asia Minor. Cities mentioned include Laodicea, Thyatira, Ephesus, Pergamum, Sardis and Smyrna.[34] By the time Pompeii perished in 79 CE, enough Phrygians had settled there to form an association.[35]

2. *Trimalchio: Profile of a Merchant*

Trimalchio, a character in the first-century novel by Petronius, illustrates how people of provincial origin could obtain wealth in shipping and commerce. Trimalchio was a slave in Asia Minor when he and his master moved to the south Italian city of Cumae.[36] Eventually he purchased his own freedom and 'conceived a passion for business'. He built five ships, loaded them with wine and sent them to Rome. Soon his business expanded to include perfumes and slaves (cf. Rev. 18.11-13).

Thus, in the figurative language of Revelation, Trimalchio began 'fornicating' with Rome. His path to success also apparently involved philandering of a more literal nature. While still a slave, he says, he not only obeyed his master, but 'I used to amuse my mistress too. You know what I mean'.[37] Even in ancient times sailors had a reputation as world-class fornicators.[38] Strabo says the temple of Aphrodite at Corinth once had thousands of courtesans. It was 'on account of these women that the city was crowded with people and grew rich; for instance, the ship-captains (ναύκληροι) freely squandered their money...'[39]

Paintings and artifacts in Trimalchio's house gave a visual survey of his career.[40] A trophy shaped like a 'ship's beak' hung in the dining room. On it was inscribed, 'Presented by Cinnamus the Steward to Caius Pompeius Trimalchio, Priest of the College of Augustus'. A large mural depicted Trimalchio presiding at a slave market. He appeared seated on

---

34. Broughton, 'Asia Minor', p. 875.

35. *IG* XIV, 701. Cited by Broughton, 'Asia Minor', p. 876.

36. Cumae was a port a few miles from Puteoli, receiving ships from Asia Minor.

37. Petronius 76.

38. For example, Horace describes the witch Candina 'often loved by sailors and traders', whose husband 'sees her get up to comply with the request of a businessman or of the shipmaster of the ship Hispana, who is ready to pay a high price for her dishonor', *Carmina* 3.6.29-32. Cited by Aubert, *Business Managers*, p. 23.

39. Strabo, *Geog.* 8.6.20. Aubert notes that male business managers in the Roman world 'were thought to have been endowed with qualitatively and quantitatively superior sexual power channeled into illicit or immoral activities', *Business Managers*, p. 22.

40. Petronius 29-30; cf. 57.6; 65.3ff; 71.12.

the 'official throne' of a *Sevir Augustalis* (a priest of the imperial cult).
His hand held a staff of Mercury, the god of commerce.

In the novel Trimalchio seizes every opportunity for advancement and
shows deference to every superior from his master to the Emperor. In
the end he becomes 'so enormously rich that he does not know himself
what he has'. A 'millionaire of millionaires', he has so many slaves that
nine out of ten have never met him.[41] He squanders money on absurd
luxuries. At a banquet, boys from Alexandria pour water chilled with
snow over the guest's hands. Other servants kneel to trim hangnails
from the feet of diners.[42]

Our interpretation of Petronius' novel must allow a margin for the
author's exaggeration and caricature. Yet the story tells of a provincial
'selling out' to Rome in a manner that may be parallel to that of the
'merchants and seamen' in Revelation. On his tombstone Trimalchio
wants 'ships in full sail' along with a picture of himself 'sitting in official
robes [of the imperial cult] on my official seat, wearing five gold
rings...'[43] Commerce combined with the imperial cult made him a
wealthy and socially prominent man.

3. *Guilds in Italy and the East*

It is likely that merchant guilds were the setting where Trimalchio attained
success, in the confluence of commerce and imperial cult.[44] Such
associations were common in the ancient world, and evidence in the
book of Revelation points toward trade guilds and merchant guilds as
important objects of early Christian debate about involvement in a pagan
society. W.M. Ramsay argued that participation in pagan societies and
guilds presented a dilemma for early believers.[45] Such associations, he
said, were an integral part of Graeco-Roman society. A prerequisite for
membership 'was professedly and explicitly the willingness to engage in
the worship of a pagan deity',[46] usually in the setting of a cultic meal or

41. Petronius 37.

42. Petronius 31.

43. Petronius 71.

44. A guild was called a *corpus, collegium, sodalitas* or *societas* in Latin. Greek
terms included συνέδριον, σύνοδος, συνεργασία and σύστημα.

45. W.M. Ramsay, 'The Letter to the Church in Thyatira', *The Expositor* 10
(1904), pp. 37-60.

46. Ramsay, *Letters to the Seven Churches*, p. 54.

group ceremony. It was 'hardly possible' for tradespeople there to be commercially viable without belonging to the guild of their trade.[47] Ramsay believed Nicolaitans (Rev. 2.6, 15) were those who said Christians could participate in pagan rituals, and therefore could be members of trade guilds and other societies.[48]

Surviving inscriptions testify to the prominence of trade guilds in Asia Minor, particularly those related to textile and metalworking industries in the cities of Revelation.[49] At Thyatira there were guilds of bronze workers, dyers, wool dealers, linen workers, leather workers, bakers and slave dealers. Pergamum had an organization of dyers; Smyrna had guilds of silversmiths, porters and ferrymen. Wool workers were organized at Philadelphia, and money changers had a guild at Ephesus. As Luke tells the story of Paul's ministry at Ephesus, silversmiths there gave an organized response to Paul's preaching (Acts 19.23-41). The tomb inscription for a certain silversmith and *neopoios* (temple maker), buried at Ephesus during the reign of Claudius, confirms that such a guild existed. The text states that responsibility for the tomb 'rests with the association of silversmiths', to whom anyone who violates the tomb must pay a fine of one thousand denarii.[50]

Although the best evidence for trade guilds in Asia Minor comes from the second and third centuries CE, *some* guilds were active during and before the New Testament era. Perhaps trade associations did not yet

47. Ramsay, *Letters to the Seven Churches*, p. 59.

48. Ramsay, *Letters to the Seven Churches*, p. 53.

49. For a survey of guild inscriptions from Asia Minor, see Broughton, 'Asia Minor', pp. 841-44. Among many other guilds represented by inscriptions, Broughton cites these at the following cities:

> Thyatira: bronze workers (*IGR*, IV, 1259; 1st–2nd cent. CE); dyers (*IGR*, IV, 1239, 1242, and 1265; 1st–3rd cent. CE); wool-dealers (*IGR*, IV, 1252; 3rd cent. CE); linen workers (*IGR*, IV, 1226; 3rd cent. CE); leather tanners (*IGR*, IV, 1216; 3rd cent. CE); leather workers (*IGR*, IV, 1169; 2nd cent. CE); bakers (*IGR*, IV, 1244; late 2nd cent. CE); slave dealers (*IGR*, IV, 1257; imperial period).
> Pergamum: dyers (?) (*IGR*, IV, 425; c. 150 CE).
> Smyrna: silversmiths and goldsmiths (*CIG*, 3154; date uncertain); porters (*AJA*, I [1885], p. 140, late 2nd cent. CE); ferrymen (?) (*IGR*, IV, 1427; date uncertain).
> Ephesus: money changers (*SEG*, IV, 541; c. 200 CE).
> Philadelphia: wool workers (*IGR*, IV, 1632; 3rd cent. CE)
> Mitylene: fullers (*IG*, XII, 2, 271; date uncertain); leather workers (*IG*, XII, 2, 109, date uncertain).
> Chios: shipowners and merchants of the harbor (*REG*, XLII [1929], p. 36; 1st cent. BCE–1st cent. CE).

50. *I. Eph.* 2212. For discussion, see Horsley, *New Documents*, IV, p. 7.

have sufficient institutional momentum to leave abundant epigraphic evidence from the first century. When John wrote Revelation, however, guilds were on the threshold of their period of maximum influence in the Graeco-Roman world.[51] Veneration of the Emperor—so ubiquitous in social and political organisations of the late first century—must also have become prominent at meetings of tradespeople. It may have been difficult for those who objected to the cult (or other pagan ceremonies) to survive in commerce and trade. During the reign of Nero, for example, an association of fishermen and fish dealers gained the right to erect a customs house at the harbor of Ephesus (see p. 96). The association presumably collected taxes on exports and imports, and was in a position to monitor all maritime traffic to and from the city. An inscription from the customs house dedicates the facility to Nero, his mother, his wife, the Roman people and the people of Ephesus.[52] While this dedication does not mention Nero's 'divine' status, it may have become offensive to devout Jews or Christians when Nero's religious self-aggrandizement became known across the Empire.

The religious nature of the customs house at Ephesus is clearly evident in a mid-second century inscription found on a statue of Isis belonging to the same association of fishermen. The statue is dedicated to Artemis, to Emperor Antoninus Pius, and 'to the city of the Ephesians, the first and greatest metropolis of Asia and twice *neokoros* of the *Augusti*, and to those who conduct business at the customs house for fishery'.[53] Horsley comments that:

> The dedication of this statue of Isis typifies the difficulty faced by pious Jews and new Christian converts in addressing themselves to earning their living in a cosmopolitan city. In order to ply the fisherman's trade in Ephesos and to sell their wares there, it was essential to gain membership of this corporation which paid dues to the city's patron deity. That is not

51. In addition to insciptions already cited, the remains of elaborate guild halls found at Ostia, Ephesus and elsewhere provide evidence that guilds reached their period of maximum influence in the second century CE. See Meiggs, *Roman Ostia*, pp. 67-71.

52. 'To Nero Claudius Caesar Augustus Germanicus the Imperator, and to Julia Agrippina Augusta his mother, and to Octavia the wife of the Imperator, and the *demos* [people] of the Romans and the *demos* of the Ephesians, the fisherman and fishmongers, having received the place by a decree from the city (and) having built the customs house for fishery (toll) at their own expense, dedicated it.' *I. Eph.* 20. Translation by Horsley, *New Documents*, V, pp. 95-114.

53. *I. Eph.* V 1503.

to say that all Jews and Christians thereby excluded themselves from such involvements: eclecticism in religious outlook leading to (from our distance in time) behavioural inconsistency was not unusual.[54]

The statue of Isis at the Ephesus harbor, associated with the customs house, may be a later example of the same blend of trade and pagan religion that John of Patmos would not accept in the first century.

Economic and Social Function of Guilds
Modern scholarship clarifies that first-century guilds were voluntary and private associations, not professional unions in the modern sense.[55] It was common to find Roman citizens, resident foreigners, freedmen and even slaves in the same guild.[56] Most evidence from inscriptions suggests they were 'purely social bodies, unconcerned with the business activities of their members'.[57] Sometimes they received members who were of a different trade, and wealthy individuals often belonged to several guilds simultaneously.[58] This suggests guilds provided a setting for general social and business interaction, rather than a forum for narrow interests of a given trade. The apparent social aspect of guilds did not, however, diminish their importance as places where entrepreneurs could make business contacts.[59] The fact that guilds represented a cross-section

54. Horsley, *New Documents*, V, pp. 106-107.

55. *Collegia*, especially in Rome, often began as 'mutual aid societies to meet basic needs of their members'. They provided a 'decent burial of the dead as well as periodic festive dinners for the living'. Garnsey and Saller, *Roman Empire*, pp. 156-57.

56. Jones, 'Economic Life', p. 45.

57. Jones, 'Economic Life', p. 43; cf. Meeks, *First Urban Christians*, p. 31. Malherbe says *collegia* 'did not exist to improve the economic condition' of their members. Nor was religious motivation central, since 'the guilds' real purpose was to provide a social life for their members'. *Social Aspects*, p. 88. A rare inscription from Tebtynis in Egypt (47 CE), however, tells of an association of salt merchants who apparently functioned as a cartel. They set prices for their product, apportioned market venues, and gathered for cultic celebrations. *Michigan Papyri* 5.245, cited by Meijer and Nijf, *Trade, Transport and Society*, pp. 75-76.

58. J.P. Waltzing, *Etude historique sur les Corporations Professionelles chez les Romains*, IV (Louvain, 1895–1900), pp. 248-51.

59. Paul relied on friends within his line of work, tentmaking. At Corinth he sought out the Jewish couple Aquila and Priscilla and stayed with them because they shared the same trade (Acts 18.1-3). The apostle also established ties with persons of prominence in the cities where he worked: at Ephesus he had friends among the 'asiarchs' (Acts 19.31). Luke portrays the apostle having the kind of useful social

of social groups only increased their potential usefulness for business relationships.[60]

The inscription by the association of fishermen at Ephesus, who erected a toll house during the reign of Nero, illustrates how guilds could bring together people from all echelons of society. Below the dedicatory text appear the names of one hundred association members who helped finance the facility. From their names Horsley calculates that up to forty-four were Roman citizens, up to forty-one were of non-servile status, and possibly as many as ten were slaves. Horsley observes:

> The range in civic status, from Roman citizens of Italic descent to slaves... provides an intriguing analogy for this similar spread in rank that is attested of the Pauline churches... A similarly high percentage of people with Latin names may be observed in NT church groups, and especially among those with some kind of connection with Paul.[61]

This analysis suggests that some Christians were in social groups where membership in a guild was possible or even likely.

Most guilds had no formal ties with local or imperial government, and Rome was vigilant lest any association in the Empire become a seedbed for political agitation. Each new guild (like any association within the Empire) needed approval from the Roman Senate or Emperor, who

and business contacts that one could establish quickly in a trade guild setting. More significant than what actually happened to Paul is the fact that Luke, writing late in the first century (and perhaps writing in Asia Minor), was ready to depict such a close relationship between the apostle and asiarchs—men who probably were government officials and who may have had ties to the imperial cult. (Magie, recognizing the ambiguity of the term, says 'the asiarchs were not provincial officials at all, but purely benefactors and unrelated to the imperial cult', *Roman Rule*, pp. 449-50. While Magie may be correct that the office of asiarch did not *necessarily* entail responsibility in the imperial cult, there is good evidence that asiarchs in fact often held government office and officiated at state religious occasions. One of the best attested is Tiberius Claudius Aristio, who appears in at least twenty-five inscriptions from Ephesus. He was asiarch in 92–93 CE and on several other occasions, and officiated as high-priest of the provincial temple of the imperial cult at Ephesus. He played a leading role in administration of the city. One inscription honoring him comes from the base of a statue found in the harbor gymnasium, a facility he helped finance. *I. Eph.* 235, 427, 461, 508, 1498. See Horsley, *New Documents*, IV, pp. 49-50, and Friesen, *Twice Neokoros*, pp. 92-112.) Luke's desire to show Paul as a friend of the asiarchs might illustrate the casual attitude toward pagan society that John considered so dangerous.

60. See Thompson, *Revelation: Apocalypse and Empire*, pp. 119-20.

61. Horsley, *New Documents*, V, p. 108. Cf. Meeks, *First Urban Christians*, pp. 47-48, 55-73.

otherwise labelled it *illicitum*.[62] Even a proposed fire brigade in Nicomedia raised the suspicions of Emperor Trajan in 111 CE, and he instructed Governor Pliny not to permit its organization.[63]

Guilds often owned a meeting hall (σχολή) or chapel *(templum)*[64] in which they conducted religious ceremonies, discussed business, hosted banquets, or just gathered to socialize. Some scholars suggest the 'lecture hall (σχολή) of Tyrannus' in which Paul preached at Ephesus (Acts 19.9) was such a guild structure. The book of Acts portrays Paul as a workman rubbing shoulders with other craftspeople. It would have been natural for the apostle to have contacts enabling him to use the meeting hall of a trade guild.[65]

Resurgence of Shipping Guilds

Associations of shippers and merchants are among the oldest guilds for which we have good evidence.[66] As early as 333 BCE merchants from Cyprus who lived in Athens built a temple to Aphrodite, and merchants from Egypt built one to Isis.[67] At the island of Delos, in the middle of

62. Meiggs, *Roman Ostia*, p. 311. For legal restrictions on societies in general, see Justinian, *Dig.* 47.22.1-3. Cf. Origen, *Contra Celsum* 1.1.

63. Trajan says even fire brigades sometimes 'have greatly disturbed the peace' in the province. He fears that 'men who are banded together for a common end will all the same become a political association before long'. Pliny, *Ep.* 10.33-34. The only associations Trajan would allow were those permitted in Rome's original treaty with a given city. In addition to controlling the guilds, Rome kept a watchful eye on trade venues: to operate a market or fair, individuals and communities needed approval from the Roman Senate or the Emperor. Such government supervision perhaps made it more likely merchants would accept imperial ideology and even cultic symbols. Inscriptions from 138 CE record that the Roman Senate granted permission for a market in Africa. *CIL*, VIII, 11, 451 and XXIII, 246. Lewis and Reinhold, *Roman Civilization*, II, p. 337.

64. In his treatment of associations at Ostia, Meiggs says it 'seems highly probable' that 'some guilds were particularly closely associated with certain temples which they built and maintained', *Roman Ostia*, p. 327.

65. Malherbe, *Social Aspects*, pp. 89-90; Thompson, *Revelation: Apocalypse and Empire*, p. 119.

66. The Greek word for 'shipper' is ναύκληρος, the Latin *navicularius*. In both languages the term usually means one who owns a ship and either uses it directly for trade or leases it out to another business person. Stoeckle, 'Navicularii', *PW*, bd. 16.2, col. 1903. Apparently the term sometimes applied to persons who merely operated a vessel. Cf. Plutarch, *De Liberis Educandis* 7.

67. E. Schürer, *The History of the Jewish People in the Age of Jesus Christ*, III.I

the Aegean Sea, an inscription from 154–53 BCE reveals there was an 'association of the Tyrian merchants and shippers of Hercules'[68] which assembled there regularly for worship and business. A similar association of traders and shippers from Berytus also met at Delos to worship Poseidon.[69] Sometime during the last century BCE or the first century CE there was a guild of ship-owners and merchants at a harbor on Chios.[70]

Most of these associations flourished before the Roman principate, and we have limited evidence of shipping *collegia* during the first century CE. An inscription from about 70 CE survives from a house of the ship-owners at Nicomedia in Bithynia.[71] The ship-owners dedicated this structure to Vespasian and may have incorporated a sanctuary to him.[72] At Amastris on the Black Sea was another building of the shippers, though we cannot be certain of its date.[73]

By the middle of the second century associations of shippers were well known in Rome and the provinces.[74] The data suggest shipping guilds were defunct or insignificant during the early principate, but emerged with new vitality in the middle of the first century and early in the second.[75] This means John wrote Revelation at a time when shippers and international merchants were moving toward greater cohesion and influence as a group.

(M. Black, G. Vermes, F. Millar and M. Goodman, eds.; Edinburgh: T. & T. Clark, 1986), p. 110.

68. κοινὸν τῶν Τυρίων Ἡρακλεϊστῶν ἐμπόρων καὶ ναυκλήρων, *I. Délos,* 1519. Cited by Schürer, *History*, III.I, p. 108.

69. *OGIS*, 591; *I. Délos*, 1520, 1772-96, 2323-27, 2611. Cited by Shürer, *History*, III.I, p. 108.

70. οἱ ναύκληροι κ[αὶ οἱ] ἐπὶ τοῦ λιμένος ἐργ[ασταί]. Broughton, 'Asia Minor', p. 841.

71. *IGR*, III, 4; cf. *CIG*, III, 3778. Cited by Broughton, 'Asia Minor', pp. 774, 837.

72. Magie says the 'ship-owners, who, thanks to the excellent harbour and the roads leading into the interior, were evidently a prosperous group, erected a 'house' to be used for the purposes of their business but perhaps containing a sanctuary to Vespasian'. *Roman Rule*, I, p. 588.

73. Broughton, 'Asia Minor', p. 777.

74. Justinian, *Dig.* 3.4.1. Cited by Stoeckle, 'Navicularii', col. 1903. Far-flung attestation of such guilds in the mid-second century suggests there must have been a period stretching back fifty or one hundred years during which the guilds developed and became effective. In Rev. 18 John seems to speak of the merchants and shippers as a recognizable group.

75. Rostovtzeff, *Roman Empire*, I, pp. 157-59; 170-71; 178.

Religious Character of Guilds

All guilds at Rome and in the East had a religious character,[76] often centered on the patron gods or goddesses of the association. By the late first or early second century, some form of the imperial cult also found expression in nearly every guild.[77] In part this stemmed from the fact that guilds typically sought wealthy and influential patrons, the very people most likely to be involved in the imperial priesthood.[78] It was common for trade guilds and merchant guilds to recognize the Emperor himself as the most revered patron. For example, the great college of artists and musicians (*synodus technitorum*) in Ephesus, which organized festivals and shows for the city, recognized both Dionysus and the reigning Emperor as patrons.[79]

The religious character of commercial institutions seems to be the aspect of Graeco-Roman society that most alarmed John. 'Fornication' was his derogatory term for any compromise with idolatrous activity. 'At stake here was the question of assimilation', posits Collins. 'What pagan customs could Christians adopt for the sake of economic survival, commercial gain, or simple sociability?'[80]

4. *Privileges for Shippers*

The imperial government had more interest in the shipping industry than in any other commercial enterprise. As we have seen, Rome was unable to feed itself and increasingly depended on the provinces for food.[81] In addition to a civilian population approaching one million, Rome had an

76. La Piana, 'Foreign Groups', p. 225; Collins, *Crisis and Catharsis*, p. 97.
77. Meiggs, *Roman Ostia*, p. 327.
78. Meiggs, *Roman Ostia*, p. 316.
79. Petit, *Pax Romana*, p. 103. John mentions that the sound of a musician and the work of an artisan (τεχνίτης) never again will be found in Rome. The role of musicians and artisans in the imperial festivals of Ephesus may have brought these persons to mind when John depicted Rome's demise.
80. Collins, *Crisis and Catharsis*, p. 88.
81. Tacitus paraphrases a letter sent by Tiberius to the Senate in 22 CE, in which the Emperor laments that 'Italy depends on external supplies' and 'the life of the Roman nation is tossed day after day at the uncertain mercy of wave and wind', *Ann.* 3.54. In his discussion of Claudius, Tacitus adds, 'in the past, Italy exported supplies for the legions into remote provinces...[but now] we cultivate Africa and Egypt by preference, and the life of the Roman nation has been staked upon cargo-boats and accidents', *Ann.* 7.43.

army to feed. A reliable *annona*, or grain supply,[82] was critical both for comfort and civil order[83] in the capital. Already under Tiberius, the 'excessive price of grain led practically to insurrection'.[84] In order to appease the population—yet not endanger the profits of shippers, Tiberius fixed the selling price of grain and guaranteed the grain merchants a subsidy of two sestertii per *modius*.[85]

Benefits Added by Claudius

When Claudius became Emperor in 41 CE, Rome had only eight days of grain supply in reserve.[86] A drought later threatened Rome's food supply, and Suetonius says Claudius was 'stopped in the middle of the Forum by a mob'. He was 'so pelted with abuse and at the same time pieces of bread, that he was barely able to make his escape to the Palace'.[87]

There was little Claudius could do directly to secure more food for the capital. Since there was no state-owned fleet to bring grain from overseas provinces,[88] Rome relied on private entrepreneurs from the provinces.[89]

82. The *annona* included grain, meat, oil and wine both for citizens of Rome and for the army. Lampe, *Die stadrömischen Christen*, p. 205.

83. Emperors placed high priority on maintaining adequate food supply for Rome. When famine threatened in 22 BCE, Augustus himself assumed control of grain administration, *Res Gestae* 5. Quaestorship of Ostia was the first important stage in the public life of Augustus's step-son, Tiberius. Near the end of his life, Augustus established the office of *praefectus annonae* to ensure adequate grain supply. Meiggs, *Roman Ostia*, p. 45. Rome regularly distributed free grain to its citizens, the object of which was *quies*, or good order. See Parker, 'Trade Within the Empire', pp. 635-57.

84. Tacitus, *Ann.* 6.13.1.

85. Tacitus, *Ann.* 2.87.

86. Seneca, *De Brevitate Vitae* 18.5. See Meiggs, *Roman Ostia*, p. 54. Claudius's preoccupation with the grain supply is evident in some of his first year's issue of coins, which portray a *modius* (corn measure) and the agricultural goddess of plenty, Ceres. Hannestad, *Roman Art*, p. 103.

87. Suetonius, *Claud.* 18.2.

88. Africa supplied grain for Rome for eight months each year, and Egypt for four months. Josephus, *War* 2.16.4 (383, 386). See Casson, *Ancient Trade*, p. 97.

89. Commerce in general 'continued to be largely in the hands of shippers of Egypt, Syria, Asia, Greece, and to some extent of South Italians'. Frank, *A History of Rome*, p. 375. Casson says 'private enterprise played a prime role' in grain shipment, and 'the state did not exercise tight control over the trade'. *Ancient Trade*, 99, p. 108. Petit says Rome took an 'official policy of non-intervention' in the economy of the Empire, but did monitor the production and distribution of grain. *Pax Romana*, p. 189. Garnsey concludes grain shippers were free agents, and did not become public

Both the crown and private citizens paid free market price for the imported grain.[90] Even if shippers belonged to a *collegium,* they still contracted individually with the Roman government for food transportation.[91] Membership in a shipping *collegium* was not mandatory during the first two centuries CE,[92] and guilds had little formal control over the activity of individual members.[93]

Claudius was the first to offer guaranteed privileges and benefits as incentive for owners to put their ships in service to the *annona.*[94] The state, he promised, would absorb the cost of any ships lost at sea. This imperial insurance must have been significant for merchants who risked maritime ventures, since shipwreck was common.[95] Tacitus records the loss of two hundred vessels within the port at Ostia during a storm in 62 CE, and another hundred lost to fire on the Tiber.[96] Trimalchio, wealthy

employees performing compulsory services until the late third or early fourth centuries. 'Grain for Rome', pp. 127-28.

90. In exceptional times the Emperor sometimes intervened with price controls. In the aftermath of the great fire at Rome in 64 CE, Nero lowered the price of grain 'to three sesterces'. Tacitus, *Ann.* 15.39. Garnsey says evidence on price controls is too fragmentary to draw firm conclusions. 'Grain for Rome', p. 127.

91. Early in the second century Rome still purchased grain on the free market from individuals. Pliny speaks of crops produced in Egypt, and says 'the imperial exchequer pays openly for its purchases' of corn, 'with prices agreed between buyer and seller'. Pliny, *Pan.* 29.4-5.

92. Stoeckle says most shippers belonged to a *collegium,* even though privileges extended to shippers were not tied to guild membership until the third century. Stoeckle, *'Navicularii'*, col. 1915.

93. Lampe, *Die stadrömischen Christen*, 206. Rostovtzeff portrays considerable state intervention in the activities of shippers. Rome exercised 'direct control' over the *annona* transportation, he says. Rostovtzeff, *Roman Empire*, I, p. 145. Such control dates from a later era than the first century.

94. Suetonius, *Claud.* 18. See Garnsey, 'Grain for Rome', p. 123. Regarding the relationship between Rome and the shippers, Casson says 'there is not the slightest trace of government control or even supervision'. Claudius 'had recourse not to the stick, only to the carrot'. *Ancient Trade*, p. 102.

95. The ship carrying Paul to Rome as a prisoner was 'an Alexandrian ship bound for Italy' (Acts 27.6). Luke reports that the pilot and the owner of the vessel were willing to set sail from Crete in the autumn, after the end of the usual navigation season, even though 'the Fast [Yom Kippur] had already gone by' (27.9-12). E. Ferguson suggests that the guarantees Claudius provided may have made this an attractive gamble. E. Ferguson, *Backgrounds of Early Christianity* (Grand Rapids: Eerdmans, 1987), p. 65.

96. Tacitus, *Ann.* 15.18.

merchant in the novel by Petronius, lost five ships during his first venture into maritime trade. 'Neptune gulped down thirty million [sestertii] in one day', he laments.[97] When a merchant ship carried the apostle Paul in chains to Rome, the craft ran aground during a storm and disintegrated (Acts 27). Elsewhere Paul reports he survived shipwreck three times (2 Cor. 11.25).[98] Wrecks littered the coastlines of the Mediterranean,[99] and prudent owners must have been grateful to the Emperor for guarantees on their investment.

Claudius also announced that Roman citizens transporting grain for an extended period of time would enjoy the tax and inheritance benefits extended to people who had several children;[100] those without citizenship could receive it.[101] Claudius said shippers who built vessels for grain transportation would enjoy large bounties *(magna commoda)* from the government, and subsequent Emperors added further benefits. Nero exempted merchants from tax on cargo ships,[102] and Hadrian freed shippers from compulsory public services (λειτουργίαι) in their home towns.[103]

97. Petronius 76.

98. Cf. Josephus, *Life* 3 (14-15). Alexandrian Jews were keenly aware of the dangers of shipwreck, as attested by the *Tr. Shem* 1.10, 2.12, 4.5, 6.16, 10.5, 11.6.

99. Parker, 'Trade Within the Empire', p. 636. R. Macmullen, *Corruption and the Decline of Rome* (New Haven: Yale University Press, 1988), pp. 8-10.

100. Suetonius, *Claud.* 19. Suetonius adds that 'all these provisions [privileges for shippers] are in force today'. The *Lex Papia Poppaea* (9 CE) provided financial and political incentives for citizens to have children. See Suetonius, *Aug.* 34; Dio Cassius, *Hist. Rom.* 55.2, 56.10; Tacitus, *Ann.* 3.25; 15.19; Gaius, *Inst.* 3.42-54; Ulpian, *Epitome* 29.3-7; Tertullian, *Apol.* 4; Lewis and Reinhold, *Roman Civilization*, II, pp. 49-52.

101. Gaius (second century) says that 'by an edict of Claudius, [Junian] Latins acquire Roman citizenship if they build a seagoing vessel of a capacity of not less than 10,000 *modii* of grain [about seventy tons], and if that ship, or another in its place, carries grain to Rome for six years', *Inst.* 1.32c. '[Junian] Latins' were a class of freedmen who enjoyed actual but not statutory freedom. The Junian Law (ca. 17 CE) regularized the status of these persons, who enjoyed limited civic rights but had the opportunity of advancing to full citizenship. Cf. Ulpian, *Epitome* 1.10-15. See Lewis and Reinhold, *Roman Civilization*, II, p. 52.

102. Tacitus, *Ann.* 13.51. Magie dates Nero's decree to 58 CE. *Roman Rule*, I, p. 563. For Vespasian's declaration of privileges to shippers (75 CE), recorded at Pergamum, see M. McCrum and A.G. Woodhead (eds.), *Select Documents of the Principates of the Flavian Emperors* (Cambridge: Cambridge University Press, 1961), p. 135, no. 458.

103. Accumulated benefits awarded to shippers by several Emperors were signifi-

Shippers Beholden to Rome

While provincial entrepreneurs kept a steady flow of grain and other products pouring into the capital, Rome saw to it that such business people realized a profit. Already in the days of Augustus, international merchants knew their personal fortunes depended on the Emperor's good graces. Suetonius relates the following incident that took place about 14 CE.

> As he [Augustus] sailed by the the gulf of Puteoli, it happened that from an Alexandrian ship which had just arrived there, the passengers and crew, clad in white, crowned with garlands, and burning incense, lavished upon him good wishes and the highest praise, saying that it was through him they lived, through him they sailed the seas, and through him that they enjoyed their liberty and their fortunes.[104]

Augustus was so pleased he gave forty gold pieces to each of his traveling companions, and made them pledge to spend the money on wares from Alexandria.

This sense of mutual benefit between Emperor and merchant prevailed throughout the first century. Maritime merchants had reason to show gratitude, since the Emperor provided benefits that made shipping possible. Claudius built the harbor and ancillary canals at Ostia[105] and put up a lighthouse.[106] At both Ostia and Puteoli he stationed a cohort of soldiers to guard against fire.[107] He built canals from the Tiber to the sea, connecting his new harbor directly to Rome.[108] Nero constructed a

---

cant enough to attract abuse. Emperor Marcus Aurelius (161-80 CE) and Verus wrote, apparently to a Greek city, that there were persons 'who on the pretext of being shippers and of trading in corn and oil to the market of the Roman people...have claimed to avoid λειτουργίαι [payments or services to the local city], although they neither sail themselves nor have the majority of their property in shipping and trade. Let their immunity be removed...'. Justinian, *Dig.* 50.6.6. Cited by Millar, *The Emperor*, p. 428.

104. Suetonius, *Aug.* 98. Charlesworth says Augustus 'was sprung from an Italian middle-class family' and did not have the 'aristocratic contempt for trade which was inborn in the consulars; he could appreciate the point of view of the merchant and middle-class business man'. *Trade Routes*, p. 10.

105. *CIL*, XIV, 85. Cited by Meiggs, *Roman Ostia*, p. 55. The official title of the Claudian harbor was *portus Augusti Ostiensis*.

106. Suetonius, *Claud.* 20.3.

107. Suetonius, *Claud.* 25.2.

108. *CIL*, XIV, 85. Cited by Meiggs, *Roman Ostia*, p. 55.

harbor for his native town of Antium[109] and attempted to cut a canal across the isthmus of Corinth.[110] Domitian rebuilt the harbor at Ostia in marble[111] and improved roads connecting Puteoli with Rome.[112] Shippers at the time of Revelation awaited a further major expansion of the Ostian harbor, a project carried out by Trajan.[113]

In addition to providing facilities for merchants, Rome gave protection from piracy and brigandage by its military presence throughout the Empire. Some scholars argue that imperial protection for merchants was more coincidental than intentional.[114] Regardless of the motive, provincials recognized the protection was real.[115] Even Philo, in 39 CE, rejoiced that Augustus had 'cleared the sea of pirate ships and filled it with merchant vessels'.[116]

Roman power provided security and stability that enabled trade to flourish, and Roman subjects who prospered responded with gratitude and cooperation.[117] It is not surprising that a merchant vessel carried Vespasian from Alexandria to Rome in 69 CE when armies of the East

109. Suetonius, *Nero* 9.

110. Suetonius, *Nero* 19.2. Caligula planned to do the same. Suetonius, *Cal.* 21.

111. Hermansen, *Ostia*, p. 9.

112. In 95 CE Domitian built the *Via Domitiana*, which provided an excellent, direct road between Puteoli and Rome. Statius, in his poem about the new road, heaps praise upon the Emperor: 'Lo! a god is he, at Jove's command he rules for him the happy world...', Statius, *Via Domitiana* 4.3.128-29.

113. Trajan also built harbors elsewhere, such as Centumcellae. Pliny, *Ep.* 6.31.15-17.

114. Raschke, 'New Studies', p. 648.

115. Roman legionaries and auxiliaries guarded major trade routes across the Eastern Desert in Egypt. Raschke says Roman troops at Egyptian towns on the Red Sea 'could have had no other purpose than to assure the safety of the trade and traders that passed through those ports and to secure the extensive imperial interest in the spice trade'. Raschke, 'New Studies', p. 648.

116. Philo, *Leg. Gai.* 146. Cf. Strabo, *Geog.* 3.2.5. Before Augustus controlled the Mediterranean, 'famine fell upon Rome, since the merchants of the Orient could not put to sea' for fear of piracy. Appian *Civil Wars* 5.8.67. Augustus later boasted he 'brought peace to the seas by freeing them from pirates'. *Res Gestae* 25. In the second century Irenaeus rejoiced that, because of Roman protection, 'we walk on the highways without fear, and sail where we will'. *Adv. Haer.* 4.30.3.

117. Trajan ruled after John wrote Revelation, but Trajan's contribution to commerce is consistent with the pattern of good relations between merchants and crown evident in Revelation 18. Pliny says Trajan 'opened roads, built harbours, created routes overland...and linked far distant peoples by trade so that natural products in any place now seem to belong to all'. Pliny, *Pan.* 29.2.

acclaimed him Emperor.[118] At Ostia the cult of Vespasian and Titus flourished for many years after these Emperors died.[119] Inscriptions or temples honoring the Emperor appeared in marketplaces and port facilities where merchants congregated. Philo cited the port of Alexandria as an example of the 'celestial honors' that many cities gave to Augustus. There residents built a precinct called the *Sebasteum*, a temple to Caesar facing the harbor. Philo says the structure was 'huge and conspicuous... embellished with porticoes, libraries, chambers, groves...and everything which lavish expenditure could produce to beautify it'.[120] It simply was good business to show loyalty to the Emperor who made maritime trade possible.

Occasionally an Emperor might even choose to reward a particular shipper with political favor, as illustrated by the following letter from Hadrian to the city of Ephesus.

> Greetings. L. Erastus is, according to him, citizen of your city, has often sailed the seas...He has specialised in transporting dignitaries and has twice sailed with me...He wants to become a member of the [city] council... If nothing stands in the way and if he is worthy of this honour, I am willing to pay the money, that councillors have to pay at their entrance.[121]

Hadrian opens this letter to Ephesus by describing himself as 'grandson of the deified Nerva' and '*pontifex maximus* [head of the college of pontiffs and of other priests in charge of the Roman state cult]'.

5. *Maritime Trade and the Imperial Cult*

Mediterranean sailors since time immemorial combined seamanship with cultic rituals. When a terrible storm threatened a ship carrying the prophet Jonah, 'the mariners were afraid, and each cried to his god' (Jon. 1.5). In addition to such times of distress, merchants and sailors also invoked the gods in permanent worship sites at many ports. In the fourth and third centuries BCE, merchants from Cyprus and Sidon built temples at

---

118. Josephus, *War* 7.2.1 (21).

119. Little evidence of a Domitian cult survives at Ostia. Meiggs ascribes this to the fact that the Roman Senate publicly damned Domitian's memory after his death. Across the Empire thousands of inscriptions bearing his name were altered or destroyed, including many throughout Asia Minor. *Roman Ostia*, p. 64.

120. Philo, *Leg. Gai.* 151.

121. *SIG*, III, 838. Meijer and Nijf, *Trade, Transport and Society*, p. 72.

Athens.[122] An inscription from Puteoli, 79 CE, states that 'the god Helios Saraptenos [that is, Baal of Sarapta between Tyre and Sidon] came on ship from Tyre to Puteoli'.[123]

In sarcastic reference to those who petition idols on board merchant vessels, Wisdom of Solomon describes a pagan seaman who 'calls upon a piece of wood more fragile than the ship that carries him'. Without condemning the profit motive or sea trade, the author says,

> ...it was desire for gain that planned that vessel...but it is your providence, O Father, that steers its course, because you have given it a path in the sea...so that even a person who lacks skill may put to sea (Wis. 14.1-4).

It is possible that maritime idols condemned in Wisdom of Solomon actually were effigies of a reigning king or Emperor, a phenomenon mentioned later in the same book.

> ...at the command of monarchs carved images were worshiped. When people could not honor monarchs in their presence, since they lived at a distance, they imagined their appearance far away, and made a visible image of the king whom they honored, so that by their zeal they might flatter the absent one as though present. Then the ambition of the artisan impelled even those who did not know the king to intensify their worship. For he, perhaps wishing to please his ruler, skillfully forced the likeness to take a more beautiful form, and the multitude, attracted by the charm of his work, now regarded as an object of worship the one whom shortly before they had honored as a human being. And this became a hidden trap for humankind, because people, in bondage to misfortune or to royal authority, bestowed on objects of stone or wood the name that ought not to be shared (Wis. 14.16-21).

Internal evidence suggests Wisdom of Solomon originated in Alexandria late in the first century BCE.[124] If this date is correct, there may have been precedent for ruler worship in maritime trade settings long before Roman Emperor worship began in earnest.

122. Schürer, *History*, III.I, pp. 109-10.

123. A.D. Nock, *Conversion: The Old and the New in Religion from Alexander the Great to Augustine of Hippo* (Lanham, MD: University Press of America, 1988), p. 66. Archaeologists have found a large number of pagan religious inscriptions in the Netherlands written by merchants trading with Roman Britain in the second and third centuries CE. These sometimes include references to the imperial house. *AE* (1973), 362, 364, 365, 370, 372, 375; *AE* (1975), 646; 647, 651; *AE* (1980), 658, *AE* (1983), 720, 721. Cited by Meijer and Nijf, *Trade, Transport and Society*, pp. 87-89.

124. See J.M. Reese, 'Wisdom of Solomon', in Mays (ed.), *Harper's Bible Commentary*, p. 821.

Pagan Themes at Mediterranean Ports

During the New Testament era, pagan symbols were common at virtually any Mediterranean port city. Cenchreae, Aegean seaport for Corinth and site of an early Christian congregation (Rom. 16.1), took its name from Cenchrias, the daughter of Poseidon and Peirene. Pausanias (second century) reports that in Cenchreae was 'a temple and a stone statue of Aphrodite, after it on the mole running into the sea a bronze image of Poseidon, and at the other end of the harbour sanctuaries of Asclepius and of Isis'.[125] Maritime merchants from Asia Minor frequented this port, transporting merchandise across the narrow isthmus to the port of Lechaion and on to Rome.[126]

Ancient authors tell of religious ceremonies and imperial honors connected with shipping. Apuleius (second century) describes how worshipers of Isis celebrated the opening of the navigation season.[127] Their leader offered 'propitious vows for the great Emperor, the Senate, the *equites,* the entire Roman people, and for the sailors and ships under the control and sovereignty of our [Roman] world'. The worship leader then uttered '*Ploiaphesia* (release ship)!' and the sailing season began.[128]

The grain trade in particular assumed a religious aura, evident on coins from Alexandria. Coins from the fourth year of Domitian's reign (84–85 CE) show Domitia Augusta wearing a crown of corn-ears, 'by which the empress is compared with or assimilated to' Demeter, goddess of fertility.[129] Reverses of coins that year portray fruit, corn-ears, poppy and a sailing boat.

When the imperial cult developed, it was natural for navigation ceremonies to incorporate honors to the Emperor. A first-century wall painting from Ostia depicts two boys pulling a cart from a moored merchant vessel toward a religious ceremony (see Figure 3). Priests at

125. Pausanias 2.2.3.

126. Strabo, *Geog.* 8.2.1. Strabo says that next to the shipway (δίολκος) across the isthmus stood the temple of the Isthmian Poseidon. *Geog.* 8.6.4; 8.6.22.

127. Navigation season in the Mediterranean was approximately from March 10 to November 10.

128. Apuleius, *The Golden Ass*, 11.17.

129. K. Scott, *The Imperial Cult Under the Flavians* (Stuttgart: Kohlhammer, 1936), p. 85. H. Koester notes that imperial coins during the Roman period 'were totally in the service of state propaganda' and frequently featured deities and temples. H. Koester, *History, Culture and Religion of the Hellenistic Age*, I (New York: de Gruyter, 1982), pp. 90-91.

Figure 3. First-century fresco from Ostia. The scene appears to be an association of boys convening for a religious ceremony, perhaps at the start of navigation season in the spring. Two lads pull a cart from the seashore, where a merchant ship rests at anchor. Another youth hands a (ceremonial?) dish to a pair of priests wearing garlands. Behind the priests is a standard with three busts, probably images of Emperors. Apparently the blend of shipping and imperial cult was important even for boys at Ostia.

Biblioteca Apostolica Vaticana, Rome. Copyright Archivi Alinari, Via Alibert 16, Rome.

the ceremony offer sacrifice under a standard bearing three images—perhaps those of Augustus, Gaius and Lucius. The ceremony appears to represent the opening of navigation season in the spring.[130]

Cultic Symbols at Italian Harbors

Any provincial shipper active in trade with Rome had regular contact with the great imperial harbors of Italy. Ostia, located at the mouth of the Tiber, was the primary port for the city of Rome. Many ships also put in at Puteoli, about 140 miles south of Ostia. From there passengers and cargo traveled by land to Rome.[131]

Religious and imperial symbols abounded at these harbors, as illustrated by a remarkably detailed coin issued by Nero in 64 CE. The coin is a sestertius portraying the harbor at Ostia (see Figure 4),[132] and it gave ordinary provincials a vivid image of the Roman port to which maritime merchants delivered cargo.[133] On this one coin appear the Emperor, merchant ships, a war galley, an individual making sacrifice, a temple and the god Neptune. The numismatic image of Ostia, pressed into the hand of countless Roman subjects, combined the very elements that John of Patmos considered an unholy configuration: commerce, pagan gods, the Roman military—and the imperial cult.

A second-century bas-relief of the harbor at Ostia provides further evidence of maritime religion (see Figure 5). A large merchant ship unloads its cargo of wine jars. Sails on the ship carry images of the she-wolf with twins, and bear the legend *V[otum?] L[ibero?]*. The latter refers to a prayer or vow *(votum)*, perhaps for the Emperor's well-being. On the cabin roof three people (perhaps the ship owner, his wife and the captain) perform a sacrifice. Next to the ship stands the god Neptune, and a small ferry boat. A gigantic lighthouse bears the statue of an Emperor; a triumphal arch depicts a chariot carrying the Emperor

---

130. See M. Rostovtzeff, *A History of the Ancient World*. II. *Rome* (London: Oxford University Press, 1938), p. 267.

131. This is the route Paul travelled as prisoner to Rome (Acts 28.13-14).

132. See Meiggs, *Roman Ostia*, p. 158 (plate xviii); Hannestad, *Roman Art*, p. 111.

133. Coins played an important role in Roman imperial ideology. Hannestad observes that 'at a time when the mass media to which we have become accustomed were non-existent', coins 'formed the most suitable medium through which to disseminate political propaganda', *Roman Art*, p. 11. Jesus pointed to a Roman coin in his discussion of debt to God and debt to Caesar (Mk 12.13-17).

Figure 4. Reverse of a sestertius from 64 CE, depicting the harbor at Ostia. At the top of the coin (the mouth of the harbor) stands a colossal statue of the Emperor holding a scepter. To the left of the statue a merchant ship enters the harbor at full sail; an oared war galley—representing the imperial fleet's responsibility for policing harbors and sea routes—embarks on the right. Just below the statue are three merchant ships with sails furled; a sailor adjusts rigging on the center vessel. Two small rowing craft move through the harbor, which is surrounded on both sides by large moles that extend to the mouth of the harbor. On the left mole, just beside the ship at full sail, is a peristyle temple with a person standing before it (making a sacrifice?). A reclining figure of Neptune lies below the whole scene, with the steering oar of a ship in one hand and a dolphin in the other. The legend reads *AUGUSTI POR[tus] OST[iensis]* ('the Ostia harbor of Augustus'). A portion of the legend appears at the bottom between the letters 'S' and 'C', which mean *S[enatus] C[onsulto]* ('by authorization of the Senate').

Nero Sestertius, *BMC*, I, p. 222, no. 132 (plate 41, no. 7). Copyright British Museum.

in victory celebration.[134] The imperial cult formally entered public life at Ostia shortly after the death of Augustus, when the town built a temple

---

134. I am indebted to Rostovtzeff for much of this interpretation. *A History of the Ancient World*, II, p. 274. Meiggs largely agrees with Rostovtzeff. *Roman Ostia*, pp. 158-59 (plate xx). He cites numismatic evidence to suggest the Emperor on the chariot may be Domitian, and speculates that the sponsor of the bas-relief was a wine merchant. Meiggs says the work could be as late as the reign of Septimius Severus (193-211 CE), but it seems to portray the harbor built by Claudius.

Figure 5. Second-century (Severan?) bas-relief of the harbor at Ostia, illustrating the interplay of religion, commerce and imperial motifs. A large merchant ship unloads its cargo. Sails on the ship carry images of the she-wolf with twins, and bear the legend V[otum?] L[ibero?]. On the cabin roof three people—perhaps the ship owner, his wife and the captain—perform a sacrifice. Next to the ship stand the god Neptune and a small ferry boat. A gigantic lighthouse behind the ship bears the statue of an Emperor; a triumphal arch (top right) features a chariot, pulled by elephants and carrying the Emperor in victory celebration. Though from the second century, the scene is little changed from the time of Revelation.

Museo Torlonia, Rome. Copyright Archivi Alinari, Via Alibert 16, Rome.

of Rome and Augustus at the Forum.[135] A priest known as the *flamen Romae et Augusti* presided over imperial cult ceremonies, which eventually honored individual deified Emperors. Vespasian is the earliest Emperor known to have had his own *flamen* at Ostia.[136]

Guilds at Ostia Penetrated by Imperial Cult

Archaeologists have information on close to forty guilds at Ostia, and there may have been more.[137] All guild sites appear to have had a place for worship, as well as a hall for meetings and banquets. Almost half of known guild houses at this port city related to navigation and the grain trade. The hall of ship-owners, probably built in the second century CE, is the 'largest and most impressive of all possible guild seats'. It includes a lavish vestibule once flanked by marble columns, and a monumental courtyard.[138]

Surviving ruins at Ostia yield abundant evidence of the blending of cult and commerce. A second-century brick temple at Ostia apparently belonged to the guild of shipwrights;[139] another may have been associated with the guild of grain measurers.[140] One inscription names a 'guild brother of the importers and merchants in the temple in the wine forum'.[141] A cult of the guild *genius* and some form of imperial cult were common to all guilds at Ostia.[142]

The interpreter of Revelation must use this evidence cautiously, since many ruins at Ostia come from the second century.[143] Yet the great

135. Meiggs says the temple to Rome and Augustus was impressive, 'almost certainly eclipsing all other Ostian temples of the day in magnificence'. *Roman Ostia*, p. 353, cf. p. 132. Cf. Zanker, *The Power of Images*, p. 310.

136. The absence of inscriptions naming priests of Augustus, Tiberius and Claudius may be a mere accident of what evidence happened to survive. Meiggs, *Roman Ostia*, p. 178.

137. Hermansen, *Ostia*, p. 55.

138. Hermansen, *Ostia*, p. 72.

139. Hermansen, *Ostia*, p. 63.

140. Meiggs, *Roman Ostia*, pp. 327-29.

141. *corporatus in templo fori vinarii importatorum negotiantium. AE* 54. Cited by Hermansen, *Ostia*, p. 60, and Meiggs, *Roman Ostia*, p. 329.

142. Meiggs, *Roman Ostia*, p. 327.

143. Meiggs, *Roman Ostia*, pp. 70, 332. However, there is very early evidence of corporate activity among maritime merchants: already under Augustus the ship-owners at Ostia (*Ostienses Naviculariei*) acted together in honoring a Roman quaestor. *CIL*, XIV, 3603.

building boom at Ostia began during the reign of Domitian, and it was part of the commercial network that John addresses in Revelation 18.[144] Structures remaining from early in the second century probably represent the full flowering of institutions already well-established at the time John was on Patmos.

Augustales Influential in Many Guilds
Perhaps the most elaborate guild in late first-century Ostia was an association promoting the imperial cult, whose members all were freedmen and took the title of Augustales.[145] These men were part of a larger association that appeared in many cities throughout the Empire, especially in Italy and the West. The organization existed to promote the imperial cult, but it also conferred status and influence upon its members.[146] It was common for businessmen to belong to several guilds at once, and upwardly mobile freedmen of many professions sought membership with the Augustales.

Membership 'considerably improved' a freedman's advance in business and trade.[147] Inscriptions at Ostia reveal Augustales rose quickly to leadership in a variety of guilds. From among their ranks came presidents of the builders, the shipbuilders and the wine importers. A president of the Augustales served both as 'curator of the ship captains of the Adriatic Sea' and chief executive (*quinquennalis*, 'five-year president') of that guild.[148] Shippers erected a statue to honor a certain imperial cult priest who was patron of the Guild of Overseers of Sea-going Vessels (see Figure 6). A similar inscription, put up by a freedman, honors a priest

144. Domitian rebuilt the Porta Romana of Ostia in marble, part of his 'complete transformation' of the city. Hermansen, *Ostia*, p. 9. Cf. Meiggs, *Roman Ostia*, p. 64.

145. The earliest inscription naming Augustales at Ostia is from shortly before 11 CE, but the institution is known elsewhere in Italy as early as 12 BCE. Meiggs, *Roman Ostia*, p. 353. Meiggs tentatively identifies the so-called 'Curia of Ostia' as the headquarters of the Augustales and dates the lavish structure to the reign of Domitian. *Roman Ostia*, pp. 219-20. Hermansen rejects the idea that the Augustales met in the 'Curia' and identifies another large structure (built c. 150–65 CE) as 'the Seat of the Augustales'. *Ostia*, pp. 79-81, 111-13. In either case, the Augustales had an early and imposing presence in Ostia.

146. Meiggs, *Roman Ostia*, p. 335.

147. Meiggs, *Roman Ostia*, p. 221.

148. A. Caedicius Successus was *curator nauclerorum maris Hadriatici, idem quinquennalis*, Meiggs, *Roman Ostia*, p. 276.

who was president of the Ostia Ship-building Guild (see Figure 7).[149]

Augustales at Ostia were men of considerable financial means, who would have been able to make business loans to shippers and other entrepreneurs.[150] In fact, Trimalchio says after his successful career as a merchant and *Sevir Augustalis* he 'retired from active work and began to finance freedmen'.[151] At Puteoli a certain freedman named C. Sulpicius Cinnamus, from the mid-first century, issued a series of *mutua* (loans) and *vadimonia* (records of security paid to continue legal action which was generated by failure to repay).[152]

It is not surprising the imperial cult had heavy influence on trade and commerce at Ostia, since members of the imperial family were popular guild patrons in that city. Numerous imperial portrait heads, busts and statues honored members of the imperial house for their gifts and patronage. A colossal head found among the ruins seems to be a portrait of Domitian.[153]

6. *Maritime Trade Offices at Ostia*

Ruins at Ostia include a plaza surrounded by small office stalls, of which sixty-one survive.[154] Representatives of the shipping industry or of guilds catering to needs of overseas merchants occupied these rooms.

---

149. Inscriptions from Puteoli provide further evidence. One reads, 'To the departed Spirits of Quintus Capitonius Probatus the elder, of the city of Rome, *sevir augustalis* in Lyon and in Puteoli, seagoing *navicularius*. His freedmen Nereus and Palaemon for their patron...', *ILS*, 7029. Cited by Meijer and Nijf, *Trade, Transport and Society*, p. 73.

150. D'Arms says by the time of Domitian, 'treasurers of the Ostian Augustales, of whom there were annually no fewer than four and at times as many as eight, paid HS 10,000 for the privilege of holding that office' (HS = sestertius). In the second century the magnificent tombstone of a rich officer (and *sevir augustalis*) in the association of Adriatic shippers occupied a plot of 2100 square feet, nearly three times the typical size of other Ostian freedmen. *Commerce and Social Standing*, pp. 129-30.

151. Petronius 76.

152. D'Arms, *Commerce and Social Standing*, p. 107. Behind the freedman, with larger financial resources, stood his patron C. Sulpicius Faustus—whose status is unknown. Faustus lent money as security on 13,000 modii (more than eighty tons) of Egyptian grain.

153. Meiggs, *Roman Ostia*, p. 66.

154. Known today as the *Piazzale delle Corporazioni*.

```
M  •  I V N I O  •  M  •  F •  P A L
            F A V S T O
D  E  C  V  R  I  O  N  I • A D L E C T O
FLAMINI • DIVI  •  TITI • DVVMVIRO
MERCATORI         •        FRVMENTARIO
Q  •  AERARI  •  FLAMINI  •  ROMAE
ET  •  AVG  •  PATRONO • COR*p*
CVRATORVM • NAVIVM • MARINAR*um*
DOMINI  •  NAVIVM  •  AFRARVM
         UNIVERSARUM *ITEM*
              *SARDORVM*
L  •  D  •  D  •  D  •  P
```

Figure 6. Inscription from Ostia honoring Faustus, priest of the imperial cult (*CIL* XIV 4142). The text reads:

> M. Junius…Faustus, decurion, appointed priest of the divine Titus, Duumvir, grain merchant, q[uaestor?] of the [public] treasury, priest of Roma and Augustus, patron of the Guild of Overseers of Sea-going Vessels. The masters of all the ships from Africa and Sardinia set up this stone from gifts they have given.

This translation reads the last line as: *L[apidem] D[e] D[onis] D[onatis?] P[osuerunt].* Mention of 'divine Titus' dates the inscription after that Emperor's death in 81 CE. This text illustrates how certain businessmen (often freedmen) rose to positions of power and influence both in the imperial cult and the shipping guilds. It also illustrates how shipmasters corporately and publicly honored a prominent imperial priest. For parallel inscriptions from Spain, cf. *CIL*, II, 1180, 1182.

```
L     •     LEPIDIO     EUTYCH^O
SEVIRO  •  AVG  •  IDEM
QVINQ        IN        COLONIA
             OSTIENSI
ET  •  IN  •  MVNICIPIO
      TVSCVLANORVM
ET  QVINQ  PERPETUO  CORPOR
   FABRVM        NAVALIVM
       OSTIENSIVM

FORTVNATVS •LIB ET• ALEXA • ACT
```

Figure 7. Inscription from Ostia honoring Eutychus, priest of the imperial cult (*CIL*, XIV, 372). The text reads.

> L. Lepidius Eutychus, priest of the imperial cult *(SEVIRO AUG[ustalis])*, also municipal official *(QUINQ[ueviro?]; QUINQ[uennalis?])* in the colony of Ostia and the city of Tusculum, and president for life *(QUINQ[uennalis?] PERPETUO)* of the Ostia Ship-building Guild.

> The last line of the inscription names the persons who put up the monument: the freedman Fortunatus, and Alexa. Eutychus was among the power elite at Ostia, carrying responsibility both in the imperial cult and the shipping industry. The inscription shows how freedmen were beholden to benefactors who represented the interests of both cult and commerce.

Remains of a late first-century temple stand at the center of the plaza,[155] a reminder that religion had a central and visible role here as well.

Shippers *(navicularii)* were primary occupants of the plaza and often shared stalls with merchants *(negotiantes)* from the same place of origin.[156] Entrepreneurs from the various provinces grouped their offices by geographic area.[157] Stalls were large enough to conduct business, but not for the stocking and sale of goods. In addition to maritime trade corporations, a wide variety of businesses related to the shipping industry had representatives at the plaza as well. Mosaics and inscriptions record the presence of shipwrights, grain measurers, receivers, bankers,[158] money changers, boatmen, caulkers, ferryboat operators and divers.

The concentration of merchant and guild offices at Ostia, in a port city where the imperial cult thrived, suggests imperial interests and ideology pervaded the shipping industry.[159] Already during the Republic, Rome stationed a *quaestor* at Ostia to supervise reception, storage and reshipment of grain from the provinces. Starting with the reign of Claudius,

155. The temple is 'late Flavian', has late first-century brickstamps, and probably was built under Domitian. Meiggs, *Roman Ostia*, pp. 65, 286.

156. Meiggs speculates that *negotiantes* ordered goods from their home districts, which the *navicularii* then transported to Ostia. Meiggs, *Roman Ostia*, p. 287.

157. Hermansen, *Ostia*, pp. 84-85.

158. The religious character of the banking industry may have been one reason John of Patmos viewed commerce with suspicion. Many cities of the Roman Empire had temple banks 'established to safeguard the money of the divinity and...to raise money to finance festivals and other expenses of the cult'. However, most commercial loans came from private banks or individuals rather than temple banks. W.E. Thompson, 'Insurance and Banking', in *CAM*, II, pp. 831-32. Individuals wealthy enough to make commercial loans probably had financial ties with pagan religious institutions or with Rome. E.g., Phoenician traders, captains and shipping agents named private Roman banker Marcus Minatius as their benefactor. R. Bogaert (ed.), *Texts on Bankers, Banking and Credit in the Greek World* (Leiden: Brill, 1976), no. 2. Tertullian writes of Christians who, in 'borrowing money from heathens under pledged securities...give a guarantee under oath', *De Idol.* 23.

159. Rostovtzeff says of the shipping guilds, there is 'little doubt that the imperial government would never have recognized...these associations had it not been for their utility to the state...', Rostovtzeff, *Roman Empire*, I, p. 59; cf. II, p. 607 n. 22.

imperial officials responsible to the *praefectus annonae* (superintendent of grain supply for the city of Rome) carried on the same work.[160]

A letter written by Tyrian shippers based at Puteoli gives some indication of the role of eastern entrepreneurs at imperial harbors. Though written in 174 CE (by which time the port of Ostia had eclipsed that of Puteoli), the letter speaks of earlier days that probably extend back to the reign of Domitian.[161] Shippers at Puteoli ask the Senate of Tyre for financial assistance to keep their offices open:

> By the gods and by the fortune of our lord Emperor. As almost all of you know, of all the trading stations at Puteoli, ours, in adornment and size, is superior to the others. In former days the Tyrians living at Puteoli were responsible for its maintenance; they were numerous and rich. But now we are reduced to a small number...[162]

This invocation of the gods and the Emperor marks yet another intersection of cult and commerce. The letter also confirms that, at the time of Revelation, some eastern shippers at Puteoli in their heyday were 'numerous and rich' (cf. Rev. 18.3, 15).

7. *Commerce and the Mark of the Beast*

Historical evidence from the ancient world indicates John of Patmos was not exaggerating when he said Rome 'glorified herself and lived luxuriously' (Rev. 18.7). Several hundred thousand people in Rome received free grain, while provincials paid for their food and sometimes went without. Elites in Rome consumed large quantities of provincial luxury goods as well as exotic products from outside the Empire.

Enterprising provincials often served as willing participants in the mechanisms of Roman consumption. In order to establish themselves in the imperial market, these entrepreneurs tied into a pyramid of reciprocal relationships that extended all the way to the Emperor. Participation in the imperial cult became an important symbol of a provincial's cooperation with his or her benefactors. Pressure to accept the cult also came

160. Meiggs, *Roman Ostia*, pp. 298-99.

161. R.M. Grant describes an inscription found at Puteoli (*OGIS*, 594), which 'contains a vow for the security of the new Emperor Domitian and refers to the place conceded by decree—to the god Helios, who sailed from Tyre to Puteoli'. Grant concludes the god 'was sent by Tyrians, presumably for Tyrians in the important trading center of Puteoli'. R.M. Grant, *Augustus to Constantine: The Rise of Christianity in the Roman World* (New York: Harper & Row, 1970), p. 20.

162. *OGIS*, 595. Cited by Meiggs, *Roman Ostia*, p. 60.

from provincial peers who were eager to continue good relations with Rome. The cult was so prevalent in the shipping industry and imperial port cities that a maritime merchant could not avoid it.[163]

Ubiquity of the imperial cult seems to be what John had in mind when he said all people, 'both small and great, both rich and poor, both free and slave' had to wear the 'mark' (χάραγμα) of the beast in order to buy and sell (13.16-17). The word χάραγμα had a range of meanings that included an official stamp on documents and the impression on coins.[164] John seems to use the term loosely as a figure of everything related to the imperial cult.

Literary Precedent for the 'Mark'

Because the 'mark' seems to have a multifaceted meaning in Revelation, we might expect that John had a variety of precedents and applications in mind. He could have drawn inspiration, for example, from apocryphal stories of the Jewish experience in Hellenistic Egypt, from a time when a mark on the body signified participation in a pagan cult and determined civic status. The author of *3 Maccabees* recounts the tale of King Ptolemy trying to force the cult of Dionysus upon Jews in Alexandria. The king set up a public inscription that read:

> None of those who do not sacrifice [to Dionysus] shall enter their sanctuaries, and all Jews shall be subjected to a registration involving poll tax and to the status of slaves. Those who object to this are to be taken by force and put to death; those who are registered are also to be branded on their bodies by fire with the ivy-leaf symbol of Dionysus, and they shall also be reduced to their former limited status (*3 Macc.* 2.28-29).

The inscription ended with a positive incentive for Jews to participate in the official cult: 'But if any of [the Jews] prefer to join those who have

---

163. From its inception, publicity about the imperial cult was widespread in the East. In 27 BCE the city of Mytilene on Lesbos voted a series of honors for Augustus, including a temple, priests, games, statues, and monthly sacrifices of a white bull on the day of Augustus's birthday. Local magistrates sent copies of their decree announcing these honors not only to Rome, but to other key cities of the Mediterranean. An (incomplete) inscription (*IGR*, IV, 39) names Pergamum, Actium, Brundisium, Tarraco, Massilia and Antioch in Syria. It is cited by Zanker, who notes, 'All these cities were important administrative or commercial centers or harbors, where the inscription would surely be read by many... There were literally hundreds of cities all around the Mediterranean that set up altars and temples to Augustus at this time'. Zanker, *Power of Images*, pp. 304-305.

164. BAGD, p. 876.

been initiated into the mysteries [of Dionysus], they shall have equal citizenship with the Alexandrians'. While the majority of Jews refused to comply, others 'readily gave themselves up, since they expected to enhance their reputation by their future association with the king' (*3 Macc*. 2.31-32).

The conscientious refusal of Egyptian Jews to conform to a pagan cult evoked popular suspicion of political disloyalty and threatened their economic status. Despite the fact that Jews 'continued to maintain goodwill and unswerving loyalty toward the dynasty' (*3 Macc*. 3.3), many of their neighbors were not convinced. Rumors circulated that the Jews 'were loyal neither to the king nor to his authorities, but were hostile and greatly opposed to his government' (3.7).

For Jews in such a precarious situation it was critical how elites in the local social and economic order responded. In this case certain 'neighbors and friends and business associates' secretly pledged to provide protection (3.10). The king responded by announcing that any Egyptians who were willing 'to give information [against the Jews] will receive the property of those who incur the punishment, and also two thousand drachmas from the royal treasury, and will be awarded their freedom' (3.28). In the end, according to *3 Maccabees*, God miraculously thwarted the evil designs of King Ptolemy, and those 'who had previously believed that the Jews would be destroyed and become food for birds...groaned as they themselves were overcome by disgrace' (6.34; cf. birds eating oppressors of Christians in Rev. 19.17-18).

If John knew of this story, he may have used the term 'mark of the beast' as a first-century parallel to the body-branding once accepted by Jews who worshiped Dionysus. Those who once wore the mark of Dionysus enjoyed access to the kind of benefits that lured some first-century Christians into the imperial cult. Ptolemy promised citizenship (rather than slavery), and there was financial advantage for those who worshiped Dionysus (exemption from poll tax). Likewise in John's day, participation in the imperial cult eased the way into citizenship and made it possible for Jews and Christians to profit in the marketplace. The tale from Alexandria depicts local business elites as sympathetic to the Jewish plight, and the author attributes this to a belief that soon 'matters would change' (*3 Macc*. 3.8). In late first-century Asia Minor, there was every reason to believe the imperial cult would exert pressure for a long time; Christians found little sympathy for their religious scruples within the political or economic hierarchy.

The 'Mark' on Coins and Documents

It would have been impossible for merchants to enter the international marketplace without handling the 'mark' on money, since many Roman coins carried impressions alluding to the imperial cult.[165] Ernest Janzen says that the beast of the Apocalypse 'has a definite financial component to it. An image (εἰκων, 13.14-15) is made of the beast and it causes all to be marked (χάραγμα, 13.16-17) if they wish to engage in buying or selling'. The ancient world used both the terms εἰκων (image) and χάραγμα (mark) to describe the process of minting coins.[166]

John may have refused to handle Roman coins simply because they normally carried the image and name of the current Emperor. Coins during the reign of Nero sometimes featured the Emperor wearing the radiate crown usually associated with divinity.[167] Scores of first-century Roman coin designs bore legends such as *IMP(erator) CAES(ar) DIVI VESP(asiani) F(ilius) DOMITIAN(us) AUG(ustus) P(ontifex) M(aximus)* ('Emperor Caesar Domitian Augustus, Son of the Divine Vespasian, Pontifex Maximus').[168] In the eyes of some devout Christians and Jews, the Emperor had come to epitomize pagan worship.[169] 'Such a refusal [to use Roman coins] is analogous to the Zealot refusal to carry, look at, or manufacture coins bearing any sort of image', Collins notes.[170] Early in the second century Ignatius of Antioch referred to

165. Already before the birth of Jesus, an *As* from Lugdunum depicted a provincial altar of Roma-Augustus. 'This coin type was minted in large quantities over an unusually long time', observes Zanker, *Power of Images*, p. 303.

166. Janzen, 'Jesus of the Apocalypse', p. 650.

167. E.g., Nero dupondii, *BMC*, I, pp. 240-42, nos. 210-24 (plate 44, nos. 1-4). The reverse of these coins bear legends such as *SECVRITAS AVGVSTI* and *VICTORIA AVGVSTI*. Cf. Domitian aureus depicting Vespasian, *BMC*, II, p. 312, no. 68 (plate 61, no. 11); and Domitian aureus depicting Titus, *BMC*, II, p. 313, no. 69 (plate 61, no. 12).

168. Domitian Sestertius, *BMC*, II, p. 356, no. 272 (plate 69, no. 3).

169. Caesar Augustus's summary of his own career illustrates the thoroughly religious nature of his office: 'I have been *pontifex maximus,* augur, one of the fifteen commissioners for sacred rites, one of the seven commissioners for religious feasts, one of the Arval fraternity, a member of the Titian society, and a *fetialis.*' *Res Gestae* 5. Easterners understood the religious role of the Emperor: the best preserved copy of the *Res Gestae* comes from the Temple of Roma and Augustus at Ancyra in Asia Minor. A bronze copy of the *Res Gestae* originally appeared on the mausoleum for Augustus in Rome (Suetonius, *Aug.* 101). The surviving copy from Ancyra renders the text in both Latin and Greek.

170. Collins, *Crisis and Catharsis*, p. 126. Cf. Collins, 'The Political Perspective

coins as bearing marks that symbolized ultimate loyalty and even raised questions of martyrdom.

> ...just as there are two coinages, the one of God, the other of the world, and each has its own stamp impressed on it, so the unbelievers bear the stamp of this world, and the believers the stamp of God in love through Jesus Christ, and unless we willingly choose to die through him in his passion, his life it not in us. (*Ign. Magn.* 5.2)

Artistic and architectural remains reveal that ancient ports in Italy and the East bore the distinct stamp of imperial religion. Shipping bills and other business documents may have carried imperial or cult emblems as well. In reference to the 'mark' of the beast in Rev. 13.16, Deissmann points to an imperial stamp affixed to documents found in Egypt from the year 48 CE. The official mark is an example, he says, of the custom 'now known to us from the papyri, of imprinting on deeds of sale and similar documents a stamp which contained the name and regnal year of the Emperor and was called, as in the Revelation, a *charagma*'.[171]

John's Refusal to be Pragmatic

Because he viewed Rome as demonic, John of Patmos apparently found the blending of commerce and imperial interests repugnant. Loyalty to Jesus Christ was a total commitment that left no room for a 'divine' Emperor. Yet veneration of a deified ruler pervaded harbors, trade venues, and commercial rituals of the late first-century Roman Empire. Even coins of the realm, without which trade was almost impossible, made blasphemous claims about the house of Caesar.

John repeatedly underscores his conviction that followers of Jesus

of the Revelation to John', *JBL* 96 (1977), pp. 252-54. Hippolytus said some Essenes (whom he identifies as Zealots or *Sicarii*) 'discipline themselves above the requisite rules of the order, so that even they would not handle a current coin of the country, saying that they ought not either to carry, or behold, or fashion an image'. *Refutatio Omnium Haeresium* 9.21. See M. Hengel, *The Zealots: Investigations into the Jewish Freedom Movement in the Period from Herod I until 70 A.D.* (Edinburgh: T. & T. Clark, 1989), pp. 190-91. C. Roth concludes that the 'anti-iconic tendency in Judaism reached its climax in the second half of the first century of the Christian era, at the time of the great Revolt against Rome'. C. Roth, 'An Ordinance against Images in Jerusalem', *HTR* 49 (1956), p. 177.

171. Deissmann reproduces the reversed likeness of an imperial stamp from 5–6 CE. The stamp reads: L λε Καίσαρος γρ[αφεῖον?], which Deissmann renders as 'In the 35th year of the Emperor, Scribe's chamber (?)'. Deissmann, *Light from the Ancient East* (New York: George H. Doran, 1927), p. 341.

must never bow to any being less than God.[172] Individuals loyal to Christ have the 'seal of God on their foreheads' (Rev. 7.3; 9.4), a figurative marking that may refer to baptism. Throughout Revelation those who wear the seal of God and those who carry the mark of the beast form mutually exclusive groups. John sees no possibility of compromise between them.

Christians and Jews[173] who adopted John's radical stance had to withdraw from guilds, and from political, religious and economic ties with Rome.[174] It is likely most Christians were not tempted to participate in the cult of the Emperor for its own sake, but merely for pragmatic financial or social reasons.[175] Christians who withdrew from all pagan cultic activities were likely to lose social and economic status. They also could face charges of disloyalty to Rome—charges John believed to be inspired by Satan, 'the accuser of our comrades' (12.10). Although such

---

172. Twice in his vision John is reprimanded for attempting to worship an angel. Both times the angel says, 'You must not do that!...Worship God!' (Rev. 19.10; 22.8-9). If heavenly beings are not worthy of worship, certainly no human could be. Cf. Est. 3.2-6.

173. Hengel (citing Hippolytus) says the Zealots were hostile to images, refused to accept pagan money, and would not enter Hellenistic cities. Thus they 'excluded themselves to a very great extent from economic life. They were unable, for example, to engage in trading'. *The Zealots*, p. 193, cf. p. 203.

174. Charles says trade guilds were the central concern of the letter to the church at Thyatira (Rev. 2.18-29). Within the Christian community 'differing views were honestly maintained as to the legitimacy of eating food sacrificed to idols'. There were many trade guilds at Thyatira, 'to one or another of which every citizen all but necessarily belonged: otherwise he could hardly maintain his business or enjoy the social advantages natural to his position'. Charles, *Commentary*, I, p. 69. Beckwith says there is nothing in the letter to Thyatira to indicate that the great issue there was withdrawal from the guilds. *Apocalypse*, p. 465. Beckwith is correct that the letter itself is not proof, but economic references elsewhere in Revelation make the question of guilds more evident. Collins says John's 'strict position on eating meat sacrificed to idols and his denunciations of "harlotry"...make it plain that he was calling upon Christians to avoid membership in guilds or other Gentile associations'. *Crisis and Catharsis*, p. 124.

175. W. Barclay notes that refusal to eat meat offered to idols 'came near to cutting off a Christian from all social fellowship with non-Christians; there were few social occasions, and almost no banquets, which he could share with the heathen world'. Even worse, a Christian's abstention from guild membership 'was equivalent to commercial suicide', *The Revelation of John*, I (Philadelphia: Westminster Press, rev. edn, 1976), p. 107.

accusations were serious, some courageous believers did 'not cling to life even in the face of death' (12.11).[176]

As the next chapter indicates, John stood within a venerable Jewish tradition of radical resistance to idolatrous Empire. Often using 'Babylon' as symbol and cipher of massive political evil, ancient Jewish prophets and apocalyptic writers of John's own day provided a rich store of literary ammunition for an attack upon late first-century Rome.

176. Collins suggests that when John speaks of believers at Ephesus bearing up 'on account of my name' (Rev. 2.3), he refers to 'formal or informal interrogation with regard to Christian faith, and thus persecution or the pressure of public opinion'. *Crisis and Catharsis*, p. 113.

Chapter 4

REPAY HER DOUBLE FOR HER DEEDS

> Fallen, fallen is Babylon the great!…her sins are heaped high as heaven,
> and God has remembered her iniquities. Render to her as she herself has
> rendered, and repay her double for her deeds; mix a double draught for her
> in the cup she mixed. (Rev. 18.2, 5, 6)

When John referred to Rome as 'Babylon', he tapped into a vein of bitterness that ran deep in Jewish consciousness.[1] Before and after the exile, Jewish prophets lambasted the Mesopotamian city for idolatry and insolence. This chapter explores the way John, in Revelation 17 and 18, appropriated and reshaped this literary tradition. Invoking the sordid reputation of ancient Babylon, however, did not provide as specific a condemnation of Rome as John sought. An examination of John's sources reveals that another city—though unnamed in the book of Revelation— also served as a prototype for the author's portrayal of Rome. This city was Tyre, the great maritime power that blended cult and commerce in ways repulsive to the prophet Ezekiel. In Revelation 17 and 18 the wicked cities of Babylon and Tyre coalesce into a perverse blend of idolatry, violence, economic exploitation, and political oppression.

1. Babylon and Rome in Apocalyptic Tradition

Babylon, great nemesis of Judah, humiliated the Jews and destroyed their temple in 587 BCE. That catastrophe was the first of a series, as one Empire after another forced itself upon the Jews in the centuries that followed. In 333 BCE Alexander the Great incorporated Palestine into his Empire, the formal beginning to centuries of hellenization in that

---

1. 'The conception of Babylon as the model archenemy of God's people…was not of John's own making, but had become a common way of speaking in Jewish circles'. Jean-Pierre Ruiz, *Ezekiel in the Apocalypse: The Transformation of Prophetic Language in Revelation 16, 17–19, 10* (Frankfurt am Main: Peter Lang, 1989), p. 386.

region. The very survival of Judaism in Palestine hung in the balance, especially during the cultural and religious rape of Judah carried out by Antiochus IV Epiphanes (175–64 BCE). Although the Maccabean revolt (167–64 BCE) marked a return to Jewish self-rule, a century of corrupt Jewish leaders brought more tyranny and religious syncretism. With the Jewish state on a downward spiral of civil war, Roman armies took Jerusalem without much struggle in 63 BCE. Palestine, along with the rest of the Mediterranean basin, remained firmly in Roman control for centuries.

Literary Expression of Anguish
Jewish literary response to this harsh history took the form of laments,[2] taunt-songs,[3] hymns of grief,[4] and prayers for divine retribution.[5] Jewish historians documented the crimes of foreign powers,[6] and storytellers recounted tales of heroic resistance.[7] Jewish cries of protest greeted each new overlord in the long parade of foreign oppressors. Babylon, though, maintained her symbolic status in Jewish tradition as archenemy.[8] Despite the fact that one million of their race lived in Mesopotamia during the first century CE,[9] Palestinian Jews never forgot the humiliation they suffered at Babylonian hands.[10]

Another wave of anguish swept over the Jewish community when Rome ravaged the second temple in 70 CE.[11] This time, however, Jews

2. E.g., Pss. 44, 74, 79; Lamentations, *4 Ezra* 3.28-36; 7.55-59.
3. E.g., Isa. 14.3-23.
4. E.g., Ps. 137.1-6.
5. E.g., Pss. 68.1-2, 21-23; 137.7-9.
6. E.g., 1 Macc. 1–2.
7. E.g., Dan. 1–6, Esther, Judith.
8. O. Kaiser says because 'Babylon was responsible for the fate of Jerusalem and the Jews, it became the symbol of world power hostile to God, and its king became the world ruler who was equally hostile to God'. O. Kaiser, *Isaiah 13–39* (Philadelphia: Westminster Press, 1974), p. 2.
9. *IDB*, I, p. 855.
10. Most authors of first- or second-century works that make Babylon an archvillain did not live in the Babylonian Jewish community. Palestine probably was the provenance of *4 Ezra* and *2 Baruch*. See introductions by B.M. Metzger and A.F.J. Klijn, *OTP*, I, pp. 520, 617.
11. The triumph celebrated at Rome in 71 CE was a particular sacrilege against the Jews. Vespasian and Titus sacrificed to the gods, then paraded the spoils of the Jewish war before huge crowds. The spoils included sacred articles from the temple in Jerusalem and a copy of the Torah. Josephus, *War* 7.5.4-5 (123-52). The Arch of

could draw from a ready store of traditional laments to express their grief. The books of *4 Ezra* and *2 Baruch,* for example, ostensibly contain theological reflections of Jews who saw Jerusalem fall in 587 BCE. In fact, these books appeared about the same time as Revelation, and express the outrage of first-century Jews over Jerusalem's fall in 70 CE.[12] Sometimes these and other first-century works use words and phrases we can trace back to specific passages in the Old Testament. More often, though, Jewish writers simply draw general themes of grief, anger and revenge from the ancient reservoir of anguish over Jerusalem's fall to Babylon.

Attitudes toward Rome in Jewish Apocalyptic Literature
Jewish apocalyptic literature from the first and second centuries CE channels a torrent of outrage against oppressors, often directed against Rome. The same Jewish milieu that shaped these works also left its imprint on John and the book of Revelation. References to wealth, trade and idolatry in other apocalyptic works give us clues to the social and theological setting of the polemic in Revelation.[13]

Many apocalyptic authors addressed themes of economic and social injustice. The author of *4 Ezra,* lamenting destruction of the temple, says 'I saw the desolation of Zion and the wealth of those who lived in Babylon [Rome]'.[14] Rome appears as a mighty eagle that suffocated dissent and dominated the earth with terror: 'no one spoke against him, not even one creature' (*4 Ezra* 11.6; cf. *T. Mos.* 10.8, Rev. 13.4). When a messianic lion calls the eagle to judgment, indictments include oppression, deceit, insolence and violence. The body of the eagle will burn (*4 Ezra* 11.37–12.3; cf. Rev. 17.16). The author rages against the obsequious fidelity of Asian society to imperial Rome:

> And you, O Asia, who share in the glamour of Babylon and the glory of her person—woe to you, miserable wretch! For you have made yourself like her... You have imitated that hateful harlot in all her deeds and devices (*4 Ezra* 15.46-48).

Titus, still standing in Rome today, depicts a triumphal procession of Roman soldiers carrying the table of showbread and the seven-branched candlestick.

12. See introduction to *2 Bar.* by A.F.J. Klijn, *OTP*, I, pp. 615-20.

13. I am indebted to H. Fuchs for pointing me to a number of the following citations in Jewish apocalyptic literature. H. Fuchs, *Der Geistige Widerstand Gegen Rom in der Antiken Welt* (Berlin: de Gruyter, 1964), pp. 60-83.

14. *4 Ezra* 3.2. Cf. *2 Bar.* 11.1-2.

This vulgar relationship between Asian society and Rome had a violent corollary in the pogroms against Jews. The Lord declares Asia would not be due such harsh punishment 'if you had not always killed my chosen people, exulting and clapping your hands and talking about their death when you were drunk' (*4 Ezra* 15.53).

The author of *2 Baruch,* probably writing early in the second century, tells of a vision in which Rome takes the shape of a haughty cedar that rules the forest with malevolent design.[15]

> Because of you, wickedness remained and has been done during all these years, but never goodness. And you possessed power over that which did not belong to you; you did not even show compassion to that which did belong to you. And you extended your power over those who were living far from you, and you keep those who are close to you in the nets of your wickedness, and you uplift your soul always like one who could not be uprooted (*2 Bar.* 36.7-9).

Baruch's vision gives an overview of history, in which divine judgment destroys a series of powerful kingdoms (presumably the Empires of Babylon, Persia and Greece). Apparently drawing from Daniel 7, the author seems to view Rome as the dreaded fourth kingdom:

> After that a fourth kingdom arises whose power is harsher and more evil than those which were before it…and it will rule the times and exalt itself more than the cedars of Lebanon. And the truth will hide itself in this and all who are polluted with unrighteousness will flee to it (*2 Bar.* 39.5-6).

Roman misrule will come to an end when the last Emperor will be bound, carried to Mount Zion, convicted and executed at a trial where the 'Anointed One' presides (40.1-2).

Sibylline Oracles 5, an early second-century work, carries an equally bitter invective against Rome.[16] Written in Egypt by a Jewish author, the book rivals Revelation 18 in its passion for vengeance. A great star will come from heaven to destroy 'Babylon' (*Sib. Or.* 5.158-59). Seething with contempt, the author addresses Rome:

> …you will remain utterly desolate for all ages yet. With you are found adulteries and illicit intercourse with boys. Effeminate and unjust, evil city, ill-fated above all… You have a murderous heart and impious spirit. Did

15. See introduction to *2 Baruch* by Klijn in *OTP*, I, pp. 616-17.
16. See introduction by J.J. Collins in *OTP*, I, pp. 390-92. *Sib. Or.* 5.47 alludes to Hadrian as the most recent Emperor ('He will have the name of a sea'—the Adriatic).

you not know what God can do, what he devises? But you said, 'I alone am, and no one will ravage me'. But now God, who is forever, will destroy you and all your people... Mingled with burning fire, inhabit the lawless nether region of Hades (*Sib. Or.* 5.163-78).

The author condemns Rome for claiming divine honors, for boasting, 'I alone am'. Arrogant Emperor Nero—the archetype of Roman decadence—will reclaim the imperial throne and declare himself 'equal to God' (*Sib. Or.* 5.33-34; cf. *Mart. Isa.* 4.1-13, 2 Thess. 2.4). As in John's vision (Rev. 18.11; 21.1), eschatological upheavals bring an end to maritime commerce with Rome: '...one day the sea will be dry, and ships will then no longer sail to Italy' (*Sib. Or.* 5.447-48; cf. 8.348).

Resentment against Rome sometimes generated a cry both for revenge and economic reparations. *Sibylline Oracles* 3, also of Egyptian origin, speaks on behalf of suffering peoples in Asia Minor.[17] Language reminiscent of Revelation depicts the drunken city of Rome on a reckless rampage of sexual exploitation.

However much wealth Rome received from tribute-bearing Asia, Asia will receive three times that much again from Rome, and will repay her deadly arrogance to her... O luxurious golden offspring of Latium, Rome, virgin, often drunken with your weddings with many suitors, as a slave will you be wed... (*Sib. Or.* 3.350-58; cf. Rev. 17.1-2, 18.3).

This work shows signs of redaction over many decades, but probably emerged in its present form late in the first century. As in the book of Revelation, the image of sexual promiscuity probably points to political and commercial alliances made by Rome with powerful people in conquered nations (cf. Ezek. 16, 23).

Sometimes in Jewish apocalyptic the polemic against Rome targeted trade networks of the Empire, reflecting the frustration of provincials who did not enjoy the benefits of commerce. *Sibylline Oracles* 8, a second-century work, satirizes powerful elites who monopolize resources of the earth.[18]

If the huge earth did not have its throne far from starry heaven, men would not have equal light but it would be marketed for gold and would belong to the rich, and God would have prepared another world for beggars (*Sib. Or.* 8.33-36).

17. See introduction by J.J. Collins in *OTP*, I, pp. 354-61.
18. Collins dates final redaction of *Sib. Or.* 8 at about 175 CE. *OTP*, I, pp. 415-17. Portions of the work may be considerably older.

Immediately following this gibe, the author says 'proud Rome' soon will burn and its 'wealth will perish' (8.37-40).

2. *Social and Economic Critique in the Book of Revelation*

Revelation stands within this apocalyptic tradition of bitter accusation against Rome. Like his Jewish contemporaries, John touches on themes that seem to reflect the frustration of marginalized people. The four horses of Rev. 6.1-8 appear to represent the suffering of conquered peoples who do not share the fruits of power: a white horse of conquest, a red horse of civil war, a black horse of famine and a pale green horse of Death.[19] John takes the vision of four horses from Zechariah (Zech. 1.8; 6.1-8) and reshapes it for a new context and purpose. In Zechariah's vision, horses patrol the earth in service to God (1.11; 6.7); in Revelation they are evil agents of Roman oppression.

The element of social injustice in Zechariah's prophecy may have inspired John to use the image of four horses as an appropriate commentary on the *pax Romana*. Returning from their patrol, the four horses of Zechariah report 'the whole earth remains at peace' (Zech. 1.11). This statement reflects the superficial serenity of international relations after the defeat of Babylon by Persia. God is not pleased, however, since the prevailing 'peace' is an unjust order. 'I am extremely angry with the nations that are at ease', God declares, 'for while I was only a little angry, they made the disaster worse' (1.15). Pagan nations rest in comfort while God's people languish in Babylon (2.7) or live miserably in Jerusalem (8.10).

In John's day, the Roman Empire brought apparent peace to the nations. This tranquility was more pacification than peace, though, since Rome promoted policies that sometimes brought suffering to vulnerable members of society.[20] A rider on one of the four horses in Revelation cries, 'A quart of wheat for a denarius, and three quarts of barley for a denarius, but do not harm the [olive] oil and wine' (Rev. 6.6, RSV). The price of grain here seems to indicate severe inflation,[21] and the cry not

---

19. The four horses represent standard end-time woes that appear in other Jewish and Christian apocalypses. Cf. *4 Ezra* 13.1-58; Mt. 24.6-8; Mk 13.7-8; Lk. 21.9-11.

20. Even Tacitus records the opinion of some persons that the *pax Romana* of Augustus was 'peace with bloodshed'. Tacitus, *Ann.* 1.10.

21. During a famine (c. 92-93 CE) in Pisidian Antioch, the governor ordered dealers not to sell grain for more than one sestertius per modius (instead of the two

to damage oil and wine may relate to an edict of Domitian in 92 CE. In that year the Empire experienced an abundance of wine and a shortage of grain. Domitian forbade anyone to plant more vineyards in Italy and ordered provincials to destroy at least half of theirs.[22] Had they obeyed Domitian's order, wealthy provincials who owned commercial vineyards might have lost income. Grain would have been cheaper for provincials, however, as more land reverted to production of staple foods. Domitian never enforced the edict, apparently fearing the wrath of people invested in the wine business.[23]

John Taps the Jewish Reservoir of Grief

While John occasionally addresses specific social and economic injustices, his primary focus remains on broader issues of power and idolatry. In addressing these topics, John drew poetry and images from the same literary reservoir used by Jewish apocalypticists.[24] Some figures and associations from the past slip unconsciously into his writing, as though embedded deeply in his thought patterns.[25] Other images, such as the beast or wicked Babylon, play such a prominent role that John must consciously have borrowed these figures because they carried a useful set of associations. Instead of alluding briefly in Revelation 18 to a range of Old Testament passages, for example, John writes a veritable midrash

sestertii profiteers demanded). See W.M. Ramsay, 'Studies in the Roman Province of Galatia, VI—Some Inscriptions of Colonia Caesarea Antiochea', *JRS* 14 (1924), pp. 179-84. Also J. Court, *Myth and History in the Book of Revelation* (Atlanta: John Knox, 1979), pp. 59-60. The price of wheat in Rev. 6.6 is one denarius per quart, or about 2.5 sestertii per quart. There are eight quarts in a modius, so a modius at this rate would have cost twenty sestertii. Thus the price of grain in Rev. 6.6 is about twenty times higher than the price set by the governor of Pisidian Antioch in 92–93 CE.

22. Suetonius, *Dom.* 7.2. Charles, *Commentary*, I, p. 167.

23. Suetonius, *Dom.* 14.2.

24. Many scholars comment on John's heavy use of the Old Testament. H.B. Swete says most of John's allusions to the Old Testament come from the following books, in descending order: Isaiah (46 references), Daniel (31 references), Ezekiel (29 references), and Psalms (27 references). H.B. Swete, *The Apocalypse of St John* (London: Macmillan, 3rd edn, 1911), pp. cxix-cxxxviii.

25. Cf. Swete, *The Apocalypse*, p. cliii. John often conflates allusions in such a lavish new configuration that it is impossible to trace his images back to a single Old Testament text. Marginal notes for Rev. 19.1-2 (Nestle-Aland, 26th edn), for example, list allusions to *Psalms of Solomon*, Daniel, Tobit, Psalms, Jeremiah, Deuteronomy and 2 Kings. Such fluent appropriation of traditional material reflects a mind steeped in—and shaped by—the Old Testament.

on specific sections of Isaiah and Ezekiel. These passages of the great prophets deal with the interplay of Empire, commerce and idolatry; they help explain John's attitude toward Rome and his reasons for rejecting economic involvement with her.

Parallels Between Rome and Ancient Babylon

There are general historical parallels between Babylon and Rome that may have brought the ancient city to John's mind. Rome destroyed the temple and now persecutes God's people (Rev. 13.10; 18.24)—just as Babylon slaughtered Jews and took them captive (2 Kgs 24.10–25.21). Rome now appears omnipotent to people of the earth (Rev. 13.4; 17.18), just as Babylon once seemed in world affairs (Isa. 47.7; Dan. 4.22).

John does not explicitly identify these parallels between the two imperial cities. However, he vents his outrage against Rome in language reminiscent of ancient Jewish curses upon Babylon. John wants God to repay Rome 'double for her deeds' (Rev. 18.6), much as Jewish exiles once said of Babylon, 'Happy shall they be who pay you back what you have done to us!' (Ps. 137.8)

Rome now dominates the earth (Rev. 14.8; 18.3), just as Babylon 'laid nations low' (Isa. 14.12). The Roman Empire takes 'blasphemous names' and receives worship from its subjects (Rev. 13.1, 4, 12; 17.3), repeating Babylon's offense of saying 'I will make myself like the Most High' (Isa. 14.14). The flesh of kings and others loyal to Rome will become a feast for vultures (Rev. 19.17-18), much as Isaiah looked for the corpse of Babylon's king to become 'loathsome carrion' (Isa. 14.19; cf. Ezek. 39.17-20). John awaits destruction of the Roman imperial cult just as Isaiah expected images of Babylon's gods to 'lie shattered on the ground' (Isa. 21.9). The imperial city of John's day deserved punishment for arrogance and seduction (Rev. 18.7, 23) as surely as did ancient Babylon.

John portrays Rome as a confident and contemptuous queen who declares, 'I am no widow, and I will never see grief' (Rev. 18.7). This recalls the prophecy of Isaiah in which Babylon proudly announces, 'I shall not sit as a widow' (Isa. 47.8). Isaiah sarcastically called Babylon a 'virgin daughter' (Isa. 47.1), perhaps because it still was unconquered. 'I shall be a mistress forever' (47.7) she declared; 'I am, and there is no one besides me' (47.8, 10). For her security Babylon relied on pagan religion and astrology, what Isaiah dismisses as 'sorceries' and 'enchantments' (47.9, 12-13). When the city finally comes to ruin, all vassals and allies who 'trafficked' with Babylon will abandon her (47.15).[26]

John intensifies Isaiah's description of a rift between the imperial capital and its allies. Rome's allies, he says, eventually will do worse than abandon her: the 'ten horns' (perhaps provincial rulers, Rev. 17.12) and the 'beast [the Empire] will hate the whore [Rome]; they will make her desolate and naked; they will devour her flesh and burn her up with fire' (17.16; cf. Bar. 4.35).[27]

Venom from the oracle against Babylon in Isaiah 13.1-22 saturates key passages of Revelation.[28] Isaiah said God will mete out such harsh judgment that Babylon

> will never be inhabited or lived in for all generations… But wild animals will lie down there, and its houses will be full of howling creatures… and there goat-demons will dance. Hyenas will cry in its towers, and jackals in the pleasant palaces… (Isa. 13.20-22).

This dreadful dose of vengeance, preserved among Jews who loved Jerusalem, spills out in the opening lines of John's dirge over Rome (Rev. 18.2; cf. Bar. 4.31-35).[29]

Strengths and Limitations of Equating Rome to Babylon
Equating Rome to Babylon gave John and his readers a familiar paradigm of oppressive power, as well as heroic models for resistance to it. There

---

26. The Masoretic text uses a participle of the word סחר, meaning 'to travel about (as a trader)'. BDB, p. 695.

27. To be put to death by fire was the punishment for the daughter of a priest who 'profanes herself through prostitution' (Lev. 21.9). Hengel observes that in the pseudepigraphal tradition, death by burning was the punishment for idolaters. Hengel, *The Zealots*, p. 188 n. 222. The description of Rome's fate in Revelation 17 would be appropriate for the offenses of both prostitution and idolatry.

28. In addition to Revelation 18, other parts the Apocalypse echo Isaiah 13: nations of the earth assemble for a great battle (Isa. 13.4; Rev. 16.12-16, 17.16, 17); every person on earth trembles at the hour of divine punishment (Isa. 13.7, 8; Rev. 6.15-17); strange phenomena affect the sun, moon and stars (Isa. 13.10; Rev. 6.12, 13; 8.12); heaven and earth tear and shake (Isa. 13.13; Rev. 6.12-14); and there is wholesale slaughter by the sword (Isa. 13.15; Rev. 6.8; 13.10).

29. John gives Jerusalem a prominent role in Revelation, but has little affection for the actual city in Palestine. In Rev. 11.8 he refers to it as 'the great city that is prophetically called Sodom and Egypt, where also their Lord was crucified'. With his Jewish background and familiarity with the Old Testament, John absorbed the bitterness Jews felt against Babylon over the destruction of Jerusalem. In Revelation he unloads that bitterness upon Rome for its idolatry and arrogance.

are so many allusions to the book of Daniel in Revelation that we must assume John consciously looked to that book for inspiration.[30] Revelation's governing metaphor of Rome as a beast (Rev. 13.1-10), for example, is an unmistakable amalgamation of the four creatures in Daniel (Dan. 7.1-28).[31]

John uses more material from apocalyptic portions of Daniel (chs. 7–12) than he does from the court tales (chs. 1–6). At least in spirit, though, the court tales stand behind John's radical stance of non-cooperation with corrupt government. Three courageous Hebrew men once refused to bow and worship an image set up by Nebuchadnezzar (Dan. 3.1-30), much as John now makes no concession to the image of the beast (Rev. 14.11, 15.2, 16.2, 19.20). All 'peoples, nations and languages' bowed to idolatrous demands of the Babylonian king (Dan. 3.7), just as provinces of the Roman Empire now accept the imperial cult (Rev. 13.7, 8). John did not expect God to deliver Christians from martyrdom (Rev. 6.9-11; 20.4) as God once spared the Hebrew men (Dan. 3.19-30; cf. 6.16-24). However, John did expect God eventually would vindicate saints who suffered, and would place them in positions of power in the kingdom of Christ (Rev. 20.4-6).

Despite all the parallels John may have seen between Babylon and Rome, certain aspects of Jewish tradition about the ancient city did not reinforce John's strategy of separation from imperial power. Jeremiah, for example, records an oracle in which God refers to the king of Babylon as 'my servant' (Jer. 27.6), and the prophet urged Jewish exiles

---

30. Nestle-Aland marginal notes for Revelation cite more than sixty possible allusions to Daniel, most from the apocalyptic chapters (Dan. 7–12). Although the court tales of Daniel (chs. 1–6) have no explicit representation in Revelation, they nevertheless may have helped shape John's language and theology. Cf. Dan. 1.12, 14 and Rev. 2.10; Dan. 5.4, 23 and Rev. 9.20; Dan. 3.4 and Rev. 10.11; Dan. 2.44 and Rev. 11.15; Dan. 2.28, 45 and Rev. 22.6.

31. G.K. Beale counts twenty-one Old Testament allusions in Revelation 13, two-thirds of which come from Daniel. He finds a 'common theological pattern which is repeated throughout both Daniel 7 and Revelation 13'. Beale concludes it is likely that 'Daniel is the most formative influence on the thought and structure of Revelation'. Beale sees both Daniel and John 'criticizing the status quo of apostasy, compromise and syncretism'. In Revelation the circumstances include 'rulers who lay claim to deity' and 'so-called Christians who agree to participate in the compromising demands of Emperor worship and of pagan society'. G.K. Beale, *The Use of Daniel in Jewish Apocalyptic Literature and in the Revelation of St. John* (Lanham, MD: University Press of America, 1984), pp. 244-45, 297-98.

to seek the welfare of Babylon. He exhorted Jews to 'pray to the Lord on its behalf, for in its welfare you will find your welfare' (Jer. 29.7). In contrast, John found no reason to seek the good of imperial Rome, and yearned for ruthless judgment on the imperial capital (Rev. 16.17-21; 18.6-8).

Perhaps even the story of Daniel was not entirely satisfactory as a precedent, since Daniel and his companions served as courtiers for the Babylonian king (Dan. 1.3-21; 2.49; 3.30). Such close cooperation with idolatrous power was unthinkable for John, who pointed fellow Christians in the opposite direction: 'Come out of her, my people, so that you do not take part in her sins' (Rev. 18.4).

3. *Tyre as a Type for Rome in Revelation 18*

The analogy between Rome and Babylon was not perfect, and in Revelation 18 John looks to another villain city when he focuses on economic aspects of Roman rule. Ancient Tyre, with its vast network of maritime trade, now takes a turn in John's line-up of imperial rogues.[32] Although John never mentions Tyre by name, portions of Revelation 18 closely resemble oracles against that city in Isaiah 23 and Ezekiel 27–28.[33] John seems to have drawn his sketch of fallen Rome with

32. Condemnation of Tyre among the Jews appears as early as the eighth century BCE. Amos says the city 'delivered entire communities over to Edom, and did not remember the covenant of kinship (ברית אחים)'. As a result, God would send fire upon Tyre to 'devour its strongholds' (Amos 1.9-10). Amos does not name the treaty-partner injured by Tyre. He may have in mind the pact between Solomon and Hiram of Tyre (1 Kgs 5.1-12; 9.10-14), or the friendship between Tyre and Israel at the time Ahab married Jezebel. See J.L. Mays, *Amos* (Philadelphia: Westminster Press, 1969), p. 34; E. Hammershaimb, *The Book of Amos: A Commentary* (New York: Schocken Books, 1970), p. 34. The connection between Jezebel and Phoenicia could help explain why John conjures up Tyre in Revelation. Both in the time of David (1 Kgs 5.1) and in the era of Jezebel, Jews had friendly relations with the Phoenicians. Eventually, under queen Jezebel, this relationship brought pagan religion into Jerusalem (1 Kgs 16.31-34). Likewise first-century Christians interacted with Rome, and John believes the exchange is bringing pagan practices into the church.

33. John draws heavily from Ezekiel throughout the book of Revelation. M.E. Boismard demonstrates there is even close correspondence between the sequence of text in Revelation and the sequence in Ezekiel. M.E. Boismard, '"L'Apocalypse", ou "Les Apocalypses" de Saint Jean', *RB* 56 (1949), pp. 530-32. J.M. Vogelgesang says there is such similarity between Revelation and Ezekiel that 'it proves beyond any doubt that John utilized Ezekiel directly'. J.M. Vogelgesang, *The Interpretation*

dust and soot from the ruins of Tyre itself.

It is surprising to find this image of ancient Tyre superimposed upon John's larger picture of wicked Babylon. The two visions in Revelation 17 and 18 relate closely in theme and structure, and Babylon is the focal point from start to finish.[34] We have seen there were many Jewish traditions about Babylon from which John could draw. He did not need to borrow vignettes of Tyre simply to show that Babylon (Rome) was wicked and idolatrous. Some aspect of Jewish tradition about Tyre was important for John's polemic against Rome.

The Commercial Nature of Ancient Tyre

Tyre's combination of economic prowess and idolatrous arrogance made it useful to John's purpose. The book of Isaiah illustrates how Tyre's commercial Empire loomed large in Jewish tradition: 'Wail, O ships of Tarshish, for your fortress is destroyed' (Isa. 23.1). In this one sentence Isaiah registers the fall of Tyre, the grief felt by her merchants and the far reach of her maritime Empire.[35] Tyre was a 'bestower of crowns', her merchants were 'princes', and her traders the 'honored of the earth' (23.8). The great city collected grain from Egypt as revenue and became 'merchant of the nations' (23.3). Power, though, led to overweening pride. Isaiah snorts at the 'exultant city' (23.7), insists God will 'defile the pride of all glory' (23.9), and repeats his notice of Tyre's demise (23.14).

of Ezekiel in the Book of Revelation (Ann Arbor: University Microfilms, 1986), p. 132; on Revelation 18 and Ezekiel 27, pp. 32-34.

34. Chapter 17 itself blends two major prophetic traditions: the Prostitute as a type of moral and spiritual degeneration, and Babylon as the epitome of a wicked city. These two traditions merge here as the Prostitute Babylon. Ruiz says 17.1 'serves as the introduction to the whole vision of the judgment of Prostitute Babylon, comprising both chapters'. Ruiz, *Ezekiel in the Apocalypse*, p. 379.

35. Tarshish is an 'unknown location famous for associations with sea traffic'. Achtemeier (ed.), *Harper's Bible Dictionary*, p. 1018. The Jonah story suggests Tarshish was in the Mediterranean (Jon. 1.3), and many scholars place it in southern Spain. 1 Kgs 10.22 says Solomon's fleet of Tarshish brought in gold, silver, ivory, apes and peacocks—suggesting Tarshish was related to trade routes in the Indian Ocean or along the east coast of Africa. Perhaps 'ships of Tarshish' simply designated 'larger sea-going vessels, regardless of their origin or ports of call'. *IDB*, IV, pp. 517-18. In any case, Isaiah set some precedent for the dirge of Rev. 18 when he condemned maritime trade ('all the ships of Tarshish', Isa. 2.16) in the same unit of prophecy that describes Judah as being polluted with 'diviners...foreigners... silver and gold...idols' (Isa. 2.5-17).

Even Isaiah's promise of Tyre's eventual restoration provided material for John to lambast Rome. Seventy years after her collapse, Isaiah says, Tyre 'will return to all her trade, and will prostitute herself with all the kingdoms of the world' (Isa. 23.17). Isaiah recognizes the intimate connection between commerce and political alliance, and says the relationship has now degenerated to a form of prostitution. In her day of restoration, though, Tyre's intercourse with nations will not gratify her own lust:

> Her merchandise and her wages will be dedicated to the Lord; her profits will not be stored or hoarded, but her merchandise will supply abundant food and fine clothing for those who live in the presence of the Lord (Isa. 23.18).

In the tradition of Isaiah, John now dismisses Roman commercial and political alliances as prostitution (Rev. 17.1-2; 18.3). Again he echoes Isaiah when he describes the New Jerusalem: saints in the city will live in the presence of God (21.3), and 'kings of the earth will bring their glory into it...People will bring into it the glory and the honor of the nations' (21.24-26).[36] Prestige and resources once monopolized by Rome will devolve upon saints under the imminent rule of God.

Tyre's Legendary Wickedness
After the exile, Jews made Tyre a byword for rapacious greed. In the book of Joel, Yahweh tells Tyre and Sidon: 'you have taken my silver and my gold, and have carried my rich treasures into your temples. You have sold the people of Judah and Jerusalem to the Greeks' (Joel 3.5-6; cf. Ezek. 27.13).[37] Such offenses will not go unpunished. In a classic case of role reversal, God will sell the sons and daughters of Tyre and Sidon as slaves to Judah (Joel 3.8).[38]

---

36. Conversion of the nations to Yahwistic faith became a common theme of post-exilic Judaism. Zechariah mentions 'inhabitants of many cities' and 'strong nations' that will come to worship at Jerusalem (Zech. 8.20-23); Tobit expects converted Gentiles 'will all abandon their idols, which deceitfully have led them into their error' (Tob. 14.6-7).

37. The book of Joel probably reached its final form between 500 and 350 BCE. J.W. Whedbee, in Mays (ed.), *Harper's Bible Commentary*, pp. 716-17.

38. In addition to Tyre, several important themes from Joel 3 reappear in Revelation. Among these are the holy war between Yahweh's warriors and armies of the nations (Joel 3.11-12, 14; Rev. 16.12-16), the sickle and wine press as symbols of divine judgment (Joel 3.13; Rev. 14.17-20), signs in the sun, moon and stars (Joel

Tyre fares no better in apocalyptic portions of Zechariah.[39] With her strong defensive situation, the city 'built itself a rampart, and heaped up silver like dust, and gold like dirt of the streets'.[40] Tyre's avarice provokes the wrath of God, who will 'strip it of its possessions and hurl its wealth into the sea, and it shall be devoured by fire' (Zech. 9.3-4; cf. Rev. 18.8-9, 21).[41]

The author of 2 Maccabees further tarnishes Tyre's reputation, naming it as the site of Jewish idolatry during the reign of Antiochus IV Epiphanes. With his program of Hellenization at full speed, Antiochus went to Tyre to celebrate the quadrennial games. Jason, high priest at Jerusalem, compromised so completely with pagan religion that he sent envoys to Tyre with three hundred silver drachmas for a sacrifice to Hercules (2 Macc. 4.18-20). Menelaus, the next high priest, compounded the sacrilege by stealing golden vessels from the temple and selling them to Tyre for personal gain (2 Macc. 4.32). Jews who met with Antiochus to protest this outrage died as martyrs at Tyre (2 Macc. 4.43-50).[42]

Early Christian literature adds to the proverbial view of Tyre as a wicked place. When Jesus berates Galilean villages for refusing to repent, he accentuates their obstinacy by declaring, 'if the deeds of power done in you had been done in Tyre and Sidon, they would have repented long ago'. Judgment awaiting the villages is so awful that Jesus can describe it only by saying it will be worse than the fate reserved for wicked Tyre and Sidon (Mt. 11.20-22; Lk. 10.13-14).

An incident recorded in Acts gave Tyre associations that may have reinforced John's negative impression of the city. Luke tells how Herod Agrippa delivered a speech to envoys from Tyre and Sidon. The

3.15; Rev. 6.12-13, 8.12), and God's dwelling in a restored Jerusalem (Joel 3.17-18; Rev. 21-22). Joel's burning desire for retribution upon enemies also finds an echo in Revelation 18.

39. Zech. 9-14 probably dates from the fifth or fourth centuries BCE. D.L. Peterson, in Mays (ed.), *Harper's Bible Commentary*, p. 747.

40. The rampart was a breakwater, 820 yards long and nine yards thick, built in the time of Hiram king of Tyre to defend the island fortress. J.G. Baldwin, *Haggai, Zechariah, Malachi* (London: Tyndale Press, 1972), p. 160.

41. The word translated 'wealth' (חיל) has a range a meanings, including 'strength', 'efficiency' and 'army', BDB, p. 298. The LXX chooses the meaning of 'strength' (δύναμις). In Rev. 18.17, though, John emphasizes the economic aspect of Rome by specifying that her 'wealth' (πλοῦτος) will perish.

42. 1 Macc. 5.15 cites the people Tyre as joining the effort to 'annihilate' the Jews.

Phoenicians shouted, 'The voice of a god, and not of a mortal'. Deification of a ruler was so abominable that 'immediately, because he had not given the glory to God, an angel of the Lord struck him down, and he was eaten by worms' (Acts 12.20-23). Josephus tells a similar version of Herod Agrippa's death, but makes no mention of envoys from Tyre and Sidon.[43] Luke features the envoys perhaps because their idolatrous praise to a ruler matched early Christian stereotypes of Phoenician paganism and misguided loyalty.[44]

Ezekiel and the Good Ship Tyre

From a wide variety of sources, these negative associations accumulated like barnacles on the reputation of Tyre among Jews and Christians. The clearest precedent for the dirge in Revelation 18 comes from the portrayal of Tyre as a stately merchant ship in Ezekiel 27.[45] The good ship Tyre once plied waters of the Mediterranean with serene self-confidence. 'I am perfect in beauty', it declared (Ezek. 27.3), revelling in its exquisite construction and adornment. Its planks, mast and oars came from Palestine. Ivory-inlaid decks came from Cyprus, its embroidered sail from Egypt (27.5-7). The strength and function of Tyre depended on these fine imports, and Tyre defended itself with mercenaries from Persia ('Paras'), western Asia Minor ('Lud') and Libya ('Put') (27.10).[46]

This reliance on the resources of allies prefigured the Roman Empire of five centuries later. Since the commercial networks of Tyre and Rome

---

43. *Ant.* 19.8.2 (343-52). Josephus places the event in Caesarea and says Herod was hailed as a god during a festival in honor of Caesar. Herod Agrippa died in 44 CE.

44. Gospel writers emphasize, however, that Jesus took his ministry of healing even to the region of Tyre. Jesus apparently quotes (satirizes?) the Jewish stereotype of Tyrians when he pauses before healing the daughter of a Syrophoenician woman: 'Let the children [Jews] be fed first, for it is not fair to take the children's food and throw it to the dogs [Gentiles, in this case Phoenicians]' (Mk 7.27; Mt. 15.26).

45. Vogelgesang demonstrates that John borrowed themes, phrases and even sequence of ideas from Ezekiel. He concludes that 'not only was John dependent on Ezekiel, but...he modeled his book on that of Ezekiel'. Vogelgesang, *Ezekiel in the Book of Revelation*, p. 69.

46. W. Zimmerli notes that Lud appears in Gen. 10.22 'and is there certainly to be equated with the Lydians of Asia Minor', i.e., people from the region of the seven churches of Revelation. *A Commentary on the Book of the Prophet Ezekiel*, II (Philadelphia: Fortress Press, 1983), p. 59. Zimmerli also understands 'Javan' (Ezek. 27.13) as a reference to the Ionians. Zimmerli, *Commentary*, II, p. 65.

covered largely the same geographic area, it is not surprising they handled the same products.[47] Trade articles listed in Ezek. 27.12-24 that reappear in Rev. 18.11-13 include gold, silver, iron, bronze, slaves, horses, ivory, purple, fine linen, jewels, wheat, oil, wine and spice.[48] Despite similarities, however, John did not mindlessly take over Ezekiel's list.[49] Rather, he scrambled the order of products and added items of particular interest to Rome: pearls, marble, silk, incense and fine-grade flour.

After enumerating products Tyre traded with far-flung places, Ezekiel focuses on merchants and mariners who managed the maritime market.[50] An ill wind sinks the good ship Tyre, and down with her go cargo, sailors, merchants and soldiers (Ezek. 27.26-27). News of the disaster races like a tidal wave along the coastlands (27.28). Grievous wailing erupts among all whose trade is on the sea (27.29-32). The loss is an economic disaster for those invested in Tyre, since her 'abundant wealth and merchandise...enriched the kings of the earth' (27.33). Allies of Tyre reel in terror; 'their kings' hair stands on end' and the merchants 'howl'.[51] Predictions of Tyre's imminent demise must have sobered Jews who took Ezekiel seriously, since Judah and Israel traded with the

47. Nor is it surprising that John would have used Ezekiel's notes on maritime commerce, since the cargo list in Ezekiel 'displays an astonishingly accurate knowledge of the commerce of the world of his day. It is confirmed by various pieces of information from other ancient sources'. W. Eichrodt, *Ezekiel: A Commentary* (Philadelphia: Westminster Press, 1970), p. 387.

48. Zimmerli says Ezekiel's list of trade articles emphasizes the consumption of Tyre. 'The list itself is purely a list of imports. In no sense does it have the aim of giving a full picture of Tyrian trade in all its comings and goings, but describes alone...what Tyre purchases through her trading agents.' Zimmerli, *Commentary*, II, p. 70.

49. There is no doubt that Rev. 18.11-13 closely parallels Ezek. 27.12-24. Vogelgesang identifies at least twenty cargo items that appear in both lists, including the distinctive phrase ψυχὰς ἀνθρώπων (souls of human beings). Vogelgesang, *Ezekiel in the Book of Revelation*, pp. 33-34. It is not surprising that ancient Tyre and first-century Rome would show interest in many of the same commercial items. Bauckham is correct that 'John has produced a highly effective description of his own' which 'gives special prominence to the merchandise' imported by Rome. Bauckham, 'Economic Critique', p. 51; cf. p. 59.

50. For discussion of Tyre's pre-Hellenistic trade network, see Hengel, *Judaism and Hellenism*, I (London: SCM Press, 1974), p. 32.

51. Translation by Zimmerli, *Commentary*, II, p. 53. The verb שׁרק usually means 'hiss', often with a connotation of derision. BDB, p. 1056.

city-state (27.17). In 594 BCE Judah even contemplated forging a political alliance with Tyre in an effort to halt the westward advance of Babylon (Jer. 27.3).[52]

Idolatrous Claims of Tyre and Rome

When John evoked Jewish tradition about Tyre to shape his indictment of Rome, he may have had in mind charges of self-deification outlined by Ezekiel.[53] The oracle in Ezekiel 28 begins with words John could have written about the Emperor of his day.

> Mortal, say to the prince of Tyre, Thus says the Lord God: Because your heart is proud and you have said, 'I am a god; I sit in the heart of the seas', yet you are but a mortal, and no god...(Ezek. 28.2).[54]

Ezekiel follows this accusation of self-idolatry with a reference to Tyre's commercial exploits: 'By your great wisdom in trade you have increased your wealth, and your heart has become proud in your wealth' (28.5).

A combination of economic success and self-aggrandizement brought Tyre to judgment. From John's perspective, the same unholy mixture will bring fire on Rome. First-century trade networks and the imperial cult centered on the city of Rome with its proud 'prince'. When John says Rome 'glorified' itself (Rev. 18.7), he uses a word (ἐδόξασεν) that appears only once elsewhere in Revelation.[55] In that occurrence, saints

52. Eichrodt, *Ezekiel*, p. 367.

53. Eichrodt notes that 'Ugaritic documents testify to the king's claim to receive worship and to be in his own person the guarantee of his people's salvation', the 'earthly embodiment of the god who dies and rises again'. *Ezekiel*, p. 390. John surely was not familiar with such Ugaritic documents, but recognized accusations of self-deification in Ezekiel's prophecy. John may have known the story of Judith, who successfully resisted when Nebuchadnezzar assumed divine status (Jdt. 6.2; 8.1–16.25).

54. Cf. Ezek. 28.6. For the long tradition of Jewish protest against rulers who claim divine status, see Isa. 14.13-14 (Nebuchadnezzar?); Ezek. 29.1-12 (Pharaoh; Ezekiel sets a precedent in calling Pharaoh a 'great dragon', cf. Rev. 12.3); Dan. 11.36-37 and 2 Macc. 9.12 (Antiochus IV Epiphanes); *Pss. Sol.* 2.29 (Pompey); Philo, *Leg. Gai.* 85-118 (Caligula); *Mart. Isa.* 4.6 and *Sib. Or.* 5.33-34 (Nero).

55. Elsewhere in the New Testament the word δοξάζω usually means praise directed to God or Jesus. Nine out of ten times Luke uses the word he follows it with τὸν θεὸν; once Luke makes Jesus the object of praise (Lk. 4.15). One occurrence in Mark and twenty-two in John all refer to God or Jesus. Matthew uses the word only once in reference to humans, when he cites Jesus' condemnation of hypocrites who seek the praise of others (Mt. 6.2). Paul is less meticulous, going so far as to

who conquered the beast stand beside the sea of glass and sing the song of the Lamb.

> Great and amazing are your deeds, Lord God the Almighty! Just and true are your ways, King of the nations! Lord, who will not fear and glorify (δοξάσει) your name? (Rev. 15.3, 4)

The great offense of Rome was taking the glory that belonged to God, the 'King of nations', and claiming it for itself. It 'glorified itself' (ἐδόξασεν αὐτὴν)[56] and gloated, 'I rule as a queen' (18.7). Any illusion of royal immunity will collapse quickly under the eschatological victory of Christ, the 'Lord of lords and King of Kings' (17.14).

Ezekiel said God would use other nations to bring judgment on Tyre:

> I will bring strangers against you, the most terrible of nations…They shall thrust you down to the Pit, and you shall die a violent death in the heart of the seas (Ezek. 28.7-8).

The 'strangers' executing judgment on Tyre apparently come from Babylon (Ezek. 30.10-11). Likewise the book of Revelation foresees a time when God will use other nations to punish Rome. Kings and nations of the Roman Empire ('ten horns' and the 'beast') will 'hate the whore' Rome. They will 'make her desolate and naked; they will devour her flesh and burn her up with fire' (Rev. 17.12-13, 16; cf. Ezek. 28.18).

Economic and Social Injustice of Tyre and Rome
Part of Tyre's guilt was that its commercial expansion led to suffering among people who did not share its wealth and power. 'In the abundance of your trade you were filled with violence, and you sinned', declares Ezekiel. Economic injustice severed Tyre's relationship with Yahweh, who hurled the guilty city from the mountain of God 'as a profane thing' (Ezek. 28.16).[57] Social or economic injustice tainted Tyre's

'glorify' his ministry (Rom. 11.13) and to speak of church members being 'honored' (1 Cor. 12.26).

56. See Ruiz, *Ezekiel in the Apocalypse*, p. 380. Ruiz notes that 'glory' in Ezekiel betokens God's presence, and δόξα is a divine attribute in Revelation, most often in the context of worship.

57. Sir. 10.7-8 illustrates the precedent in wisdom literature for John's view of divine judgment on the pride and greed of rulers: 'Arrogance is hateful to the Lord and to mortals, and injustice is outrageous to both. Sovereignty passes from nation to nation on account of injustice and insolence and wealth.' Other ancient authorities add here, 'Nothing is more wicked than one who loves money, for such a person puts his own soul up for sale'. Cf. 10.14-18.

Empire: 'By the multitude of your iniquities, in the unrighteousness of your trade, you profaned your sanctuaries' (28.18).[58]

John shares the sentiment of this oracle when he sees a great millstone cast into the sea.[59] With his eye on Rome, John says by 'such violence Babylon the great city will be thrown down' (Rev. 18.21; cf. Ezek. 28.16, Jer. 51.63-64). John follows this prophecy with a reference to Rome's vibrant cultural and commercial life: musicians, artisans, millers, marriage, and merchants will cease to exist in the imperial capital (Rev. 18.22-23). Rome's violent end matches the crimes it perpetuated on Christians and other hapless victims: In Rome 'was found the blood of prophets and of saints, and of all who have been slaughtered on earth' (18.24).

Sooner or Later the Evil City Will Fall
Steeped as he was in Jewish history and prophecy, John certainly knew Tyre did not fall as quickly as Ezekiel expected. Ezekiel himself tells how Nebuchadnezzar exhausted his army in a long and unsuccessful siege of the fortified city (Ezek. 29.18-20).[60] Even though Tyre made concessions to Babylon after thirteen years, and lost its colonies later in the sixth century, it still remained active in trade and shipping.[61]

With its incomparable defensive position on a rocky island just off the coast, Tyre was arrogant about its security.[62] Few enemies ever attempted a siege, and in 332 BCE Alexander the Great became the first

58. Bauckham says 'it is to focus his indictment of Rome for her *economic* exploitation...that John reapplies to Rome Ezekiel's oracle against Tyre... Tyre was the middleman through whom all trade passed, and grew rich on the profits of its trade. Rome, on the other hand, was where all the expensive goods John lists ended up'. Bauckham, *The Bible in Politics*, pp. 92, 94.

59. In reference to some items on the bill of lading in Revelation 18, Bauckham says, 'the trade was probably perceived by most provincials who, like John, did not benefit from it, as directly exploitative, drawing resources to Rome which were needed in the provinces (such as wheat and slaves), or using local labour to extract expensive products at little benefit to local people (for example, marble)'. Bauckham, 'Economic Critique', p. 78.

60. Babylonians besieged Tyre from 586/5 to 573/2 BCE.

61. Tyrians brought cedar trees to help build the second temple at Jerusalem (Ezra 3.7). To the rebuilt Jerusalem they brought 'fish and all kinds of merchandise and sold them' in Judah (Neh. 13.16).

62. When Tyre refused to receive him, Alexander the Great said 'You indeed, relying on your situation, because you live on an island, despise this army of foot-soldiers...'. Quintus Curtius, *Historiae* 4.2.5. Cf. Arrian, *Anab.* 2.18.2.

to bring Tyre to utter defeat.[63] With extreme effort, his Macedonian army mounted a siege by constructing a causeway between Tyre and the mainland.[64] Eventually the Tyrians suffered terrible defeat: six thousand killed in battle, two thousand crucified,[65] and thirty thousand sold as slaves.[66] With Tyre's colonies 'distributed over almost the whole world', news of the catastrophe spread far and wide.[67] Memory of Tyre's ruin lingered in the Graeco-Roman world, the prominent example of an 'unconquerable' city that finally met its match. Anyone who knew the story of Tyre's collapse would recognize John's logic in using the ancient city as a type for Rome. Both cities usurped the place of God, and some day both would bow under divine judgment.

4. Nero Redivivus *as Agent of Judgment*

As if drawing venom from every possible source for his attack on Rome, John seems to go beyond biblical and apocalyptic traditions to incorporate the *Nero redivivus* myth that circulated widely in the East.[68] Of course if John wrote Revelation in the last decade of the first century, it was nearly thirty years since Nero committed suicide. Some Easterners, however, still nurtured the notion that Nero would come back to life (or emerge from hiding) and retake the imperial throne at the head of a Parthian army.

Having been a devotee of Greek culture, and having favored certain sectors of eastern society with gifts and attention, Nero remained popular among some Greeks long after his death. This helped fuel fantasies that Nero would reappear to take the throne. Roman historians tell of imposters who pretended to be Nero in short-lived revolt attempts.[69]

63. Eichrodt, *Ezekiel*, pp. 367-68.

64. Arrian, *Anab.* 2.18.1-24.6 and Quintus Curtius, *Historiae* 4.2.1-4.21.

65. Quintus Curtius, *Historiae* 4.4.17.

66. Arrian, *Anab.* 2.24.5.

67. Among these were colonies at 'Carthage in Africa, Thebes in Boeotia, Gades on the Ocean'. Quintus Curtius, *Historiae* 4.4.19.

68. For an argument that the *Nero redivivus* theme already influenced Mark, and for general comments on the subject, see M. Hengel, *Studies in the Gospel of Mark* (London: SCM Press, 1985), pp. 14-28. Hengel notes (p. 21) that Mark 13 is more concerned about apostasy within the church than about persecution from outside. John of Patmos, a generation later, shared the same concern that false teachers and apostasy were primary threats to the church (Rev. 2.2, 20-24).

69. Tacitus, *Hist.* 2.8, 9; Dio Cassius, *Hist. Rom.* 64.9; Suetonius, *Nero* 57.

Some Jewish and Christian authors of the late first and early second centuries allude to this popular theme and summon the ghost of Nero to play a prominent role in their vision of the end times. One Jewish tradition held that Nero would return as an incarnation of Beliar to 'lead men astray', including 'many faithful, chosen Hebrews' (*Sib. Or.* 3.63-70).[70]

Nero's Legendary Alliance with Armies of the East

Several times John of Patmos seems to evoke this popular idea of Nero's return, as many modern commentators have noticed.[71] The beast of Empire 'rising out of the sea' has seven heads (Emperors; cf. Rev. 17.9, 10), and 'one of its heads seemed to have received a death-blow, but its mortal wound had been healed'(13.3); this might be a reference to *Nero redivivus*. Other passages of Revelation seem to reflect a belief that disastrous rebellion and destruction will rain down on the Roman Empire from the East. The sixth trumpet of John's vision marks release of 'four angels who are bound at the great river Euphrates'. These angels, perhaps heavenly patrons of the Parthian nation, will kill a third of humankind with a cavalry force of two hundred million (9.13-19; cf. 16.12).

The possible role of *Nero redivivus* in Rome's fall becomes a bit more evident toward the end of John's Apocalypse. The 'beast', which represented an Empire in Revelation 13, now seems to represent a charismatic leader:

> The beast that you saw was, and is not, and is about to ascend from the bottomless pit and go to destruction. And the inhabitants of the earth…will be amazed when they see the beast' (17.8).

Apparently the beast now is Nero reincarnated, who will rally the forces of ten other political leaders to stage a successful strike against Rome after failing to conquer the Lamb.[72]

---

70. Cf. *Sib. Or.* 2.167; *Mart. Isa.* 2.4; 4.2.

71. Charles says John expected Nero to return as a 'supernatural monster from the abyss rather than as a mere mortal', *Commentary*, I, xcvii. Caird similarly speaks of a 'new monstrous Nero' who will issue from the reigning imperial line to inflict a terrible persecution, *Commentary*, 219. The best recent analysis of the Nero motif in Revelation is by Bauckham, *The Climax of Prophecy*, pp. 384-452.

72. Bauckham calls attention to a quote from Philostratus (*Life Apoll.* 4.38), in which Apollonius of Tyana arrives at Rome during the reign of Nero and describes the Emperor as a 'beast' (θηρίον). 'I know not how many heads it has', says Apollonius, '…but to this extent it is more savage than the beasts of mountain and forest…', *The Climax of Prophecy*, p. 410.

> ...the ten horns that you saw are ten kings who have not yet received a
> kingdom, but they are to receive authority as kings for one hour, together
> with the beast. These are united in yielding their power and authority to the
> beast; they will make war on the Lamb, and the Lamb will conquer them...
> And the ten horns that you saw, they and the beast will hate the whore
> [Babylon/Rome; cf. 17.18]; they will make her desolate and naked; they
> will devour her flesh and burn her up with fire. For God has put it into
> their hearts to carry out his purpose by agreeing to give their kingdom to
> the beast, until the words of God will be fulfilled (17.12-17).

This enigmatic passage seems to foretell a time when the imperial
patronage structure will come unhinged, when provincial elites of the
East will turn against Rome. Just as evil itself first took shape as a
rebellion *within* the spiritual realm created by God (12.7-9), a plague of
insubordination will erupt within the Roman Empire dominated by
Satan. This rebellion is evil, of course, since conspirators will 'make war
on the Lamb'. Nevertheless God will use the very kings who fawned on
Rome as agents of divine retribution (cf. Isa. 44.28–45.3; Jer. 1.14-19).

It is not surprising that John follows treatment of the *Nero redivivus*
theme in chapter 17 with an examination of economic implications in
chapter 18, since that same combination appears elsewhere in Christian
apocalyptic literature. *Sibylline Oracles* 4, written about 80 CE, mentions the 'great king' (Nero) who will 'flee from Italy like a runaway
slave unseen and unheard over the channel of the Euphrates' (*Sib. Or.*
4.119-120).[73] After the eruption of Vesuvius (79 CE), Nero will cross the
Euphrates with a vast army (*Sib. Or.* 4.130-39; cf. Rev. 9.13-19) to
avenge Rome's mistreatment of Asia.

> Great wealth will come to Asia, which Rome itself once plundered and
> deposited in her house of many possessions. She will then pay back twice
> as much and more to Asia, and then there will be a surfeit of war (*Sib. Or.*
> 4.145-48).

John may not have read this particular passage, but he is familiar with
the general notion of Nero's return and recognizes that destruction of
Rome will have dramatic economic and political implications. Instead of
Roman imperial wealth flowing back to Asia, as the author of *Sibylline
Oracles* 4 hopes, John awaits the day when 'kings of the earth will bring
their glory' into the New Jerusalem (Rev. 21.24).

John's apparent use of the *Nero redivivus* legend left no room for
doubt about his attitude toward Rome. Having condemned Rome with

73. For the date of *Sib. Or.* 4, see introduction by J.J. Collins, *OTP*, I, pp. 381-83.

the vitriolic language of 'beast', 'harlot' and 'Babylon', he now depicts armed rebellion against the imperial government as equally depraved. Nero was a hero in the eyes of some Greeks, but the vicious persecution he unleashed against Christians at Rome in 64 CE surely made his name anathema to anyone in the church. If idolatrous Domitian held the throne when John wrote Revelation, and if the only serious political challenge against Rome would come from someone like Nero, John cherished no hope for redemption of the great power from Italy.

With its images of dragon and beasts, Revelation paints such a compelling image of evil personified that it became a standard reference point in patristic literature for the emerging theme of the Antichrist. Although John never actually uses the word 'Antichrist' in his Apocalypse, his portrait of the beast contains virtually all standard characteristics of the Antichrist that appear in second- and third-century Christian works.[74] Revelation is a literary fusion of at least two major mythological themes: (1) the classic serpent 'combat myth' so familiar in the ancient East (known in Hebrew scriptures as Leviathan and Behemoth; cf. Rev. 13),[75] and (2) the new *Nero redivivus* legend. Whereas most Antichrist literature of the first through third centuries attacks *internal* opponents of the church,[76] Revelation is unusual in using Antichrist themes to condemn *external* opponents.[77]

A Vigorous Rejection of Roman Rule

Like other Jewish and Christian apocalyptic writers, John reshaped well-known literary tradition to portray heroes and villains of the first-century world. His choice of Babylon as a prototype for Rome accents the depth of his anger at the Empire of his day. Babylon was the worst rogue in the Jewish gallery of historic enemies, and few of John's readers would have misunderstood the intended slur when he applied the name to Rome. Nor would any reader knowledgable in Hebrew literature have failed to recognize John's allusions to Tyre, complete with its maritime Empire and self-deifying ideology.

74. Jenks, *Origins and Early Development*, pp. 248-54. Jenks dates Revelation to 68–69 CE, and (p. 256) credits it for providing 'a powerful stimulus for a whole new way of conceiving the reality of evil from a Christian perspective'.

75. For full treatment of this aspect, see A.Y. Collins, *The Combat Myth in the Book of Revelation* (Harvard Dissertations in Religion 9, Missoula, MT: Scholars Press, 1976).

76. E.g., 1 Jn 4.1-6.

77. Jenks, *Origins and Early Development*, p. 254.

By equating Rome to Babylon, John expressed strong visceral rejection of the Italian city and its claim to universal dominion. By calling up the ghost of Tyre, he associated Rome with the unholy blend of cult, commerce and social injustice that brought terrible retribution upon that ancient city. By weaving the *Nero redivivus* legend into his work, John seemed to expect that a demented Emperor might someday return to mete out vengeance on the very city the Emperor once held at his command.

Having identified some of the Jewish literary and legendary precedents for John's condemnation of Rome, I now go on to assess the degree to which some Jews and Christians of the ancient world were willing to accommodate themselves to a pagan environment. With his keen interest in matters related to Jewish identity and the Jerusalem temple, it seems likely that John was aware of the wide range of Jewish strategies for economic, political and social survival under Roman rule. In the following chapter we see that some Jews cooperated with Rome in ways that John must have found unacceptable. We also see a vigorous Jewish tradition of refusal to participate in any form of idolatry or syncretism. John of Patmos embraces the latter stance and urgently calls upon his readers to do the same.

Chapter 5

THE BLOOD OF PROPHETS AND OF SAINTS

...in you was found the blood of prophets and of saints, and of all who
have been slaughtered on earth (Rev. 18.24).

The Jewish literary tradition from which John drew so heavily is only
part of the ethos that shaped his Apocalypse. He also absorbed the living
memory of two minority religious communities maintaining monotheistic faith under a great pagan power. Being both Jew and Christian,[1]
John personally was familiar with the responses of both traditions
toward claims and demands of imperial Rome.

This chapter examines the three-way relationship between Jews,
Christians and Rome as a context for understanding John's concerns
about cult and commerce. Christians who looked to Jewish precedent in
relating to Rome found a wide range of experiences and strategies, from
total alienation to economic or political cooperation. Both John's
message and his literary genre (Jewish apocalyptic) place him within the
tradition of radical Jews who rejected Roman rule. Some of John's
opponents in the seven churches, however, apparently followed the
example of more pragmatic Jews who found ways to cooperate with the
great imperial power.

Jewish merchants who took a pragmatic approach to Rome thrust
themselves into settings rife with pagan symbols and imperial cult
influence. This chapter reviews evidence that imperial officials sometimes
made allowances for Jewish religious scruples against syncretism. The
practical effect of this in commercial settings may have been to lessen
the pressure on conscientious Jewish merchants to participate in cultic
activities they found objectionable. As Christianity separated from Judaism
late in the first century, however, Christian merchants would have lost
any such privileges. By the time John wrote Revelation, it is likely

---

1. See discussion of authorship on pp. 31-33.

Christian merchants had to participate fully in religious ceremonies of the guilds and ports—or abandon international commerce entirely.

1. *Jewish Experience on John's Mind*

Jewish experience with Rome loomed large in John's world view: He used the city of Jerusalem (defeated by Rome in 70 CE) as an image of Christ's imminent reign on earth (Rev. 21.2, 9, 10, 23). Despite his appropriation of Jewish hopes and symbols, John is caustic when he mentions Jews in Asia Minor. He refers bitterly to the 'slander on the part of those who say that they are Jews and are not, but are a synagogue of Satan' (2.9; cf. 3.9). In the same spirit he calls the Jerusalem of his day the 'great city that is prophetically called Sodom and Egypt, where also their Lord was crucified' (11.8).

Although tension sometimes ran high between Jews and Christians late in the first century, the two groups shared many theological and sociological traits.[2] Both remained monotheistic in a polytheistic environment; both rejected idolatry and suffered occasional persecution; both worshipped the God of Abraham and claimed the Hebrew scriptures; both had reservations about the imperial cult and struggled to avoid assimilation into pagan society. The sub-apostolic church (c. 70–135 CE) in the East so closely resembled the Jewish community that Frend refers to it as the 'Christian synagogue'.[3] These sociological and theological similarities make it likely that Jews and Christians grappled with the same issues in responding to the lure—and danger—of commerce in a pagan environment. An understanding of how Jewish merchants related to the imperial economy helps define the options for participation that Christian merchants also were likely to consider.

Several factors make it easier to describe the social and economic location of Jews in the late first-century world than to do the same for Christians. Jews had related to Rome for almost three centuries by the

---

2.   Illustrated by parts of the Gospels, including Mt. 15.1-9; 23.1-39; and Jn 9.1-41. See Frend, *The Rise of Christianity*, p. 144.

3.   Frend, *The Rise of Christianity*, pp. 119-60. Frend summarizes the period by saying 'Between 70 and 135 Christianity became a religion based very largely on the geography and organization of the Hellenistic synagogue'. He says 'the life, thought, and organization of the church can be understood only within the framework of Hellenistic Judaism'. *The Rise of Christianity*, p. 120. Jas 2.2 refers to the Christian worship gathering as a 'synagogue' (συναγωγή).

time John wrote Revelation. Important literary and archaeological evidence of that interaction survives, in contrast to scarce evidence on the relatively brief experience of Christians. Christians not only had a much shorter tenure in the Empire, but largely remained hidden within the Jewish subculture for several decades. First-century Greeks and Romans usually cared little about (what appeared to them as) minor differences between Jews and Christians.[4] They rarely noticed followers of Jesus or mentioned them in literature. These factors conspire to give us little direct data on Christians during the first century, aside from documents produced by the Christian community itself.

Proximity of Jews and Christians

Christians surely did not follow every Jewish precedent in matters of cult and commerce. However, geographical and sociological proximity of the two groups meant that Christians entering the marketplace must have been aware of—and sometimes influenced by—attitudes and practices of their theological cousins.[5] By the time John wrote Revelation, the Jewish nation in Palestine had experienced nearly the full spectrum of possible political relationships with the great power from Italy. Once a friend and ally of Rome, Judea became a vassal state and eventually suffered terrible defeat when it rebelled (66–70 CE).[6] As Jews cautiously reestablished themselves within the Empire, Christians outside Palestine needed to find their own identity as a faith community distinct from

---

4.   E.g., Gallio, proconsul of Achaia (c. 51 CE), treated the dispute between Jews and Christians at Corinth as a Jewish internal affair (Acts 18.12-17). The Romans gradually made a distinction between the two groups, however, as attested by Nero's targeted persecution of Christians at Rome in 64 CE.

5.   Judaism gave birth to Christianity (Rev. 12.1-6), and the movement grew most quickly in the very cities where diaspora Jews had their largest representation. Scholarly estimates of the size of the Jewish population at Ephesus range from 7,500 to 75,000. See Robinson, *The Bauer Thesis*, pp. 114-15; Meeks, *First Urban Christians*, p. 34. Philo says Jews were 'very numerous in every city' of Asia and Syria. *Leg. Gai.* 245.

6.   The long history of Jewish-Roman relations began during the Maccabean revolt (167–64 BCE), when Jewish patriots made a league of friendship with the emerging Roman power. Josephus, *War* 1.1.4 (38). Judas Maccabeus sent an envoy to Rome 'to establish friendship and alliance', 1 Macc. 8.17-30; cf. 12.1-4. Josephus says Hyrcanus the high priest and Antipater, 'the governor of the Jews', supported Julius Caesar in his military campaign against Pompey in Egypt in 48 BCE. *Ant.* 14.8.1 (127).

Judaism. It was an insecure time for both groups. Both Jews and Christians felt pressure—from within and without—to conform to political, social and religious conventions of the Roman Empire.

As the following pages suggest, some first-century Jews carried on trade with Rome, honored the Emperor or served within the hierarchy of imperial government. Others rejected Rome's claim to legitimate authority, avoided contact with imperial institutions or bitterly condemned Rome for idolatry. The book of Revelation registers a similar range of responses to Rome within the Christian churches of Asia Minor and addresses the same economic and political questions that faced the Jewish community. If no Christians of Asia Minor had been drawn into pagan cult and commerce, John probably would not have addressed these themes at such length.

The 'Synagogue of Satan'

Mobility and 'cross-fertilization' among Jewish and Christian communities was common in the East. Paul and his fellow missionaries traveled extensively throughout the diaspora, and countless rabbinic references indicate such movement was common in Jewish circles.[7] Prominent leaders of the Hellenistic Christian church—notably Paul—once played influential roles in the Jewish community. Crispus, an 'official of the synagogue' (ἀρχισυνάγωγος) at Corinth, became a Christian (Acts 18.8, cf. 1 Cor. 1.14).[8] Several writings of the early church in Asia Minor document a concern that some Christian communities might revert to full practice of Judaism.[9]

Christians adopted much of their theology and ethics from Jewish tradition, and it is likely Jewish experience influenced Christians who engaged in trade.[10] Early in his Apocalypse John twice refers to Jews, using language with economic and social implications.

---

7. E.g., Apollos was a native of Alexandria, moved to Ephesus, and ministered in Achaia (Acts 18.24-28). Aquila was a native of Pontus who lived in Rome, moved to Corinth with his wife Priscilla, then settled in Ephesus (Acts 18.1-23; cf. Rom. 16.3; 1 Cor. 16.19; 2 Tim. 4.19). After years of traveling in the East, Paul planned to visit Rome on his way to Spain (Rom. 15.24, 28).

8. Theissen marshals epigraphic evidence to argue that synagogue rulers usually were men of means who enjoyed high social status even beyond boundaries of the Jewish community. Theissen, *The Social Setting of Pauline Christianity*, pp. 74-75.

9. Gal. 2.14; *Ign. Magn.* 8.1, 10.3, *Ign. Phld.* 6.1

10. The Christian Sibylline books, which proliferated for centuries in the early church, illustrate continuing Jewish influence on Christian thought. A. Momigliano

> And to the angel of the church in Smyrna write…I know your affliction
> and your poverty, even though you are rich. I know the slander on the part
> of those who say that they are Jews and are not, but are a synagogue of
> Satan. Do not fear what you are about to suffer. Beware, the devil is about
> to throw some of you into prison… Be faithful until death…(Rev. 2.8-10)

> And to the angel of the church in Philadelphia write… I know that you
> have but little power, and yet you have kept my word and have not denied
> my name. I will make those of the synagogue of Satan who say that they
> are Jews and are not, but are lying—I will make them come and bow down
> before your feet… (Rev. 3.7-9)

Vituperative language about a 'synagogue of Satan' might stem from a
belief that Jews helped persecute Christians.[11] John's larger use of symbolism, however, suggests that he mentions Satan here as a way of high-
lighting commercial or political relationships some Jews had with Rome.
This is implicit later in his Apocalypse, when John examines the source
of Rome's imperial power: the first beast (the Emperor or the whole
Empire) received 'his power and his throne and great authority' from
Satan himself (13.2). By using the epithet 'synagogue of Satan' in his
letters to Smyrna and Philadelphia, John implies that certain Jews in those
cities are in the same category as Rome—that is, in league with Satan.

The Jewish community itself was capable of raising an equally caustic
polemic against its own members who yielded to Rome's seduction. A
late first-century Jewish writer in Egypt called Nero 'Beliar', and said
the wicked Emperor 'will…lead [people] astray, and he will lead astray
many faithful, chosen Hebrews, and also other lawless [people] who
have not yet listened to the word of God' (*Sib. Or.* 3.63-70).[12] If this
devout Egyptian Jew thought *many* members of his faith community
showed an idolatrous loyalty to Nero, it is possible that John came to the
same conclusion about Jews in Asia Minor.

---

says appearance of these works 'probably implies some exchange between Jews and
Christians and certainly presupposes a Christian interest in what the Jews thought
about the Roman Empire'. A. Momigliano, *On Pagans, Jews, and Christians*
(Middletown, CT: Wesleyan University Press, 1987), pp. 139-40.

11. The author of Acts depicts Jews as harassing people who accepted Jesus as
the Messiah, and tells of a Roman proconsul who took no action when 'all of them'
(presumably the Jews) beat a Christian sympathizer named Sosthenes 'in front of the
tribunal' (Acts 18.17. Note, however, that the Western text—not the preferred
reading—adds 'all of *the Greeks*' beat Sosthenes.)

12. For discussion of date, authorship and provenance of this prophecy, see introduction to *Sibylline Oracles* 3 by J.J. Collins, *OTP*, I, pp. 354-61.

There is no question of anti-Semitism in the book of Revelation. John himself almost certainly was a Jew and he counts Jews from every tribe of Israel among the people of God (Rev. 7.4-8). The central concern of Revelation is compromise with idolatrous Rome, and John equally condemns Jews and Christians who show signs of diluting their faithfulness to God. Christians at Thyatira, for example, who compromise their faith will be thrown out 'in great distress' or struck dead (2.22, 23).

If commerce and pagan cult related closely in the first-century Roman Empire, it is not surprising that conscientious Christians at Smyrna suffered poverty (2.9). This is exactly the circumstance we would expect among people who refused to take part in pagan ceremonies that were an integral part of the economy. In addition to their financial distress, Christians at Smyrna endure 'slander' (literally 'blasphemy', βλασφημία) from those who claim to be Jews. John says the devil is about to throw some believers into prison (2.10), a circumstance that might be related to the 'slander' from parts of the Jewish community. Thompson notes that the word 'slander' (βλασφημία) is strong language, since elsewhere in Revelation John uses the term for activity of the beast and the whore (13.1, 5, 6, 17.3).[13] John's choice of words suggests Christians of Smyrna were in conflict with Jews (and perhaps fellow Christians) who compromised in some way with Rome or the imperial cult.[14]

While the letter to Smyrna highlights financial costs of radical loyalty to Jesus, the letter to Philadelphia reveals the political price. Believers at Philadelphia have 'little power' (3.8)—also the logical predicament of steadfast monotheists in a setting where social and political advance depended on ties to the imperial cult. Even the type of judgment God will visit upon persecutors suggests Christians in Philadelphia suffered status deprivation: 'those of the synagogue of Satan who say that they are Jews and are not, but are lying' will 'come and bow down' at the feet of believers (3.9). Though excluded from powerful religious and

---

13. Thompson, *Revelation: Apocalypse and Empire*, p. 173.

14. Christians at Smyrna who wrote the account of Polycarp's martyrdom (c. 155 CE) placed heavy blame on the Jews. When Polycarp declared his Christian faith in the arena, 'all the multitude of heathen and Jews living in Smyrna cried out with uncontrollable wrath and a loud shout, "This is the teacher of Asia...the destroyer of our Gods, who teaches many neither to offer sacrifice nor to worship"', *Mart. Pol.* 13.1; cf. 17.2. Had he been willing to 'swear by the genius of Caesar', the aged bishop could have saved his life. Polycarp, *Mart. Pol.* 8.2; 9.2; 10.1.

political circles of Asia Minor, believers eventually will have favored status in the eschatological kingdom.[15] Christ says the person who conquers will be a 'pillar in the temple of my God', and will wear the name of the new Jerusalem (3.12). In other words, Christians will participate fully in the established cult of the new Jerusalem, and will hold full citizenship.[16] John and his circle of radical Christians enjoyed neither of these marks of status in the cities of Asia Minor.

What, then, was the political and economic status of the Jews with whom Christians at Smyrna and Philadelphia found themselves in conflict? Just as there was great diversity within the early Christian church, there also was a wide range of attitudes toward Rome within the Jewish diaspora. There is evidence that certain parts of the Jewish people in the Empire related more closely to Rome than John would have found acceptable. A long history of dealings with Italy made it difficult for Jews—and Jewish Christians—to extricate themselves from Rome when imperial institutions fostered economic oppression or came under control of the imperial cult.

2. Jewish Political and Economic Relations with Rome

Generations of political ties with Rome enabled most Jews of Asia Minor to establish communities and function well in the imperial society. As early as 49 BCE, Rome granted exemption from military service to the 'Jews who are Roman citizens and observe Jewish rites and practise them in Ephesus'.[17] The temple of Roma and Augustus at Pergamum displayed an edict of Augustus that granted Jewish rights.[18] The

15. Thompson, *Revelation: Apocalypse and Empire*, pp. 173-74.
16. Cf. Phil. 3.20, 'But our citizenship (πολίτευμα) is in heaven...' Cf. Heb. 11.10, 16. Heb. 13.14 says 'For here we have no lasting city, but we are looking for the city that is to come'. Tertullian told his Christian reader, 'you are a foreigner in this world, a citizen of Jerusalem, the city above', *De Cor.* 13.
17. *Ant.* 14.10.13 (228-30); cf. 14.10.16 (234); 14.10.19 (240). See Schürer, *History*, III.I, p. 22. The apostle Paul, native of Tarsus, is an example of a Jew who apparently enjoyed Roman citizenship from birth (Acts 22.28).
18. The actual site of the original inscription is not certain. Schürer says many scholars placed it in Galatia 'because of the instruction at its conclusion that the text should be exhibited in *Ancyra,* the capital of Galatia. However, 'Αγκύρη is not more than a conjecture... The manuscripts all have αργυρη, and the context demands a reference to the site of the temple of Roma and Augustus in *Asia,* namely Pergamum'. *History*, III.I, pp. 34-35.

inscription noted that 'the Jewish nation has been found well disposed to the Roman people' and 'may follow their own customs' in accordance with the law of their ancestors.[19] Josephus recites a long litany of privileges extended to diaspora Jews, using the terminology of benefactor (εὐεργέτης),[20] friendship (φιλία)[21] and loyalty (εὔνοια).[22] Ephesus, Pergamum, Sardis[23] and Laodicea each had Jewish communities that enjoyed special privileges.[24] These included the right to practice religion unhindered, license to send the temple tax (*didrachmon*) to Jerusalem and freedom from military service.

Such privilege always was vulnerable to the whims of Rome, as illustrated by Jewish experience under Claudius. In response to pogroms against Jews in Egypt, the Emperor sent a letter to the city of Alexandria in 41 CE requesting 'that the Alexandrians conduct themselves more gently and kindly toward the Jews...and that they do not inflict indignities upon any of their customs in the worship of their god'. Claudius stated matter-of-factly that Jews 'enjoy their own affairs and have the benefit of an abundance of many good things...'[25] Luke reports, though, that a few years later Claudius himself 'ordered all Jews to leave Rome' (Acts 18.2).[26]

Cooperation between Romans and Jews
In the first century CE, some high Roman officials in Asia Minor—even priests of the imperial cult—favored the Jewish community with donations. An inscription from Acmonia in Phrygia mentions 'the synagogue

19. *Ant.* 16.6.2 (162-63). The book of Esther depicts Jews as already having a unique legal relationship to Empire under Persian rule: Haman said to King Ahasuerus, 'There is a certain people scattered and separated among the peoples in all the provinces of your kingdom; their laws are different from those of every other people, and they do not keep the king's laws...', Est. 3.8.

20. *Ant.* 14.10.23 (257).

21. *Ant.* 14.10.6, 26 (205, 266).

22. *Ant.* 14.10.7 (212).

23. The Jewish community at Sardis was powerful and well-established since the third century BCE. Josephus records that Antiochus III resettled two thousand families of Mesopotamian Jews at Sardis. *Ant.* 12.3.4 (148-53).

24. *Ant.* 14.10.10-26 (219-67); 16.6.1-7 (160-71).

25. Garnsey and Saller, *The Roman Empire*, pp. 83-86.

26. Dio Cassius says there was a prohibition against Jewish gatherings in Rome already in 41 CE, but no expulsion at that date. *Hist. Rom.* 60.6.6.

built by Iulia Severa'.[27] Coins from Acmonia during the reign of Nero name Iulia Severa as 'high priestess' (of the imperial cult).[28] Her son entered the Senate under Nero and was legatus to the proconsul of Asia.[29] In view of her religious office, Iulia Severa cannot have been a practicing Jew herself.[30] Rather, Schürer suggests, she built the synagogue for the Jews as their patroness. 'The Jewish community in Acmonia therefore had friends in the highest social circles at that time.'[31]

27. τὸν κατασκευασθὲ[ν]τα ο[ἶ]κον ὑπὸ Ἰουλίας Σεουήρας. *IGR*, IV, 655; *MAMA*, VI, 264. Cited by Schürer, *History*, III.I, p. 31. Cf. Lk. 7.2-5.

28. *CIG*, III, 3858. Cited by S. Applebaum, 'The Legal Status of the Jewish Communities in the Diaspora', in S. Safrai and M. Stern (eds.), *The Jewish People in the First Century*, I (Philadelphia: Fortress Press, 1974), p. 443. Coins mentioning Iulia Severa usually read *ΕΠΙ [ΑΡΧ] CΕΡΟΥΗΝΙΟΥ ΚΑΠΙΤΩΝΟC ΚΑΙ ΙΟΥΛΙΑC CΕΟΥΗΡΑC*, 'during the high priesthoods of Servenius Capito and Iulia Severa'. See W. M. Ramsay, *Cities and Bishoprics of Phrygia*, I (Oxford: Clarendon Press, 1895), no. 530, pp. 638-40. An inscription from Phrygia reads Ἰουλίαι Σ[εο]υήραι ἀρχιερείαι καὶ ἀγωνοθέτ[ιδι]. *Cities and Bishoprics*, I, no. 550; cf. no. 551, p. 647. Iulia Severa's second husband was Tyronius Rapo (*CIG*, III, 3858). Applebaum says, 'that he was a Jew by origin (though also a pagan priest) seems to be proved by the inscription of his relative G. Tyronius Cladus [*CII*, II, 771]. The Iulli Severii, moreover, appear to have been distantly related to the Herods. It is clear then, that some Hellenized Jews of Asia had by this date obtained not only Roman citizenship...but that they had achieved high office in the city in the course of a process of assimilation which in some cases, apparently, involved apostasy'. Applebaum, 'The Legal Status', p. 443.

29. P.R. Trebilco, *Jewish Communities in Asia Minor* (SNTSMS, 69; Cambridge: Cambridge University Press, 1991), pp. 59-60.

30. M. Stern says we should not think of Iulia Severa as a full proselyte, but rather as 'one who displayed in some way sympathy for Judaism'. A relative of her husband entered the Roman Senate during the reign of Nero. M. Stern, 'The Jewish Diaspora', in Safrai and Stern (eds.), *The Jewish People in the First Century*, I, p. 150 n. 7. So also Trebilco, *Jewish Communities*, p. 59. Collins argues that Iulia Severa possibly may have been Jewish. Collins, 'Insiders and Outsiders in the Book of Revelation', in J. Neusner and E.S. Frerichs (eds.), *To See Ourselves as Others See Us: Christians, Jews, 'Others' in Late Antiquity* (Chico, CA: Scholars Press, 1985), p. 195.

31. Schürer, *History of the Jewish People* 3.1, p. 31. Later inscriptions indicate there was a general trend toward extensive Jewish participation in the political and economic life of Acmonia. By the third century Jews there 'took the highest responsibilities and offices in civic life and...had the economic means and appropriate social status to fulfil these obligations'. Thompson, *Revelation: Apocalypse and Empire*, p. 140. Already in the first century the author of Acts could depict the Roman centurion Cornelius as being 'well spoken of by the whole Jewish nation' (Acts 10.22).

During the same era, some Jews in Palestine apparently cooperated enough with Rome to attain equestrian status. In 66 CE the Procurator Florus, in an act of indiscriminate reprisal, slaughtered some 3600 Jewish men, women and children. Josephus was horrified that Florus crucified many of his victims, but seems especially appalled that such fate should befall Jewish men of high standing in the Roman social order:

> Florus ventured that day to do what none had ever done before, namely, to scourge before his tribunal and nail to the cross men of equestrian rank, men who, if Jews by birth, were at least invested with that Roman dignity.[32]

Equestrian status was supposed to exempt those who held it from punishment by whipping or crucifixion.[33]

Jewish Protest against Accommodation
Literature from first-century Palestine indicates that Jewish attitudes toward Rome ranged from vitriolic condemnation to warm embrace. It is likely—though not certain—that John himself came from Palestine.[34] He wrote in a Semiticized Greek, and had keen interest in Jerusalem and the temple (Rev. 11, 21, 22).[35] If he did not personally experience Jewish society in Palestine, surely he knew Jews in Asia Minor who did. Jewish experience in Palestine under Roman rule helps explain the range of attitudes toward the Roman Empire we find in Asia Minor late in the first century.[36]

32. *War* 2.14.9 (305-8).

33. Mere citizenship afforded a measure of protection, as attested by the account in Acts of Paul's imprisonment in Jerusalem. When the presiding tribune examined Paul by flogging, Paul asserted his rights: 'Is it legal for you to flog a Roman citizen who is uncondemned?' he demanded. The tribune was afraid, 'for he realized that Paul was a Roman citizen and that he had bound him' (Acts 22.22-29).

34. Eusebius (citing Papias) says the author of Revelation either was John the apostle or the presbyter John, one of the 'Lord's disciples'. *Hist. Eccl.* 3.39.4-6. In either case, Eusebius gives John's origin as Palestine.

35. See S. Thompson, *The Apocalypse and Semitic Syntax* (Cambridge: Cambridge University Press, 1985), and Charles, *Commentary*, pp. cxlii-clii.

36. The Babylonian Talmud records a conversation between three rabbis (ca. 135 CE) which captures the breadth of Jewish attitudes toward the Empire: 'Rabbi Judah began and said: 'How excellent are the deeds of this [Roman] nation. They have instituted market places, they have instituted bridges, they have instituted baths'. Rabbi Jose was silent. Rabbi Simeon ben Yohai answered and said: 'All that they have instituted they have instituted only for their own needs. They have instituted market places to place harlots in them; baths, for their own pleasure; bridges, to collect toll.' Rabbi

Jewish society in first-century Palestine, like other provincial regions, formed a social pyramid in which the upper strata allied themselves with the Roman rulers. The Similitudes of Enoch (*1 En. 37–71*, late first century CE) depict powerful Jewish elites as compromising their faith and oppressing less fortunate members of society.[37] The author saw Palestine as conforming to the same elitist pattern that prevailed in other provinces of the Empire. At the top of the social pyramid were 'kings of the earth' and 'mighty landowners' (48.8)[38] who combined idolatry and economic exploitation: 'All their deeds are oppression. Their power (depends) upon their wealth...their devotion is to the gods which they have fashioned with their own hands' (46.7). In a callous display of syncretism, such idolaters 'like to congregate' in Jewish houses of worship with the faithful (46.8).[39]

We cannot use these tendentious statements as proof that most or even many Jews compromised their loyalty to Yahweh. The Zealot movement, of course, represented the polar opposite of these upwardly mobile Jews. Although recent scholars emphasize the diverse and *ad hoc* nature of the Jewish resistance movement, Hengel's book *The Zealots* marshals compelling evidence of themes that repeatedly appear in the rebel movements between 6 CE and the great revolt of 66–70 CE.[40] 'Zeal' for Yahweh and his law was the undergirding passion of these

Judah reported the conversation to government officials, who declared that 'Judah who exalted shall be exalted; Jose who remained silent shall be banished to Sopphoris; Simeon who reproached shall be put to death'. *Sab.* 33b. Lewis and Reinhold, *Roman Civilization*, II, p. 414.

37. Scholarly opinion on the date of the Similitudes ranges from the second century BCE to 270 CE. I accept the arguments of scholars who date the Similitudes late in the first century. See M.A. Knibb, 'The Date of the Parables of Enoch', *NTS* 25 (1979), pp. 345-59, and C.L. Mearns, 'Dating the Similitudes of Enoch', *NTS* 25 (1979), pp. 360-69. At the SNTS Pseudepigrapha Seminars (1977–78), members agreed the Similitudes 'were Jewish and dated from the first century CE'. The book of *1 Enoch* as a whole originated in Judea and was in use at Qumran before the beginning of the Christian era. *OTP*, I, pp. 6-8.

38. *1 En.* 63.12 adds 'governors' and 'high officials' to the list of elites.

39. A textual variant of this verse in the Ethiopic version of *1 Enoch* implies the idolaters were not themselves part of the worshiping community. See R.H. Charles, *The Book of Enoch* (London: SPCK, 1917), p. 65, and *OTP*, I, p. 35, note t.

40. E.g., R.A. Horsley and J.S. Hanson go so far as to say that 'the old "Zealot" concept [of a sustained, monolithic rebel movement] has been shown to be a historical fiction, with no basis in historical evidence'. Horsley and Hanson, *Bandits, Prophets, and Messiahs: Popular Movements at the Time of Jesus*, p. xiii; cf. pp. 240-41.

freedom fighters, and zeal precluded any compromise with the values, cult or political structures of pagan Rome.[41] In contrast to the Zealot minority, however, certain other Jews scrambled as high as possible up the social and political pyramid of provincial society—a precedent John would have considered unacceptable for his Christian readers.

Talmud and the 'Wicked Roman Government'
Because of its relatively late date of redaction (late second century and following), we must be cautious about drawing heavily from rabbinic literature to sketch the outlines of Jewish attitudes toward Rome in the first century. Nevertheless, the Talmud and other rabbinic sources arguably preserve some traditions and attitudes that crystalized during the New Testament era. Even these traditions we must interpret with care, since rabbinic literature by design includes a much wider diversity of opinions than does, for example, the canonical New Testament.[42]

With these caveats in mind, it is still possible to sketch broad outlines of rabbinic attitudes toward Rome, and offer anecdotal evidence that Jewish perspectives on the Empire were diverse. Perhaps most telling of a negative view is the frequent use of names such as Edom, Esau, Amalek, Seir and Tyre (all despised foes of the Jews) as epithets for Rome. Other common rabbinic references to the imperial rulers are 'the wanton government', 'the fourth kingdom' (cf. Dan. 7.7-28), and 'the wicked Roman government'.[43]

41. See especially *The Zealots*, pp. 146-228. Hengel notes the Zealot pattern of retreating into the desert as a way for the faithful to separate themselves from pagan influences and pressures. He says there probably is 'a relationship' between this Zealot practice and the image of the woman in Revelation 12 (who represents the people of God) fleeing into the wilderness. *The Zealots*, p. 251. If John of Patmos took inspiration from Zealot practice (which seems likely), we would expect him to share the Zealot determination not to associate with any political, social or economic institutions of Rome.

42. J. Neusner sets a worthy example for other scholars when he rejects the notion that 'to define what "Judaism" says about a subject, we merely collect, arrange, and so compose into neat collection defined by the topic at hand all typically pertinent sayings from all times and places and documents'. J. Neusner, *The Economics of the Mishnah* (Chicago: University of Chicago Press, 1990), p. xiii. The diversity of Jewish thought, and the relationship of any given opinion to its context, make it impossible to articulate a 'typical' Jewish conviction in many areas of belief and practice.

43. See M.D. Herr, 'Rome, In Talmudic Literature', *Encyclopedia Judaica*, XIV, col. 243.

There was divided opinion among the rabbis as to whether Rome ever was (or could be) an instrument of divine service. One tradition held that Rome was born in idolatry: 'On the day that Jeroboam brought the two golden calves, one into Bethel and the other into Dan, a hut was built [on the site of Rome], and this developed into Greek Italy.'[44] A similar legend dated Rome's foundation to the era when a king of Israel unwisely established links with pagan royalty of Egypt: 'When Solomon married Pharaoh's daughter, Gabriel descended and stuck a reed in the sea, which gathered a sand-bank around it, on which was built the great city of Rome.'[45]

The roots of such contempt for Rome rest in part in experiences of Rome as an unreliable partner, alternately protector and oppressor. The Talmud states that the Roman government issued laws that prescribed death for anyone who did *not* kill Jews upon finding them and later threatened the same for anyone who *did* kill Jews.[46] Sometimes particular religious practices—such as wearing of the *teffillin*—incited Rome to threaten Jews with capital punishment.[47] This capricious and violent nature of the Empire provoked some rabbis to describe Rome as an animal. In language reminiscent of Revelation 13, one tradition says 'The Holy One, blessed be He, will say to Gabriel...rebuke the wild beast [Rome]...'[48]

This same text continues with *economic* critique of Rome's opulence, describing the city as having 365 thoroughfares, each thoroughfare with 365 palaces, each palace with 365 storeys, each storey with 'sufficient to provide the whole world with food'. With ill-concealed revolutionary design, the rabbis invoke a prophecy that God some day would effect a more just distribution of such wealth: 'Her merchandise and her wages will be dedicated to the Lord; her profits will not be stored or hoarded, but her merchandise will supply abundant food and fine clothing for those who live in the presence of the Lord' (Isa. 23.18).[49] There is both resentment about economic injustice and a conviction that wealth comes from God in the statement of one rabbinic school that 'two *stater*

44. *Sab.* 56b.
45. *Sanh.* 21b.
46. *Git.* 55b.
47. *Sab.* 49a. Apparently Rome sometimes forbade Jews to study and practice the Torah. Rabbi Akiba persisted and was executed. *Ber.* 61b.
48. *Pes.* 118b.
49. The Isaiah prophecy originally referred to Tyre.

weights of fine gold came down into the world, one of which went to Rome and the other to the rest of the world'.[50]

Along with such impassioned polemic against Rome in the Talmud, there are occasional examples of rabbis who insisted the Empire's authority issued from God. 'Brother Hanina', intoned one teacher, 'knowest thou not that it is Heaven that has ordained this [Roman] nation to reign? For though she laid waste His House, burnt His Temple, slew His pious ones and caused His best ones to perish, still is she firmly established!'[51] That is faint endorsement, to be sure, and the same tractate follows immediately with examples of contradictory advice on the appropriate level of Jewish involvement in Roman society. Some rabbis admonished the faithful to avoid (gladiatorial) stadiums and (army) camps as places of sorcery and as the 'seat of the scornful'. Similarly, some objected to theatres and circuses 'because entertainments are arranged there in honour of the idols'. Other rabbis, however, cited special circumstances in which it was acceptable for Jews to appear at such venues.[52]

Radical loyalty to one God is unwavering in the Talmud, and this gives us the best measure of rabbinic attitudes toward the imperial cult. The rabbis tell of seven brothers whom the authorities brought one by one before the Emperor: 'They brought the first before the Emperor and said to him, Serve the idol. He said to them, It is written in the Law, *I am the Lord thy God.* So they led him away and killed him.' Each son in turn quoted scripture, refused to bow to the image, and suffered martyrdom.[53] Apparently in an attempt to save the last brother, the Emperor said, 'I will throw down my seal [bearing the Emperor's image] before you and you can stoop down and pick it up, so that they

50. *Git.* 58a.

51. *'Abod. Zar.* 18a. Desecration of the Temple in 70 CE could not be justified or forgiven in the eyes of devout Jews. Their outrage spawned lurid descriptions of the transgression, including an account of general Titus fornicating in the Holy of Holies on top of an open scroll of the Law. *Git.* 56a. Rumors persisted that the Romans held in storage at Rome both the holy vessels of the temple and the curtain of the Holy of Holies. *Me'il.* 17b; *Yom.* 57a; cf. *Pes.* 119a. In fact, the Arch of Titus at Rome does portray soldiers carrying temple vessels from Jerusalem in triumphal procession.

52. *'Abod. Zar.* 18b. One rabbi in this text, without elaborating, says, 'There is a difference in the case of calling to do business'. This sounds like a rationale that could have justified considerable engagement—perhaps commerce—in pagan settings.

53. The first son quoted Exod. 20.2, the others in succession quoted Exod. 20.3; 22.20; 20.5; Deut. 6.4; 4.39; 26.17,18.

will say of you that you have conformed to the desire of the King'. But the last brother was executed after saying, 'Fie on thee, Caesar...if thine own honour is so important, how much more the honour of the Holy One, blessed be He!'[54] This story illustrates the desire of some rabbis to dissuade Jews from accepting *any* compromise with idolatry. Such a determined stance would have led adherents to avoid any involvement in the imperial cult.

One scholar summarizes by saying rabbinic authors, in the diversity of their views on Rome, 'are no different from their contemporaries, as can be seen by comparison with the evaluations of the Greeks, the Church Fathers, and even the Romans themselves'.[55] The point for this study is that, while many Jews (and perhaps many Christians) took a dim view of the imperial power, others had a more positive opinion and even found ways to participate in certain economic or social structures of the Roman Empire.

Roman Influence on Jewish Worship

Despite a deep concern in Jewish tradition about idolatry and syncretism, Rome sometimes was able to influence Jewish religious practice. Philo records this striking account of imperial representation at the temple in Jerusalem.

> Indeed so religiously did he [Caesar Augustus] respect our interests that supported by wellnigh his whole household he adorned our temple through the costliness of his dedications, and ordered that for all time continuous sacrifices of whole burnt offerings should be carried out every day at his own expense as a tribute to the most high God. And these sacrifices are maintained to the present day...[56]

Roman involvement in Jewish religious institutions occasionally appears elsewhere in the first century CE. Luke tells of Jewish elders at Capernaum who urged Jesus to heal the slave of a Roman centurion. 'He is worthy of having you do this for him', they said, 'for he loves our people, and it is he who built our synagogue for us' (Lk. 7.4-5).[57]

54. *Git.* 57b.
55. Herr, *Encyclopedia Judaica*, XIV, col. 243.
56. *Leg. Gai.* 157 (cf. 317-18). Josephus says 'the whole Jewish community' bore the expense of daily sacrifices on behalf of Caesar. *Apion* 2.6 (77).
57. A critic might dispute the historicity of Luke's version of events involving Romans. For our purposes, though, it is enough to demonstrate that a Christian writer, late in the first century, believed such close ties existed between imperial representatives and the Jewish community.

In a similar vein Josephus tells of a speech purportedly made in Jerusalem by the aged high priest Ananus during the Jewish revolt of 66–70 CE. Ananus says Jews should find Roman rule acceptable, since they see 'in our Temple courts the very votive offerings of the Romans' and recall that the 'Romans never overstepped the limit fixed for the profane' in the Jerusalem temple.[58]

Inscriptions from Rome suggest that some Jews there honored imperial officials by naming synagogues after them. There was both a 'synagogue of Augustesians' (συναγωγὴ Αὐγουστησίων)[59] and a 'synagogue of Agrippesians' (συναγωγὴ Ἀγριππησίων)[60] in the capital city. These two synagogue names apparently derived from Caesar Augustus and his son-in-law Marcus Vipsanius Agrippa (whom Caesar was grooming to be his successor). Augustus and Agrippa might have been patrons of the communities in question, perhaps having owned certain Jews in them as slaves.[61] Smallwood says naming a synagogue after Augustus 'testifies to the gratitude which the Diaspora felt for his measures to guarantee their religious liberty'.[62]

Josephus articulates the logic that permitted some Jews to honor the Roman Emperor.

---

58. *War* 4.3.10 (181-82). In *War* 5.13.6 (563) Josephus says 'the Roman sovereigns ever honoured and added embellishment to the temple' in Jerusalem.

59. *CII*, I.2, nos. 284, 301, 338, 368, 416, 496. Cited by Schürer, *History*, III.I, p. 96. Cf. E.M. Smallwood, *The Jews Under Roman Rule: From Pompey to Diocletian* (Leiden: E.J. Brill, 1976), p. 138, and Meeks, *First Urban Christians*, p. 206 n. 161.

60. *CII*, I.2, nos. 365, 425, 503. Cited by Schürer, *History*, III.I, p. 96.

61. Schürer cites Phil. 4.22 (οἱ ἐκ τῆς Καίσαρος οἰκίας) as a parallel in the Christian church. *History*, III.I, p. 96. H.J. Leon says it is 'highly probable that the [synagogue] congregation was named for the Emperor Augustus, who was a true friend of the Jews'. There is no evidence, however, that members of the congregation ever were slaves or freedmen of the imperial house. Agrippa 'is known to have befriended the Jews and may have been the patron of the congregation and even the builder of its synagogue. While this view is not improbable, it must still remain conjecture'. Possibly the synagogue was named after a Jewish king, Agrippa I or Agrippa II. H.J. Leon, *The Jews of Ancient Rome* (Philadelphia: Jewish Publication Society, 1960), pp. 11, 141-42.

62. Smallwood, *The Jews Under Roman Rule*, p. 138. Augustus went so far as to inscribe the following proclamation of Jewish rights on the pillar of a temple of the imperial cult in Asia Minor: 'As for the resolution which was offered by [the Jews] in my honour concerning the piety which I show to all men…I order that it and the present edict be set up in the most conspicuous part of the temple assigned to me by the federation of Asia in Ancyra.' Josephus, *Ant.* 16.6.2 (165).

> ...our legislator [Moses], not in order to put, as it were, a prophetic veto
> upon honours paid to the Roman authority, but out of contempt for a prac-
> tice profitable to neither God nor [mortals], forbade the making of
> images... He did not, however, forbid the payment of homage of another
> sort, secondary to that paid to God, to worthy [humans]; such honours we
> do confer upon the Emperors and the people of Rome. For them we offer
> perpetual sacrifices...[63]

Roman Emperors also received recognition at synagogues in Alexandria.
Philo tells of a pogrom Jews in that city suffered during the reign of
Caligula. Hooligans destroyed synagogues, including 'tributes to the
Emperors which were pulled down or burnt at the same time, the
shields and gilded crowns and the slabs and inscriptions...'[64]

Despite such anecdotal evidence of compromise, there were limits to
how far most Jews would go in honoring Caesar or Rome. When Pilate
brought 'effigies (εἰκόνας, cf. Rev. 13.14) of Caesar which are called
standards (σημαῖαι)' into Jerusalem, aggrieved Jews thronged to
Caesarea from Jerusalem to demand their removal. When the procurator
threatened the protesters with death for rejecting the imperial standards,
a large number of them fell prostrate to the ground, 'extended their
necks, and exclaimed that they were ready rather to die than to transgress
the law' of their ancestors.[65]

In similar fashion, Jews of Jerusalem united in opposition when Caligula
demanded that his statue stand in the temple at Jerusalem as an object of
worship.[66] Seething with contempt for Caligula and his cult, Philo says,

> the created and corruptible nature of man was made to appear uncreated
> and incorruptible by a deification which our [Jewish] nation judged to be
> the most grievous impiety, since sooner could God change into a man than
> a man into God.[67]

---

63. *Apion* 2.6 (75-77).

64. *Leg. Gai.* 20 (133). Apparently the synagogues did not previously contain
imperial statues, since desecration of synagogues during the pogrom included
installment of images of Gaius. *Leg. Gai.* 20 (134-35).

65. *War* 2.9.2-3 (169-74).

66. Josephus writes, 'The Jews said [to Caligula], "We offer sacrifices twice
every day for Caesar, and for the Roman people"; but that if he would place the
images among them, he must first sacrifice the whole Jewish nation; and that they
were ready to expose themselves, together with their children and wives, to be slain'.
War 2.10.4 (197).

67. *Leg. Gai.* 118.

Philo understood that radical monotheism put Jews in a precarious position when Emperor worship became popular. He says Caligula

> ...looked with disfavour on the Jews alone because they alone opposed him on principle, trained as they were we may even say from the cradle, by parents and tutors and instructors and by the far higher authority of the sacred laws and also the unwritten customs, to acknowledge one God who is the Father and Maker of the world.[68]

These examples of Jewish conviction and resistance to the imperial cult indicate that many Jews would brook no compromise with idolatry.[69] For every Jewish merchant who flirted with idolatry in order to trade with Rome, there must have been many others who accepted financial loss rather than give even token allegiance to a 'divine' Emperor.

The great revolt of 66–70 CE could have put diaspora Jews in a precarious political position, but ultimately little changed in their relations with Rome.[70] In 71–72 CE, however, Emperor Vespasian made one change that affected Jews throughout the Mediterranean world: he ordered Jews to send their annual temple tax (δίδραχμον, cf. Mt. 17.24) to Rome instead of Jerusalem.[71] Money that traditionally supported the Yahweh cult at Jerusalem[72] now officially went to the temple of Jupiter Capitolinus, the god who triumphed through Roman armies over the Lord of Israel.[73] Smallwood notes the symbolic importance of this change.

---

68. *Leg. Gai.* 115.

69. Hengel says a primary concern of Judas the Galilean, in his revolutionary movement early in the first century, was to 'narrow down and intensify the first commandment'. In late Judaism, 'Lord' meant virtually the same thing as 'God'. Thus the Zealot's confession of faith was 'I am Yahweh, your Lord... You shall have no other lords except me!' Hengel attributes this concern to the burgeoning cult of Emperor worship. *The Zealots*, pp. 98-99.

70. See Smallwood, *The Jews Under Roman Rule*, pp. 356-88.

71. Romans called this new source of revenue from the Jews the *fiscus judaicus*. Josephus, *War* 7.6.6 (218). Dio Cassius says Rome levied the tax on 'Jews who continued to observe their ancestral customs'. *Hist. Rom.* 65.7.2. *CIL*, VI, 8604 mentions an official called *procurator ad capitularia Iudaeorum*. See J. Juster, *Les Juifs dans l'Empire Romain: Leur condition juridique, économique et sociale*, I (Paris: Librairie Paul Geuthner, 1914), pp. 282-86; and M. Ginsberg, 'Fiscus Judaicus', *JQR* 21 (1930-31), pp. 281-91.

72. Cf. Exod. 30.13-16; Neh. 10.32-33; Josephus, *Ant.* 18.9.1 (312).

73. Josephus, *War* 7.6.6 (218).

> The effect of this measure was that Judaism remained a *religio licita* only
> for those people who declared their allegiance by paying the *didrachmon,*
> soon to be known as the 'Jewish tax', to Rome, and thus purchased the
> privilege of worshipping Yahweh and contracting out of the imperial cult
> by a subscription to Jupiter.[74]

John of Patmos, with his heightened sensitivity to the meaning of
symbols, must have found this arrangement abhorrent. Such a *modus
vivendi* between diaspora Jews and Rome could have helped generate
John's caustic comments about a 'synagogue of Satan' (Rev. 2.9; 3.9).

In the wake of a catastrophic revolt against Rome in 66–70 CE,
virtually all Jews late in the first century must have known that radical
monotheism could create a serious political dilemma. Apparently some
Jews dealt with this problem by practicing their religion quietly in the
private sphere while participating publicly in social and economic life of
pagan society. During the reign of Domitian, certain Jews in Rome
'were prosecuted who without publicly acknowledging that faith yet
lived as Jews, as well as those who concealed their origin and did not
pay the tribute levied upon their people'.[75] Just as some hid their identity in order to avoid the *didrachma* tax, others may have hidden their
identity in order to participate in pagan social or commercial institutions.

3. *Jewish Role in International Commerce*

Although Palestinian Jews remained primarily an agricultural people
down to the Christian era, they began to play a role in Mediterranean
sea trade early in the Hasmonean era.[76] In the mid-second century BCE,
Simon 'took Joppa for a harbor, and opened a way to the isles of the

---

74. Smallwood, *The Jews Under Roman Rule*, p. 345. Tertullian observed that the
fiscus judaicus won the Jews a 'tribute-liberty' that enabled them to worship freely.
Apol. 18.

75. Suetonius, *Dom.* 12.2. The comment by Suetonius is a reversal of the statement by John, 'those who say that they are Jews and are not' (Rev. 2.9, 3.9). The two
authors could be talking about the same phenomenon, namely Jews who dualistically
separated private religion from public life. Suetonius, viewing them from the 'public'
side, insists they were Jews and had to pay the Jewish tax. John, reflecting the
'private' dialogue within the Judeo-Christian community, insists their compromise
with pagan society disqualifies them as Jews.

76. Hengel notes there is some evidence of diaspora Jews involved in wholesale
trade before 310 BCE, but these 'certainly form an exception'. *Judaism and Hellenism,*
I, p. 34.

sea' (1 Macc. 14.5; cf. 14.34).[77] Alexander Janneus later extended Jewish control of the Mediterranean coastline from Dora in the north to Rhinocorura on the border with Egypt.[78] Jews thus dominated principal land trade routes that connected Mesopotamia and Arabia with Egypt and the Mediterranean trade routes (see Figure 8).

This control of land routes and ports in Palestine meant cities of Asia Minor and the eastern Mediterranean basin as a whole 'were forced to accept Red Sea and Arabian wares from Judaean harbours and perhaps through Jewish middlemen operating in Delos and such Asiatic ports as Miletus, Ephesus, Smyrna and Tarsus'.[79] Although Roman conquest diminished Jewish territory in 63 BCE, by the reign of Herod the Great Jews again controlled the ports of Gaza, Anthedon, Joppa and Strato's Tower (later Caesarea).[80] Hence Jewish merchants 'continued to enjoy a slice of the oriental luxury trade'.[81] Using words reminiscent of Revelation 18, Applebaum says this transit trade in luxury goods 'benefited a relatively small group of specialist merchants' as well as the

77. Already when Judas Maccabeus made an alliance with Italy, the Jews were enough of a maritime people that Rome made them promise not to supply enemies of Rome with ships (1 Macc. 8.26). Jewish pirates operated throughout the eastern Mediterranean. *Ant.* 14.43, cf. Strabo, *Geog.* 16.2.28 (759). Hengel notes that a tomb in Jerusalem from during the reign of Alexander Jannaeus shows a naval galley pursuing a ship. Her captain is standing at the prow with his bow drawn. *The Zealots*, p. 28 n. 38. Jews resumed piracy at the beginning of the Jewish War. *War* 9.2 (416). For a general discussion of Jews in maritime trade, see R. Patai, 'Jewish Seafaring in Ancient Times', *JQR* 32 (1941–42), pp. 1-26. Jacob's blessing on Zebulun (Gen. 49.13) reflects the long-standing interest of Palestinian Jews in shipping.

78. *Ant.* 13.15.4 (395-96).

79. S. Applebaum, 'Economic Life in Palestine', in *The Jewish People in the First Century*, II (Philadelphia: Fortress Press, 1976), pp. 667-68. Applebaum describes the wares handled by Jewish middlemen as 'highly profitable luxury articles such as incense, perfumes, spices, silk, precious stones, gold, expensive textiles, animal skins, and rare woods'—a cargo list strikingly similar to Rev. 18.11-13. Ben Sira (second century BCE) was concerned about the moral compromises of Jewish merchants: 'A merchant can hardly keep from wrongdoing, nor is a tradesman innocent of sin…As a stake is driven firmly into a fissure between stones, so sin is wedged in between selling and buying'. Sir. 26.29–27.2; cf. 42.2-5.

80. *War* 1.20.3 (396-97); *Ant.* 15.7.3 (217). Josephus says Jews even launched a large number of pirate ships out of Joppa during the revolt of 66–70 CE. *War* 3.9.2-4 (414-31).

81. Applebaum, 'Economic Life', p. 668.

imperial treasury, the kings and the ports.[82] The Roman Senate endorsed Jewish participation in maritime trade, declaring in the second century BCE that 'it shall be lawful' for Jews of Pergamum 'to export goods from their harbours'.[83]

During the early Roman imperial era, Jewish merchants reached to the far corners of the Roman Empire selling wine, spices, perfumes and perhaps textiles. Guilds of Jewish artisans emerged in Alexandria, and Jewish bankers seem to make their first appearance at this time. 'Judaism never had any religious or ethical objection to buying and selling goods for profit', one scholar observes, 'so this diversification was simply a result of changed economic opportunities'.[84]

Jewish Merchants in the East

Philo provides a glimpse of Jewish involvement in trade when he describes a pogrom that temporarily disrupted the Jewish community in Alexandria. Jewish tradespeople lost their wares, and 'no one—husbandman, shipper (ναυκλήρου),[85] merchant (ἐμπόρου),[86] artisan (τεχνίτου)[87]—was allowed to practise his usual business'.[88] Philo lists shippers and merchants among those who suffered most, suggesting international trade was an important activity among Alexandrian Jews.[89]

82. Applebaum, 'Economic Life', p. 677.

83. *Ant.* 14.10.22 (249-50). A story in the Midrash suggests Jewish merchants of the second century CE continued to view Romans as protectors. A Jewish trader, carrying chests full of money on a ship operated by Gentiles, overheard a plot by the sailors to kill him and take the money. The trader threw the money into the sea. 'When they landed, he went and charged them before the Emperor's proconsul, who imprisoned them...' *Eccl. R.* 3.6.

84. M. Tamari, *'With All Your Possessions': Jewish Ethics and Economic Life* (New York: The Free Press, 1987), pp. 65-66.

85. Cf. Acts 27.11. There are numerous instructions for sailors in the Talmud, including one that indicates they were absent from their wives for long periods of time: R. Eliezar said 'Men of independence' had to fulfill conjugal duties 'every day', while sailors had the same obligation only once in six months. *Ket.* 61b.

86. Cf. Rev. 18.3, 11, 15, 23.

87. Cf. Rev. 18.22 and Acts 19.24, 38.

88. *Flaccus* 57. My translation. See H.I. Bell, 'Anti-Semitism in Alexandria', *JRS* 31 (1941), pp. 1-18.

89. *B. Bat.* 73a offers instructions for those who sell ships. An inscription from Upper Egypt reads, 'Thanksgiving to the God! Theodotos son of Dorion the Jew who was saved from the sea'. V. Tcherikover says 'It must be assumed that he [Theodotos] was a merchant accustomed to sea voyages', *Hellenistic Civilization and the Jews* (Philadelphia: Jewish Publication Society, 1959), pp. 338-39.

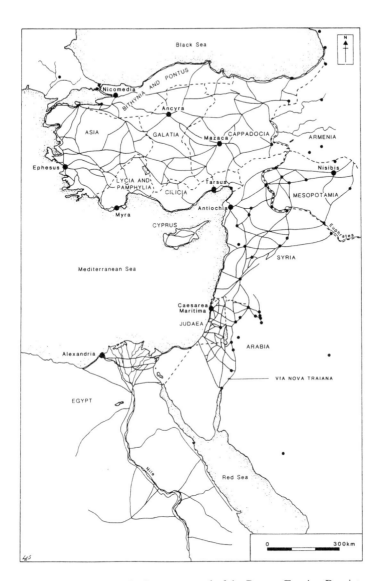

Figure 8. Map of land routes in the eastern end of the Roman Empire. By virtue of its geographic location, Judaea played a key role in international commerce. Merchant vessels coming from China, India, or the east coast of Africa had to unload at a Red Sea port. Merchandise then travelled by land to Mediterranean ports—either across the desert to the Nile and down to Alexandria, or up to Caesarea Maritima in Judaea. The latter port also received caravans from Syria and Mesopotamia.

Illustration after John Wacher, *The Roman World*, I (New York: Routledge & Kegan Paul, 1987), p. 272. Used by permission of Routledge.

Some provincial Jews cooperated closely with the Roman government in administrative affairs. Philo's own brother, Alexander, was a customs superintendent ('Alabarch') on the Arabian side of the Nile.[90] He also was a close friend of Emperor Claudius, and served as 'guardian' for the Emperor's mother.[91] He had financial relations with Puteoli, from which city he promised to release a loan to Agrippa I.[92] Josephus says Alexander was among the wealthiest of his countrymen and a devout Jew.[93] Philo's brother may have participated in what Applebaum describes as 'maritime trade based on the Alexandria-Delos-Puteoli triangle'.[94]

Rabbinic tradition holds that Johanan ben Zakkai, guiding light of Jewish spiritual reorganization following the disaster of 70 CE, 'spent forty years in trade'.[95] During the second century CE, prominent religious leaders of the Jewish community in Palestine engaged in commerce with the Far East.[96] With a large community of co-religionists still in

90. *Ant.* 18.6.3 (159); 18.8.1 (259). Josephus says Alexander was both well born and rich, *Ant.* 20.5.2 (100). Another Jew named Demetrius also served as Alabarch. *Ant.* 20.7.3 (147). See Schürer, *History*, III.I, pp. 136-37. Applebaum says 'The nature of the distinguished post of Alabarch...is obscure. All that can be said is that it was a rich man's function in the municipal administration of Alexandria. It is generally thought to have been the control of customs, perhaps on the Nile'. Applebaum, 'The Social and Economic Status of the Jews in the Diaspora', in S. Safrai, M. Stern *et al* (eds.), *The Jewish People in the First Century,* II (Philadelphia: Fortress Press, 1976), p. 705. Cf. Strabo, *Geog.* 17.1.16. See Tcherikover, *Hellenistic Civilization and the Jews*, p. 339.

91. *Ant.* 19.5.1 (276).

92. *Ant.* 18.6.3 (160). Applebaum says this financial relationship with Puteoli 'can only be interpreted to mean that one of the family's sources of income was commerce'. 'Economic Life', p. 706.

93. *Ant.* 20.5.2 (100).

94. Applebaum, 'Economic Life', p. 706.

95. Yohanan ben Zakkai 'spent forty years in trade, served as disciple of sages for forty years, and spent forty years as sustainer of Israel'. *Sifre* 357.14; cf. *Sanh.* 41a. The *Sifre* statement sounds legendary, since it compares the one hundred and twenty years of Yohanan to the lives of Moses, Hillel and R. Aqiba. Regardless of accuracy, the reference to involvement in trade suggests second-century Jews saw commerce as a respectable line of work for the influential rabbi.

96. *Gen. R.* 77.2 records an incident that happened when 'R. Hiyya the Elder, R. Simeon b. Rabbi, and Rabban Simeon b. Gamaliel were occupied in trading in silk in the area of Tyre'. *Gen. R.* probably was redacted c. 400 CE. J. Neusner, *Genesis Rabbah: the Judaic Commentary to the Book of Genesis*, III (Atlanta: Scholars Press, 1985), p. x. There are several references in the Talmud to rabbis owning or leasing

Babylonia, it was convenient for Jewish merchants in Palestine to make commercial links with Mesopotamia.[97]

4. *Cult and Commerce among Jewish Merchants*

Early in the first century CE there was a Jewish community at Puteoli, at that time principal port for trade between Rome and the East.[98] When Paul came to Italy late in the reign of Nero, there was a Christian community at Puteoli as well (Acts 28.13-14). The early presence of Jews and Christians in Ostia and Puteoli indicates they were surrounded by maritime trade, perhaps active in it themselves.[99] At Ostia are remains of a first-century synagogue, evidence of a substantial Jewish community.[100] An inscription from the ancient building mentions both the 'well-being of Augustus', and the ark (κειβωτος) for holding scrolls of the Torah.[101] This citation of Torah ark and Emperor in one inscription illustrates the desire of some practicing Jews to show deference to Roman rulers.

ships: R. Dimi (*B. Bat.* 22a); R. Eleazar b. Harsom received from his father a legendary 'one thousand boats on the sea' (*Yom.* 35b).

97. Rabbi Hiyya himself was born in Babylonia, and rabbinic writings refer to him as 'the Babylonian'. *Ket.* 5a; *Gen. R.* 26.4.

98. Josephus, *Ant.* 17.12.1 (328); *War* 2.7.1 (104). Smallwood says the Jewish community at Puteoli 'can safely be assumed to have grown up round a nucleus of traders, but there is no evidence for the date of its foundation'. Smallwood, *The Jews Under Roman Rule*, p. 129 n. 28. Josephus relates an incident that seems to indicate some Jews at Puteoli had close ties with the imperial family. As a young man he arrived by ship at the imperial port. There he 'became acquainted with Aliturius, an actor of plays, and much beloved by Nero, but a Jew by birth; and through his interest became known to Poppea, Caesar's wife...', *Life* 3 (16).

99. A Jewish freedman at Puteoli named Acibas, of the first or second century CE, set up a tombstone to his pagan master P. Caulius Coeranus, a *negotiator ferriarum et vinariariae*. *CIL*, X, 1931; *CII*, I, 75. Cited by Applebaum, 'Social and Economic Status', p. 722.

100. Schürer, *History*, III.I, p. 8. A.T. Kraabel, 'The Diaspora Synagogue: Archaeological and Epigraphic Evidence since Suhenik', *ANRW*, II, 19.1 (1979), pp. 497-500. Applebaum says the first-century synagogue at Ostia was 'sufficiently substantial to argue a well-to-do element of the [Jewish] community, which it is natural to interpret as engaged in the import and export business of the harbour town'. Applebaum, 'Social and Economic Status', p. 722.

101. The inscription is part Latin, part Greek: *Pro salute Aug[usti]*, οἰκοδόμησεν κὲ αἰπόησεν (sic) ἐκ τῶν αὑτου δομάτων καὶ τὴν κειβωτὸν ἀνέθηκεν νόμῳ ἁγίῳ Μίνδις φαῦστος με[...]. *AE* 77 (1967). Schürer, *History*, III.I, p. 82.

Herod's Syncretism

Herod the Great set a precedent for religious syncretism that must have been familiar to any maritime merchant carrying goods out of Palestine. Even as he launched a spectacular restoration of the temple in Jerusalem, elsewhere in Palestine Herod financed diverse projects tied to the imperial cult. Josephus says there was 'no suitable spot within his realm' which Herod 'left destitute of some mark of homage to Caesar'.[102] When he built a harbor at Strato's Tower (Caesarea) on the Mediterranean coast, cult and commerce blended in elaborate fashion.

> On an eminence facing the harbour-mouth stood Caesar's temple, remark-able for its beauty and grand proportions; it contained a colossal statue of the Emperor, not inferior to the Olympian Zeus...and another of Rome, rivalling that of Hera at Argos. The city Herod...accordingly gave the name of Caesarea.[103]

There was a large and wealthy Jewish community at Caesarea in the first century, and Christian missionaries reached the city early (Acts 8.40, 12.19).[104] At Caesarea Peter had his famous encounter with the Roman centurion Cornelius. Cornelius, a 'God-fearing man' and 'well spoken of by the whole Jewish nation', became a Christian (Acts 10.22). This story graphically portrays the meeting of Roman, Jewish and Christian influences in a Hellenistic port city.[105] If Jewish merchants could work

---

102. *War* 1.21.4 (407). Jews in Rome paid homage as well. During the official mourning period in Rome at the time of Caesar's funeral, 'foreigners went about lamenting each after the fashion of his country, above all the Jews'. Suetonius, *Jul.* 84.

103. *War* 1.21.7 (414).

104. Shortly before the Jewish Revolt there was a disturbance in Caesarea between Jews and Syrians. Josephus says the Jews 'had the advantage of superior wealth and physical strength'. *War* 2.13.7 (268). The Jews felt secure, 'drawing confidence from their wealth and consequently despising the Syrians' who were 'inferior in wealth' (*Ant.* 20.8.7 [175-76]). Gentiles of Caesarea slaughtered some 20,000 Jews at the outbreak of war in 66 CE; others from the city fled or became galley slaves. *War* 2.18.1 (457). For a thorough study of Caesarea in the first century, see L.I. Levine, *Caesarea under Roman Rule* (Leiden: Brill, 1975), pp. 15-33.

105. Horsley observes that Cornelius 'appears to have had no difficulty reconciling his duties *qua* centurion, which must have involved participation in the pagan rituals that were an unavoidable part of life in the Roman army, with his frequent attendance at the local synagogue and regular worship of the Jewish God'. G.H.R. Horsley and S.R. Llewelyn, *New Documents Illustrating Early Christianity* (6 vols.; North Ryde: Macquarrie University, 1981-92), II, p. 104. Perhaps more to the point, the author of

out of Caesarea, a syncretistic environment in their homeland, there would be little to dissuade them from visiting the ports of Italy.

5. *Rabbinic Concern for Idolatry in Commerce*

Juxtaposed to this Jewish entrepreneurial experience is a tradition of devout Jews who objected to international trade, at least to the extent it involved contact with Gentiles and pagans. The rabbinic schools to which Hillel and Shammai belonged declared as ritually unclean a wide variety of ordinary and luxury imports.[106] The Mishnah shows concern about the close relationship between cult and commerce, and prohibits Jewish merchants from doing any business at all with Gentiles during their pagan religious festivals. Festivals included in this rabbinic censure were Kalenda (the Roman New Year), Saturnalia, Kratesis (commemorating Roman conquest of the East), the anniversary of the Emperor's accession to the throne, the Emperor's birthday or the anniversary of his death.[107] The rabbis advised merchants to conduct business outside rather than inside any city that contained idols, a directive that would have applied to Ostia, Ephesus, Caesarea and countless other Mediterranean cities.[108] Jewish traders were not to sell Gentiles either frankincense or other items used in sacrifice to idols.[109]

Beyond this focus on cultic purity was a long-standing prophetic concern about the spiritual hazards of commerce and wealth. Hosea sounded a theme that other Hebrew prophets echoed: 'A trader, in whose hands

Acts had no hesitation in portraying Cornelius as active in both the Roman army and a Jewish synagogue.

106. These included metal implements, wheat from Alexandria and luxury glass articles imported from Alexandria, Tyre and Sidon. The Mishnah prohibited sale of cattle, corn and wine to Gentiles. During the revolt of 66 CE, Jews at Jerusalem prohibited use of all foreign oil and foodstuffs on grounds of impurity. See Hengel, *Judaism and Hellenism*, I, p. 53.

107. *'Abod. Zar.* 1.8a.

108. *'Abod. Zar.* 1.11b. Cf. Hippolytus, who says of the radical Essenes (whom he identifies as Zealots), 'no one of those goes into a city, lest (by so doing) he should enter through a gate at which statues are erected, regarding it a violation of law to pass beneath images', *Refutatio Omnium Haeresium* 9.21.

109. *'Abod. Zar.* 1.13b, 14b. Tertullian advises the same for Christian traders, since 'idolatry is more easily carried on without the idol, than without the ware of the frankincense-seller', *De Idol.* 11.

are false balances, he loves to oppress. Ephraim has said, "Ah, I am rich, I have gained wealth for myself..." ' (Hosea 12.7; cf. Amos 8.4-6, Jer. 6.13, 8.10).

Roman Concessions to Jewish Scruples

Despites such warnings from their own tradition, evidence suggests some Jewish merchants did enter pagan settings for trade. They may have done so because Rome made specific concessions *(de jure* or *de facto)* to Jewish religious scruples. An edict by Emperor Claudius states that Jews in Alexandria suffered under Caligula because 'they refused to transgress the religion of their [ancestors] by addressing him as a god'.[110] Claudius restored privileges granted to Jews since the days of Augustus, and decreed that Jews throughout the whole world were free to observe their traditional customs.[111] Schürer says that, beginning with the reign of Claudius, 'no serious suggestion was ever made of compelling Jews to participate in the imperial cult'. Romans treated freedom from this obligation as an ancient right of the Jews, 'a circumstance through which they enjoyed particular advantage by comparison with Christians'.[112] Philo reports that Jews in Rome won concessions that allowed them Sabbath observance. When distribution of free grain fell on the Jewish holy day, government officials held back the portion reserved for the Jews so they could claim it the following day.[113]

If Rome had such respect for Jewish religious convictions, it is possible conscientious Jewish merchants were able to enter Roman ports without overt participation in ceremonies of the imperial cult. At the time of Revelation, however, the situation for Christian merchants may have been more difficult. The earliest Christian merchants, by virtue of their Jewish roots, would have operated under privileges already gained by

---

110. *Ant.* 19.5.2 (284).

111. *Ant.* 19.5.3 (286-91).

112. Schürer, *History*, III.I, p. 122. When Tacitus discusses Christians in connection with the great fire of Rome in 64 CE, he introduces the sect as a recent and undesirable development that emerged in Judaea. *Ann.* 15.44. He also shows contempt for the Jews, but in doing so gives further evidence that Jews enjoyed (or claimed) exemption from certain religious practices: 'the earliest lesson they receive is to despise the gods, to disown their country,...they set up no statues in their cities, still less in their temples; this flattery is not paid their kings, nor this honour given to the Caesars', *Hist.* 5.5.

113. *Leg. Gai.* 158.

the Jewish community.[114] By the end of the first century, however, Romans understood that Christians were a separate group alienated from Judaism.[115]

With manifest tension between Jews and Christians late in the first century,[116] Jewish merchants could not have been eager to share with Christians any special cultic status they had gained in trade venues. The Romans, who long had tolerated Jewish religious peculiarities, could not have been happy to see the proselytizing Christian movement spring from Judaism. It was one thing to tolerate a monotheistic faith that largely remained within the confines of an ethnic minority. It was something else to see a movement like Christianity—with its apocalyptic outlook and critical view of power—attracting thousands of Greeks and Romans in provinces of the East.

Separation from Judaism Made Christians Vulnerable
It is hardly surprising that a religious community as large and scattered as diaspora Judaism would produce some people who operated in the ambiguous area between strict monotheism and pagan polytheism. Jewish merchants had traded for centuries in ports and marketplaces filled with temples to many gods, facing daily the pressures and attractions of polytheism. Evidence in rabbinic texts suggests that conscientious

114. Luke records an episode that illustrates the tendency of Romans in the middle of the first century to view Christians as a subgroup of Judaism: Gallio, proconsul of Achaia (c. 51 CE), treated the dispute between Jews and Christians at Corinth as a Jewish internal affair (Acts 18.12-17).

115. In explaining why Titus wanted to destroy the Jerusalem temple in 70 CE, Tacitus says it was 'a prime necessity in order to wipe out more completely the religion of the Jews and the Christians; for…these religions, although hostile to each other, nevertheless sprang from the same sources; the Christians had grown out of the Jews: if the root were destroyed, the stock would easily perish'. Tacitus, 'Fragments of the Histories' 2, in *Tacitus: History*, II (LCL, London: Heinemann, 1931), pp. 220-21.

116. Examples of this tension in the NT include Luke's account of Stephen's sermon in which Stephen blames Jews for murdering the 'Righteous One' (Acts 7.52-53), and accounts in the fourth Gospel of synagogue officials excommunicating members who acknowledged Jesus as Messiah (Jn 9.22; 12.42; 16.2). A decisive political divergence occurred when followers of Jesus fled Jerusalem in 68 CE instead of supporting the Jewish revolt against Rome. Eusebius, *Hist. Eccl.* 3.5.3; cf. Lk. 21.20-24. Pharasaic Jews of the late first century added a sentence to the 'Eighteen Benedictions' recited in synagogues, calling down a curse upon 'Nazarenes' and heretics—categories that probably included Christians. *Ber.* 29a.

merchants sought ways to avoid compromising their exclusive loyalty to Yahweh. Roman imperial officials understood that Judaism was a venerable religion, and knew that refusal to join imperial cult ceremonies did not necessarily imply disloyalty to the Emperor.

After the disastrous Jewish revolt of 66–70 CE, however, diaspora Jews were especially vulnerable to suspicions of disloyalty. The author of the fourth Gospel, writing late in the first century, registers the concern about political allegiance that centered on Jesus. When Pilate sought to release Jesus, 'the Jews cried out, "If you release this man, you are no friend of the Emperor. Everyone who claims to be a king sets himself against the Emperor"' (Jn 19.12; cf. 19.15). Luke records another incident in which Jews were quick to place suspicion of disloyalty on Christians. 'These people who have been turning the world upside down have come here also', charged Jews at Thessalonica. 'They are all acting contrary to the decrees of the Emperor, saying that there is another king named Jesus' (Acts 17.6, 7).

Perhaps reflecting more the circumstances of his own rather than Paul's day, Luke articulates the kind of charges that could have made it difficult for Christian merchants to operate in the Roman world. Radical Christians such as John did 'turn the world upside down', inverting the Roman social pyramid by giving supreme allegiance to a crucified Galilean instead of the Emperor. Jews throughout the Mediterranean knew it was dangerous to associate with the Christian movement: according to Luke, when Paul arrived as a prisoner in Rome, Jews there reported that 'with regard to this sect we know that everywhere it is spoken against' (Acts 28.22).

As late first-century Christianity developed a negative image among Jews and Romans, it must have been increasingly difficult for conscientious Christian merchants to stay in the international market. No longer protected from pagan or imperial cult pressures by virtue of being Jewish,[117] and perhaps facing hostility from their Jewish counterparts, Christian merchants were economically and politically vulnerable. Some Christians—including those at the industrial city of Laodicea— actually prospered in this precarious environment (Rev. 3.17). John believed such Christians achieved their comfortable status by apostasy, and urged them to repent (3.19).

Although repentance probably would mean losing financial and politi-

---

117. See E. Judge, 'Judaism and the Rise of Christianity: A Roman Perspective', *AJJS* 7 (1993), pp. 82-98.

cal status in the Roman world, John did not expect Christians to be left homeless. The next chapter surveys the lasting security which John believed faithful followers of Jesus would enjoy in the New Jerusalem, both in the present and in the age to come.

Chapter 6

A HEALING OF THE NATIONS

> And I saw the holy city, the new Jerusalem, coming down out of heaven from God, prepared as a bride adorned for her husband. And I heard a loud voice from the throne saying, 'See the home of God is among mortals'... And the city has no need of sun or moon to shine on it, for the glory of God is its light, and its lamp is the Lamb. The nations will walk by its light, and the kings of the earth will bring their glory into it. Its gates will never be shut by day—and there will be no night there. People will bring into it the glory and the honor of the nations (Rev. 21.2, 3, 23-26).

John does not end his Apocalypse with the ghastly demise of Rome, and it would be inappropriate for this study to do so. John's vitriolic attack upon Rome should be seen in the brilliant light of an eschatological 'New Jerusalem' that he believes soon will rule the earth (Rev. 21–22). Although he does not elaborate, it is clear this city has social and economic dimensions that redress failures of the Roman Empire. Ultimately, John yearns for a 'healing of the nations' (22.2), not for the obliteration of human society. This hope triumphs in John's view of the future, and the New Jerusalem may be a reality he already has begun to experience within the alternative society of those who name Jesus as Lord. John claims citizenship in this New Jerusalem, not in the Roman Empire—and calls his readers to do the same. Allegiance to a new society under the rule of Christ enables John and his readers to withstand idolatrous social and economic pressures of the dominant culture in which they live.

1. A Convergence of Pressures on Christians

I have argued that Christian communities of Asia Minor probably experienced more internal *desire* to conform to pagan society than external *pressure* in the way of persecution. Certainly a few Christians—John himself, Antipas (2.13) and souls under the altar (6.9-11; cf. 20.4)—suffered hardship or death in their conflict with Roman officials and provincial society. Other Christians, however, accommodated sufficiently to social and political norms that they could live in the cities of Asia Minor without serious harassment or suffering. These people, with their desire for social acceptance and financial security, participated in various levels of political and economic life of the Roman Empire. Some perhaps avoided external pressures of persecution by making concessions to Roman ideology and the imperial cult. These incurred the wrath of John and other radical believers who took a hard stance against any show of loyalty to the 'beast' from Italy.

Withdrawal from Economy Difficult for Christians
In John's world view, the imperial cult came to epitomize all that was unjust or idolatrous about Rome. The cult in any form became a 'red flag' that demarcated whole areas of society John thought Christians should avoid. The cult not only had high visibility on a hill at Ephesus; increasingly, it also penetrated economic institutions of the whole Mediterranean world. In John's view it was not sufficient for Christians simply to avoid entering imperial temples in the cities of Asia Minor; Christians also needed to withdraw from international commercial venues where Emperor worship was common practice.[1]

Such economic withdrawal was difficult in port cities and industrial areas of western Asia Minor, where the local economy drew much of its strength from commercial ties with Rome. The fact that Jews had engaged in maritime trade for centuries only compounded the dilemma: the Jewish diaspora was the seedbed of early Christianity, giving shape to basic theological and sociological expressions of the Christian movement. First-century Jews were active in maritime trade with Rome, and it was natural for Christians to do the same. When Christianity made a definitive break from Judaism, however, Christian merchants probably lost any special exemptions from the imperial cult that Jews had enjoyed in commercial settings.

Thus late first-century Christian merchants who participated in maritime or export trade felt pressure from several sides. In order to survive in the international marketplace it was essential to cooperate with—if not actually join—trade guilds or harbor institutions that supported the

---

1.   Other Jewish and Christian voices of John's day called for withdrawal from the Roman economy and institutions. The author of *4 Ezra* wrote, 'Let him that sells be like one who will flee; let him that buys be like one who will lose; let him that does business be like one who will not make a profit... Those who conduct business do it only to be plundered' (*4 Ezra* 16.41-47; cf. 1 Cor. 7.29-31).

imperial cult. While financial forces pushed Christian merchants toward concessions to the cult, the monotheistic faith of Christians made cultic activities of the guilds and harbors anathema. The resulting tension put Christian merchants in an awkward position, and must have made them unpopular among pagan merchants who were grateful to Rome for opening the way to commercial success.

It was Rome that made the seas safe for commerce, Rome that provided privileges and services for the shippers. Christian merchants who earned a living in maritime trade, yet refused to accept the imperial cult, must have appeared ungrateful to their pagan associates. Since the imperial cult *gradually* penetrated commerce in the first century, there must have been merchants who made their capital investment before the blending of cult and commerce became an urgent issue. Such people may have owned businesses, ships or warehouses. At what point did international commerce become so tainted with the imperial cult that Christians had to withdraw? This was a matter of subtle theological discernment; first-century Christians (and Jews) disagreed on where to draw the line.

Cowards and Liars in the Apocalypse

In view of his allusions to persecution and martyrdom, it is likely John wrote Revelation during some episode of local persecution; there is no reason to believe he simply imagined suffering and violence. Nor is there evidence such hardship was widespread among Christians. The pathos of Revelation issues from John's deep desire to awaken the church to a conflict of loyalties that many readers apparently do not yet recognize or even see on the horizon.[2] There is urgency to his message, since John

---

2.   In this regard Revelation may have parallels to the sociological context of the court tales in Daniel 1–6. P.R. Davies argues that the historian 'finds little evidence of religious persecution or enforced emperor-worship in the eastern diaspora under Neo-Babylonians, Persians or Seleucids. These tales of conflict have been manufactured for ideological reasons. These reasons may be quite complex, but we can presume that the preservation of distinct values and identity by a subculture in an imperial cultural milieu, whether hostile or not, requires conflict in order to sustain itself; lack of conflict aids assimilation'. P.R. Davies, 'Daniel in the Lions' Den', in L. Alexander (ed.), *Images of Empire* (Sheffield: Sheffield Academic Press, 1991), p. 161. Regardless of whether or not the court tales were 'manufactured', they must have been retold for generations by people who actually suffered no persecution. Likewise vivid conflict portrayed in Revelation could have helped shape the identity and convictions of believers who experienced no overt conflict with Rome.

and a few other believers are suffering and even have their lives in danger. Yet some Christians to whom John writes, by their apathy or lack of spiritual perception, unwittingly serve as accomplices to the idolatry and oppression of Rome.

John may have had compromised Christians in mind when he wrote this cryptic warning near the end of his Apocalypse.

> But as for the cowardly, the faithless, the polluted, the murderers, the forni-cators, the sorcerers, the idolaters, and all liars, their place will be in the lake that burns with fire and sulfur, which is the second death. (Rev. 21.8; cf. 22.15)

From John's lonely vantage point as a persecuted prophet, the 'cowardly' (δειλοῖς) may be Christians who were not brave enough to confess their faith publicly and accept the consequences.[3] The 'faithless' could be those who changed loyalties under pressure; the 'polluted' (ἐβδελυγμένοις) those who accommodated in some way to pagan worship.[4] People who informed on radical Christians, leading to their arrest and martyrdom, may be 'murderers' (φονεῦσιν) in the eyes of John.[5] In the tradition of Hebrew prophecy, 'fornicators', 'sorcerers', and 'idolaters' may be syncretists who claimed loyalty both to Christ and Caesar;[6] 'liars'

---

3. In *Mart. Pol.* 4, the verbal form of the same root (δειλιάω) describes the cowardly response of a Christian who recanted when faced with wild beasts in the arena at Smyrna.

4. First-century Christians associated the word βδέλυγμα with pagan desecra-tion of the temple at Jerusalem (probably by the Romans, 70 CE: Mt. 24.15; Mk 13.14). When Jesus said it was impossible to serve both God and money, he con-cluded by saying 'what is prized by human beings is an abomination (βδέλυγμα) in the sight of God' (Lk. 16.15). In Rev. 17.4, the harlot Rome holds in her hand a cup full of 'abominations' (βδελυγμάτων). All these references are consistent with John's use of βδελύσσομαι ('abhor') to include Christians who share in acts of idolatry for commercial gain. Rom. 2.22 uses the verb form in reference to abhorrence of idols.

5. The same Greek word for 'murderers' is used to describe religious authori-ties who killed Jesus (Acts 7.52) and other prophets of the kingdom of heaven (Mt. 22.7).

6. It probably is in the context of John calling idolatry and syncretism 'fornication' that we must understand John's reference to 'virgins' in Rev. 14.4. The 144,000 redeemed saints on Mount Zion are those who 'have not defiled themselves with women, for they are virgins; these follow the Lamb wherever he goes'. It is unlikely John was a misogynist, as some modern critics suggest, or that he was advo-cating sexual abstinence. The women with whom believers could defile themselves were Rome (represented by the goddess Roma or the great prostitute Babylon) or the

(ψευδέσιν)[7] could be apostates who, under questioning, denied ever having followed Jesus.[8] John had no patience—and little compassion—for people who showed less than complete loyalty to Jesus.

2. *Nonviolent Response to Social Injustice*

While this study has focused on cultic aspects of imperial rule, a complete assessment of John's message must consider his condemnation of Roman violence and economic exploitation. The imperial cult put a glamorous, mystical veneer on an Empire built on the backs of conquered nations and millions of slaves. Christians were only a small minority among countless victims of the great imperial beast. The dirge in Revelation 18 ends with John backing off from the scene to take a panoramic view of the carnage: 'in you was found the blood of prophets and of saints, and of all who have been slaughtered on earth' (Rev. 18.24).

It is not adequate to say John rejected Roman rule solely because of the imperial cult. Nor is it adequate to say early Christians avoided participation in the army for the same simple reason. In both cases, imperial religion provided a means of expressing loyalty to an economic and political system that violated Christian standards of love and justice. Something more than cultic abominations tainted commercial networks of the Empire: Revelation makes repeated allusions to the greed and selfish opulence of Rome and her merchants (18.3, 7, 11-16, 19). Despite terrible plagues that came upon the earth in John's vision, people 'did not repent of their murders or their sorceries or their fornication or their *thefts*' (9.21). Rome coopted and rewarded provincial elites who subdued the local population and directed regional economies toward appetites of Italy.[9] In the spirit of the great Hebrew prophets, John could have condemned Rome on grounds of social injustice alone.

---

heretical teacher Jezebel, 'who refuses to repent of her fornication' (2.20-23).

7.   In his vision of the Lamb on Mount Zion (Rev. 14.1-5), John sees the faithful thousands who 'follow the Lamb wherever he goes'—suggesting complete fidelity in belief and praxis. In their mouth 'no lie was found', perhaps implying they claimed no dual loyalty. For the long Jewish tradition of connecting sorcery and fornication (often with mention of Balaam), see Hengel, *The Zealots*, p. 186.

8.   Cf. Pliny, who says some defendants in his courtroom 'denied they were, or had ever been, Christians'. *Ep.* 10.96.

9.   This is a colonial arrangement that has seen parallels in almost every century. Nicholas Wolterstorff examines the role of modern business interests from America and western Europe in developing nations. 'The profits from these enterprises do not

Rejection of the Zealot Model

John's utter reliance on God is the foundation of his strategic response to a situation of systemic evil. He longs for Rome's demise, but never issues a call for violent revolution. In contrast to the Zealot model of armed resistance,[10] faithful Christians must respond with patient endurance rather than violence: 'If you are to be taken captive, into captivity you go; if you kill with the sword, with the sword you must be killed' (Rev. 13.10). While the world follows a beast with all its power and violence, Christians follow a gentle and (seemingly) powerless Lamb—confident that God's love will triumph in the end. A great multitude of the faithful stand on Mount Zion with the Lamb (14.1-5), and an angel proclaims from mid-heaven, 'Fallen, fallen is Babylon the great!' (14.8). The collapse of Rome will be God's doing, not something humans engineer.

As if to emphasize a strategy of patient obedience to Jesus rather than revolution, John adds, 'Here is a call for the endurance of the saints' (14.12). In its pacifism Revelation parts dramatically from the Jewish tradition of heroic armed revolt against imperial oppression. Maccabean rebels slaughtered their foes and plundered the enemy, then 'went up to Mount Zion with joy and gladness, and offered burnt offerings, because they had returned in safety; not one of them had fallen' (1 Macc. 5.48-54). In contrast to this tradition of violent heroism, in Revelation it is a Lamb 'standing as if it had been slaughtered' (5.6) that leads God's people to triumphant celebration on Mount Zion. Jesus, during his earthly ministry, engaged beastly powers from a position of apparent weakness and vulnerability. Despite apparent defeat through political execution on the cross, God vindicated Jesus' lamb-like stance with resurrection power.

---

entirely return to the core. They are shared with investors and administrators from the middle and upper classes in the semiperiphery.' The United States, he argues, 'supports repressive regimes that declare themselves in favor of free enterprise and prove hospitable to American businesses. While United States citizens themselves enjoy great freedom of speech and action, their government effectively undermines these freedoms for many others by combatting opposition to the oppressors in friendly periphery states'. N. Wolterstorff, *Until Justice and Peace Embrace* (Grand Rapids: Eerdmans, 1983), p. 95. This, perhaps, is a modern version of the 'fornication' John condemns in Revelation 18.

10. Hengel says there may be an anti-Zealot polemic in Jesus' promise that 'the meek' will 'inherit the earth'. These words 'were in very sharp contrast to the Zealot teaching and must have struck the Zealots, who called for retributory violence as a response to all injustice, as a form of enthusiasm'. *The Zealots*, p. 309; cf. p. 379.

Jesus the Example in Confronting Evil

John may have taken a nonviolent stance toward the evil of a corrupt Empire, but he was not passive. By featuring the 144,000 who 'follow the Lamb wherever he goes' (Rev. 14.4), John highlighted the life and example of Jesus the Lamb. Bringing together enemies and crossing social, economic or political barriers was the very substance of Jesus' earthly ministry. Among his circle of twelve disciples, for example, Jesus counted both a tax collector (Lk. 5.27) and a Zealot (Lk. 6.15; Acts 1.13). Before joining the band of disciples, the first was a collaborator with Rome and the second was an armed revolutionary. These two men should have hated each other, but something about the kingdom of God transcended their political formation and brought them together for a larger purpose. Jesus did not hesitate to rebuke political leaders (Lk. 13.32), and he decisively rejected the Roman philosophy of government (Lk. 22.25). However, he also had compassion on the slave of an enemy centurion (Lk. 7.1-10), and freely forgave the soldiers who executed him (Lk. 23.34).

Far from being passive in the face of evil, Jesus taught his followers to assert themselves creatively into a situation of oppression. Disciples were to turn the other cheek, go the second mile and love the enemy (Mt. 5.39, 41, 44). All of these were responses designed to throw the oppressor off guard and to claim the dignity and moral authority of the victim.[11] There is no indication that Jesus sought to humiliate the enemy; surprise leading to reflection was a more likely objective. Ultimately Jesus sought to win over the person perpetrating evil and to redeem them for the kingdom of God. Paul caught something of this strategy in his instructions about feeding the enemy and overcoming evil with good (Rom. 12.21).

For John, isolated on the island of Patmos, such a strategy of engaging and subverting the powers may have been difficult. Geographically removed as he was from the fault line in Asia Minor between the kingdom of Rome and the kingdom of Jesus, John mostly thought in broad symbolic terms rather than in specific practical detail. To make his point about the importance of allegiance to Christ, he polarized all of humanity into those who follow the beast and those who follow the Lamb. The beast fills followers with greed and idolatry—a way that leads to death and a lake of fire. The Lamb inspires followers with hope and love—a way that leads to life and the New Jerusalem.

11. See 'Jesus' Third Way: Nonviolent Engagement' in W. Wink, *Engaging the Powers* (Minneapolis: Fortress Press, 1992), pp. 175-93.

It is important to view such radical dualism in the light of a future when harmony and wholeness are restored. Just as the author of Colossians expected Christ to 'reconcile to himself all things, whether on earth or in heaven' (Col. 1.20), John anticipates the day when humanity and all the cosmos will be re-created (cf. Acts 3.21). Although cowards, idolaters and other faithless people may perversely head for the lake of fire (Rev. 21.8), salvation ultimately is widely inclusive (21.24-26). Excluded are the 'dogs and sorcerers and fornicators and murderers and idolaters, and everyone *who loves and practices* falsehood' (22.15). The choice of language here suggests a willful and persistent rejection of God's invitation to a restored humanity.

For John, the good news of salvation is open to 'anyone who wishes to take the water of life as a gift' (22.17). He never suggests that people who cooperated with idolatrous pagan institutions are beyond redemption. He does say the New Jerusalem is a place where corruption itself will find no foothold: 'nothing unclean will enter it, nor anyone who practices abomination or falsehood' (21.27). People who love greed and violence more than the kingdom of God will have excluded themselves.

Roots of John's Bitter Anger at Rome
Some modern readers express disquiet at John's apparently vindictive (or even envious!) attitude toward Rome and those who cooperated with the corrupt Empire.[12] The call for Rome's irrevocable destruction in Revelation 18–19 is so intense that it almost seems to preempt the grace of God.

If John in fact was a Jew (which seems almost certain), he surely would have felt the pain of Jerusalem's destruction (70 CE) and the attending humiliation of his people. The Romans, by the ubiquitous propaganda of coin inscriptions, let everyone in the Empire know that Jews had been brought low for their rebellion. More than two dozen coin designs from the reigns of Vespasian through Domitian carried the words *IVDAEA DEVICTA* ('Judaea defeated') or *IVDAEA CAPTA* ('Judaea captive').[13] Most coins of the series portray Judea as a woman,

---

12. See, e.g., discussion by Collins, *Crisis and Catharsis*, pp. 168-75.

13. F.W. Madden, *History of Jewish Coinage and of Money in the Old and New Testament* (London: Bernard Quaritch, 1864), pp. 183-97. In *BMC*, II, see Vespasian *as*, p. 173, no. 736A (plate 30, no. 4); Vespasian *sestertii*, pp. 184-85, no. 755 (plate 32, no. 5), nos. 761-65 (plate 33, nos. 1-4); p. 196, no. 796 (plate 37, no. 1); p. 197, no. 800 (plate 37, no. 7); p. 202, no. 812 (plate 39, no. 1); p. 206, no. 826 (p. 40, no. 1);

seated and weeping under a palm tree—with a triumphant Roman soldier (sometimes the Emperor) standing nearby. A few coins also depict a Jewish man with hands bound behind his back. In addition to bearing blasphemous imagery of the Emperor as divine, these coins were a constant reminder to Jews of their ill treatment at the hands of Rome.

Historical circumstances of Domitian's final years as Emperor might help explain the flood of feeling flowing through John's pen. While it may be true that Domitian was no more a tyrant than several other Emperors of his century, he nevertheless was extremely harsh to people who got in his way. Suetonius—admittedly a partisan writer—says Domitian executed many senators at Rome and 'became an object of terror and hatred to all'.[14]

Many elites in Rome hated Domitian for his cruelty and capricious rule. A few years after Domitian's death, Pliny described a catharsis of rage against the Emperor that erupted upon news of his assassination. The tone of Pliny's words is reminiscent of Revelation 19:

> ...those innumerable golden images [of Domitian], as a sacrifice to public rejoicing, lie broken and destroyed. It was our delight to dash those proud faces to the ground, to smite them with the sword and savage them with the axe, as if blood and agony could follow from every blow. Our transports of joy—so long deferred—were unrestrained; all sought a form of vengeance in beholding those bodies mutilated, limbs hacked in pieces, and finally that baleful, fearsome visage cast into the fire, to be melted down, so that from such menacing terror something for [human] use and enjoyment should rise out of the flames.[15]

It is ironic that a member of the imperial elite gave a response to Domitian that parallels the cry of a powerless exile on Patmos.

Despite any superficial similarities, however, John and Pliny looked at the world through very different eyes. John's critique of Roman power cut to the very roots of the Empire; Pliny merely rejoiced to have a single branch trimmed. Pliny saw statues of a bad Emperor lie broken and destroyed; John expected to see Rome itself dashed into the sea (Rev. 18.21). Pliny delighted to see mutilated pieces of an imperial statue; John awaited the day when the entire imperial hierarchy—from

---

Vespasian *asses*, p. 210, no. 845 (plate 40, no. 11); p. 213, no. 862 (plate 42, no. 1); Titus *sestertii*, pp. 256-57, nos. 162-170 (plate 48, nos. 8-10); Titus *as*, p. 294, no. 308 (plate 57, no. 4).

   14. *Dom.* 10, 14.
   15. *Pan.* 52.

kings and captains to their slaves and free supporters—would be dis-membered and fed to the birds (19.17-18). In Pliny's account, 'public rejoicing' burst forth at Domitian's demise; in John's vision, a great multitude cried, 'Hallelujah! Salvation and glory and power belong to God' (19.1).

Rage in the Jewish Lament Tradition
John vented his anger against Rome in tones reminiscent of the lament poetry in the Psalms. 'O daughter Babylon, you devastator!' the psalmist wrote, 'Happy shall they be who pay you back what you have done to us! Happy shall they be who take your little ones and dash them against the rock!' (Ps. 137.9) Poets of Israel did not flinch at registering the full range of human emotion, and there is no reason to expect John—immersed as he was in the Hebrew scriptures—to filter out his rage. Bernhard Anderson points out that authors of the lament psalms 'cry to God out of the depths in the confidence and certainty that he has the power to lift a person out of the "miry bog" and set his feet upon a rock (Ps. 40.1-2)'. Hence the laments are really 'expressions of praise—praise offered to God in the time of his absence'.[16]

Read in the light of Hebrew poetic tradition, Revelation comes into focus as a visceral response to injustice on a grand scale. The bile of the book pours out as a catharsis of emotion, offered to God as the only one capable of redressing the situation. Traditional Hebrew lament psalms move through a progression that includes address to God, complaint, confession of trust, petition, words of assurance, and a vow of praise.[17] All these elements appear in the poetry of Revelation, now pitched in an apocalyptic key. John may be angry, but he expresses his rage in prayer and leaves retribution to the hand of God.

3. *A Just Society in the New Jerusalem*

The story of Noah's flood ends with a rainbow and the promise of a new relationship between God and mortals (Gen. 8.20–9.17; cf. Rev. 4.3; 10.1). Revelation parallels this hope with the description of a New Jerusalem that will rule justly where Rome miserably failed.[18] John sees

16. B.W. Anderson, *Out of the Depths* (Philadelphia: Westminster Press, 1970), p. 56.
17. Anderson, *Out of the Depths*, p. 57.
18. In his encomium *To Rome* in the mid-second century, Aelius Aristides uses

the holy city 'coming down out of heaven from God' (Rev. 21.2, 10)—emphasizing that it is an *earthly* reality, not a place where saints go when they die. Use of a present active participle ('coming down') suggests that John saw the city's arrival as imminent, perhaps something God's people already experienced in a provisional way. The mention of 'all nations' (21.24; 22.2) indicates that more is involved than mere restoration of the Jewish capital in Palestine: New Jerusalem is a metaphor of all humanity living in harmony with God and one another (cf. 5.9; 14.6).

Presence of God through the Risen Christ
In practical terms, what did John have in mind when he envisioned a future of world peace mediated through the New Jerusalem? How could such a great transformation of world economy and power take place? True to apocalyptic convention, John expected a dramatic theophany at the end of time, accompanied by cosmic upheaval and universal acknowledgement of God's sovereignty.

Yet there are reasons to believe John may have thought of the New Jerusalem as being in part a present, tangible reality. The risen Christ appears standing among the golden lampstands of the seven churches (Rev. 1.12). Given John's high Christology, it is possible that he understood this mystical presence of Christ as partial fulfilment of the New Jerusalem prophecy that 'the home of God is among mortals' (21.3).[19] Christ already dwelt with believers in Asia Minor; he would 'come in to eat' with any church that would 'open the door' (3.20). Actual Christian *communities* took shape in the early church, made up of people who gathered together in their common experience of knowing the risen Christ.

Though a faithless world did not acknowledge or honor Jesus, John understood him to be 'the ruler of the kings of the earth' (1.5). Followers

---

language that parallels John's choice of city as a metaphor for the Roman Empire. Aristides also describes the Emperor as an omniscient just judge, in language that John would have reserved for God alone on judgment day: '[The Emperor] governs the whole world as if it were a single city... Under the Roman Empire, neither the plaintiff nor the defendant need submit to an unjust decision. Another great judge remains from whom justice is never hidden. At that bar there is profound and impressive equity between small and great, obscure and eminent, poor and rich, nobleman and commoner'. *To Rome* 36-39, cited by Lewis and Reinhold, *Roman Civilization*, II, pp. 411-12. Cf. Rev. 20.11-15.

19. See, e.g., the virtual merger of God and Lamb in Rev. 22.1.

of Jesus across the Roman Empire took this literally, insisting that their highest political and religious loyalty belonged to the crucified and risen Christ (e.g., Acts 17.7; cf. Jn 19.12). An actual network of Jesus' disciples, consisting of people who made real changes in their political allegiance and economic priorities, superimposed itself upon the vast Roman world.

John could not have believed that cosmic salvation already was complete or that the New Jerusalem already was fully realized. His statement that 'death will be no more', that 'mourning and crying and pain will be no more' (Rev. 21.4), simply did not reflect the reality of a persecuted church and corrupt world. Yet pivotal phrases in the final chapters of Revelation echo expressions of realized eschatology elsewhere in early Christian literature.

John hears the one seated on the throne say, 'See, I am making all things new' (21.5). Paul's encounter with the risen Lord had led him to observe that 'if anyone is in Christ, there is a new creation; everything old has passed away; see, everything has become new' (2 Cor. 5.17). For Paul, apocalyptic transformation on a cosmic scale was not only a future event of physical change; it also was a *radical shift of perspective* that happens in the minds and hearts of people who follow Jesus. All of creation looked new after Paul encountered the risen Lord; all lesser values and priorities, all fears of death or human power, had passed away.

John of Patmos heard the one seated on the throne announce, 'To the thirsty I will give water as a gift from the spring of the water of life' (Rev. 21.6). The fourth Gospel records Jesus saying, 'let the one who believes in me drink' (Jn 7.38; cf. 4.7-15). The Gospel writer understood the 'living water' of divine presence to be a reality for all who confessed Jesus as Messiah. John of Patmos, drinking in the love and hope that he enjoyed by mystical union with Christ, may have quenched his own spiritual and political thirst with waters from the New Jerusalem.

Ezekiel and Economic Justice in the Reign of God
Just as John borrowed images from Ezekiel to describe the wicked city of Babylon (Rome),[20] he now uses the Temple Vision of Ezekiel 40–48 as a paradigm for a fresh portrait of God's redeemed city. Ezekiel described a restored Jerusalem in which kings no longer would be 'whoring' in idolatry (Ezek. 43.7), where princes would 'put away violence and

20. See pp. 156-61.

oppression' (45.9), where merchants would operate with 'honest balances' (45.10). Although John makes only a brief survey of the New Jerusalem, he seems to share Ezekiel's hope for a political order of righteousness and justice.

We get some notion of John's idea of economic justice from his description of the jewel-studded New Jerusalem. Precious stones adorning the city's foundation closely match those on the ephod of the high priest in the tabernacle (Exod. 28.17-20; see Figure 9). Perhaps John meant to suggest that the New Jerusalem fulfills some cultic function of the ancient tabernacle or temple. It is more likely, though, that John tailored his list of jewels to match those worn by the king of Tyre in his primal state before the fall (Ezek. 28.13).

References to Ezekiel proliferate in the final chapters of Revelation, and Tyre features large in John's treatment of Babylon.[21] Ezekiel describes the king of Tyre as once having been innocent and good 'in Eden, the garden of God'. Laden with precious jewels, the noble king was 'on the holy mountain of God' and was blameless until 'iniquity was found in you' (Ezek. 28.12-15). His besetting sin was commerce tied to violence (28.16), compounded by idolatrous pretense (28.5, 6, 9, 17).

Now, in the New Jerusalem, John sees heaven and earth restored to the pristine state of Eden before the fall. From his vantage point on the holy mountain of God (Rev. 21.10), John witnesses the arrival of a newly-created city of justice and peace. In contrast to the poison fruits of violence and greed that fed the cities of Tyre, Babylon and Rome, the New Jerusalem has trees that bring a 'healing of the nations' (22.2). One measure of the enormous scope of healing is that 'kings of the earth'— erstwhile villains of the Apocalypse—will 'bring their glory' into the holy city (21.24). Apparently the king of Tyre—archetype of idolatry and economic exploitation—proffers his glory in the form of jewels for the foundation of the city! Or, if God in fact destroyed the wicked king (Ezek. 28.18-19), at least the king's ill-gotten wealth now becomes the inheritance of all peoples who stream into the New Jerusalem.

---

21. One indication of this is the relative number of marginal references in the Nestle-Aland Greek New Testament (26th edn). In chapters 17–22 of Revelation, the editors cite more than thirty-five references to Ezekiel. For Exodus they cite only two (one of which is Exod. 28.17-20).

		Rev. 21.19-20	*Exod. 28.17-20* *(Septuagint)*	*Ezek. 28.13* *(Septuagint)*
1	jasper	ἴασπις	ἴασπις	ἴασπιν
2	sapphire	σάπφιρος	σάπφειρος	σάπφειρον
3	chalcedony	χαλκηδών		
4	emerald	σμάραγδος	σμάραγδος	σμάραγδον
5	onyx	σαρδόνυξ	ὀνύχιον	ὀνύχιον
6	carnelian	σάρδιον	σάρδιον	σάρδιον
7	chrysolite	χρυσόλιθος	χρυσόλιθος	χρυσόλιθον
8	beryl	βήρυλλος	βηρύλλιον	βηρύλλιον
9	topaz	τοπάζιον	τοπάζιον	τοπάζιον
10	chrysoprase	χρυσόπρασος		
11	jacinth	ὑάκινθος		
12	amethyst	ἀμέθυστος	ἀμέθυστος	ἀμέθυστον
	carbuncle		ἄνθραξ	ἄνθρακα
	silver			ἀργύριον
	gold			χρυσίον
	ligure		λιγύριον	λιγύριον
	agate		ἀχάτης	ἀχάτην

Figure 9. The twelve jewels in the foundation of the New Jerusalem (Rev. 21.19-20), with parallels from Exodus and Ezekiel. The twelve stones John mentions (upper table, first two columns) closely parallel stones on both the ephod of the high priest in the tabernacle (Exod. 28.17-20) and the king of Tyre in his primal state before the fall (Ezek. 28.13). The preponderance of allusions to Ezekiel in the final chapters of Revelation suggests John had Ezekiel 28 in mind when he described jewels of the New Jerusalem. Ezekiel said the king of Tyre once wore these jewels until in 'the abundance of your trade you were filled with violence, and you sinned'. Then God 'cast you as a profane thing from the mountain of God' (Ezek. 28.16). In John's New Jerusalem, rulers of the earth enter the holy city (Rev. 21.24) and jewels of the king of Tyre are restored to the mountain of God in a community of economic justice.

Isaiah and Socio-Economic Restoration

In addition to drawing heavily from Ezekiel, John seems to have found inspiration for his view of creation restored from the Zion tradition of Isaiah. John launches into his New Jerusalem passage by evoking Isaiah's statement that God will make 'a new heaven and a new earth' (Rev. 21.1; cf. Isa. 65.17; 66.22). Isaiah's vision of the future describes the new era in socio-economic terms: infant mortality—perennial bane of the poor—will be gone, and the elderly will live out their years (Isa. 65.20). There will be sufficient economic and political security for people to build houses and enjoy the fruits of agriculture (65.21-22). Jerusalem will be a place of joy, and Yahweh 'will extend prosperity to her like a river, and the wealth of the nations like an overflowing stream' (66.12).

Having tied his vision of the future to Isaiah's poetry, John alludes to other passages from that prophet that include economic factors. John's statement that God will 'wipe every tear' from the eyes of his redeemed people points back to the Isaiah Apocalypse (Isa. 24–27). In that breath-taking preview of cataclysmic judgment, Isaiah catalogs humanity according to socio-economic polarities: slave/master, maid/mistress, buyer/seller, lender/borrower, creditor/debtor (24.2). The Isaiah Apocalypse follows immediately upon a section that deals, yet again, with Tyre's rapacious international trading network (Isa. 23). The terrors of Isaiah 24–27 seem to issue at least in part from God's wrath at idolatry and economic oppression. God, who is a 'refuge to the poor, a refuge to the needy in their distress' (25.4), intervenes to destroy the economic predator. Having rooted out exploitative economic systems, God restores international relationships by inviting all peoples to Mount Zion for a feast of 'rich food' and 'well-aged wines' (25.6).

Isaiah expected Jerusalem to mediate salvation for all nations (Isa. 2.2). War itself would come to an end as nations 'beat their swords into plowshares' and no longer jockeyed for territorial control (Isa. 2.4). Both Isaiah and John of Patmos wrote of a glorious future, and both saw the present as a bleak blend of idolatry, military exploitation and economic injustice. Isaiah condemned a fallen society full of illicit alliances with other nations, obscene accumulation of wealth, massive investment in war *materiel,* and stupid reliance upon idols.[22] Isaiah captures in his dark visage 'all the ships of Tarshish' (2.16)—a focus on maritime commerce that John later repeats in his condemnation of Rome.

These signs of hubris and sin, however, fade rapidly for both Isaiah and John when they anticipate God's reign emanating from Jerusalem. (Second) Isaiah expects that divine restoration will transform Jerusalem into a jewelled urban paradise (Isa. 54.11-12; cf. Rev. 21.11, 18-21). Isaiah awaits a future when Zion will delight in both justice and plenty. He says of Jerusalem, 'the abundance of the sea shall be brought to you, the wealth of the nations shall come to you'. Nations shall willingly 'bring gold and frankincense, and shall proclaim the name of the Lord' (Isa. 60.6). John draws us back to this oracle by repeating Isaiah's

---

22. '…they clasp their hands with foreigners. Their land is filled with silver and gold…their land is filled with horses, and there is no end to their chariots. Their land is filled with idols…', Isa. 2.6-8.

insistence that gates of Jerusalem 'shall always be open' so that nations can bring in their wealth (Isa. 60.11; Rev. 21.25).

Incomparably Better than Any Roman City
John's description of the New Jerusalem suggests no one on earth could miss its arrival: in dazzling splendor the holy city descends from heaven. By any standard the restored Jerusalem is huge, measuring twelve thousand stadia in length, in width and in height (Rev. 21.16). Twelve thousand stadia converts to fifteen hundred miles (twenty-four hundred kilometers), big enough to fill the entire Mediterranean basin and most surrounding lands claimed by Rome. Probably, John is not thinking of literal distances when he computes the size of the new city. It is best to leave measurements of the city as 'twelve thousand stadia', because twelve is the number both of the tribes of Israel and the apostles of the Lamb (21.12, 14). The community of God's people, at times seemingly limited to twelve Jewish tribes or to a small band of disciples, someday will cover the world.

By reporting that the New Jerusalem is *a thousand times* twelve stadia, John calls attention to its extravagant scope and enormous capacity. Far from being a small place for only a chosen few, the redeemed city can accommodate all peoples of the world, with room to spare. If Rome was impressive for its size and splendor, the reign of God will be infinitely greater.

Not surprisingly, the New Jerusalem of Revelation mirrors key features of the ideal city in Greek and Roman thought. The quadrangular shape of the holy city (Rev. 21.16) suits the grid street pattern found so often in Greek and Roman urban areas. Roman city planning, in its simplest form, is evident in the north African settlement of Thamugadi (see Figure 10). Although Thamugadi dates from the second century and could not itself have had any influence on John of Patmos, it reflects an ideal that apparently circulated widely in the Roman world.[23]

Like the New Jerusalem, Thamugadi was a perfect square, with a large avenue bisecting the town.[24] The main thoroughfare was a colonnaded street, perhaps analogous to the tree-lined river-street of the New Jerusalem (22.1-2). Whereas three gates gave entrance to Thamugadi

23. E.J. Owens, *The City in the Greek and Roman World* (London: Routledge, 1991), p. 110.
24. According to Herodotus (1.178), Babylon was a square. Cited by Charles, *Commentary*, II, p. 163.

from the north, John's holy city has three gates on all four sides. Like so many Roman towns, there was a forum and theater at the heart of Thamugadi. These standard venues of public commerce and ceremony presumably have their counterparts in the New Jerusalem, where God and the Lamb have a throne and people gather for worship (22.3,4).

Long before John wrote Revelation, Aristotle gave a full description of the ideal city, and emphasized that water was an essential factor.[25] Thamugadi evidently had abundant water, with baths at several sites inside and outside the city. Likewise, the New Jerusalem has its own plentiful supply. A 'river of the water of life' issues from the divine throne and flows 'through the middle of the street of the city' (22.1-2).

Extending a mile on all sides of Roman towns and cities was the *pomerium,* a boundary within which city laws applied and within which no strange cults or other detestable practices could enter.[26] The same is true for the New Jerusalem: 'nothing unclean will enter it, nor anyone who practices abomination or falsehood, but only those who are written in the Lamb's book of life' (21.27).

Even inscriptions on the foundations and gates of the New Jerusalem are in keeping with Roman custom. There are countless examples of public inscriptions from the Roman imperial era that record the philanthropy of individuals who funded municipal works or otherwise served as patrons of a city. From first-century Spain, for example, comes this memorial.

> To Quintus Toreus Culleo son of Quintus, imperial procurator of the province of Baetica—because he at his own expense repaired the town walls dilapidated through old age; gave a plot to build baths…[27]

Similarly, the walls of the New Jerusalem bear inscriptions honoring patrons and benefactors of the city. Twelve city gates each display the name of one tribe of Israel. Twelve foundations for the city walls bear names of 'the twelve apostles of the Lamb' (21.12-14). Thus the holy city honors and remembers those who gave their lives in service or in martyrdom to the God whom Christians worship.

---

25. Aristotle, *Politics* 1330b-1331b. Cited by Owens, *The City in the Greek and Roman World*, pp. 4-5.

26. See Livy, *History of Rome* 1.44. Cited by Lewis and Reinhold, *Roman Civilization*, I, p. 56.

27. *CIL*, II, 3270. Cited by Lewis and Reinhold, *Roman Civilization*, II, p. 348.

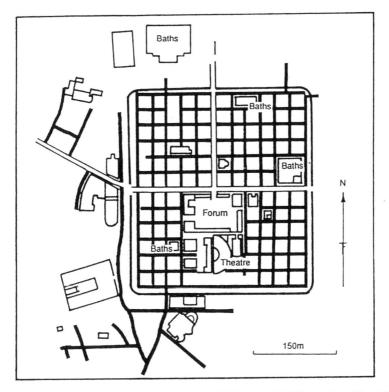

Figure 10. The second-century settlement of Thamugadi (Timgad) in Numidia, northern Africa, provides a simplified example of the ideal in Roman city planning. Like the New Jerusalem described by John, it was a square walled city (Rev. 21.12, 16); it had three gates on the north side (21.13) and a main thoroughfare through the middle (22.2); multiple baths suggest it supplied residents with abundant water (21.6; 22.1, 14, 17).

Illustration from E.J. Owens, *The City in the Greek and Roman World* (London: Routledge, 1991), p. 135. Used by permission of Routledge.

Along with similarities between the New Jerusalem and typical Roman cities, there are striking differences. No self-respecting Roman city was without one or more temples, usually connected to the forum or marketplace. Inhabitants of the New Jerusalem have no need of an ordinary temple, since 'the Lord God Almighty and the Lamb' actually reside there (21.22). There is no need for a religious building, since the people of God themselves constitute a 'temple' where God dwells (3.12; cf. 1 Cor. 3.16-17; Eph. 2.21). In contrast to most ancient cities, which were poorly illuminated at night, the holy city is a place of continuous light (Rev. 21.23, 25; 22.5; cf. Mt. 5.14).

While it is possible to relate aspects of New Jerusalem's configuration to the ideal Roman city, this should not detract from the influence of Jewish literary tradition on John's concept of urban planning. John's holy city may have been quadrangular (or more precisely, cubic) because the holy of holies in Solomon's temple was a perfect cube (1 Kgs 6.20; 2 Chron. 3.8). Just as God was wholly present in the inner sanctuary of Solomon's temple, God now is wholly present in all of the New Jerusalem. It is likely that a river issues from John's New Jerusalem because Ezekiel saw the same (Ezek. 47.1-12). Probably there were three gates on each wall, with names of the twelve tribes of Israel on them, because that is what appeared in Ezekiel's vision (Ezek. 48.30-34). Perhaps the best conclusion to draw is that John leaned heavily on Jewish sources, but described the New Jerusalem in language and symbols that had relevance for first-century Christians surrounded by Roman urban culture.

4. Faith Community as a Taste of the New Jerusalem

John's underlying metaphor of the faith community as a delightful city finds parallel elsewhere in early Christian literature. The author of Hebrews tells believers they 'have come to Mount Zion and to the city of the living God, the heavenly Jerusalem' (Heb. 12.22; cf. 11.10, 16). While such language has a certain other-worldly flavor, something of that heavenly city seems to press itself upon the present: the author of Hebrews goes on to describe a tangible church *community* in which mutual love, hospitality, and fidelity are paramount (Heb. 13.1-5).

Jesus and the Promise of Plenty 'in this Age'

If John actually understood the New Jerusalem as a present reality of radically new power relationships, one might expect inspiration for this to have come from a memory of Jesus. In fact, Jesus spoke of a new kind of society that his followers were to live out immediately. In contrast to the 'kings of the Gentiles' who dominated society, Jesus' disciples were to serve (Lk. 22.25-27; cf. Phil. 2.5-11). He told them it would be difficult for a rich man to enter the kingdom of God, and instructed his followers not to 'store up treasures on earth' or to worry about tomorrow (Mt. 6.19-21, 34).

Not surprisingly, disciples who lived out these radical instructions felt financially and socially vulnerable. Simon Peter once articulated his worry: 'Look, we have left everything and followed you' (Mk 10.28).

Jesus responded by assuring Peter there was social and economic security in the kingdom here and now:

> Truly I tell you, there is no one who has left house or brothers or sisters or mother or father or children or fields, for my sake and for the sake of the good news, who will not receive a hundredfold now *in this age*—houses, brothers and sisters, mothers and children, and fields with persecutions— and in the age to come eternal life (Mk 10.29-30).

We do not have to postulate some *deus ex machina* event in order to explain how marginalized people come to possess family and fields. People who follow Jesus *share what they have.* Jesus' comments about receiving 'a hundredfold now in this age' follow immediately upon his encounter with a wealthy prospective disciple. Jesus told the candidate, 'sell what you own, and give the money to the poor' (Mk 10.21).

Far from offering an individualistic 'gospel of wealth' that plagues the modern Western church, Jesus promoted an egalitarian economic system that functioned as an alternative to the selfishness and inequities of the ancient market economy. Jesus and his disciples practiced a common purse (Jn 13.29; cf. Lk. 8.3), and the first Christian community shared all things in common (Acts 4.32). There is little evidence to suggest that most New Testament churches literally pooled material resources in a common purse. Yet a genuine practice of sharing, even on an international level, remained the expectation. Paul invested a great deal of time and energy in collecting funds from far-flung Gentile congregations for the destitute Jewish church at Jerusalem.[28] James said that feeding and clothing needy fellow church members was a test of true faith (Jas 2.14-17).

Corporate Imagery of 1 Peter
The author of 1 Peter, writing to Christians in Asia Minor, understood believers in a corporate sense as constituting a 'spiritual house' built upon Jesus Christ the cornerstone (1 Pet. 2.4-8). As if to answer the pervasive cultic and political lure of organizations tied to imperial Rome, the author of 1 Peter calls Christians 'a royal priesthood, a holy nation' (1 Pet. 2.9). John H. Elliott says,

> The universal, egalitarian, and socially determined form of communal salvation which these collective terms implied characterized Christianity as

---

28. Gal. 2.10; Rom. 15.25-28; 1 Cor. 16.1-4; 2 Cor. 8–9; cf. Acts 11.27-30.

an attractive alternative to the options presented by Judaism, the collegia, the mystery cults and the theoretical place of belonging which inclusion in a universal Roman *patria* was supposed to have offered.[29]

Elliot argues that 1 Peter addresses Christians who literally were 'resident aliens' (πάροικοι, 1 Pet. 2.11)—the technical term for an actual class of marginalized people who had little social, political or economic status.

We have seen that not all readers of Revelation were powerless; some apparently basked in wealth and social acceptance. Yet those who rejected the values and institutions of Rome as decisively as John of Patmos soon must have found themselves stripped of all status and economic power in wider society. The Christian church may have been the only base of financial and social security these people had. Those who became 'aliens' because of loyalty to Jesus did not simply need a secure future in heaven; they needed a home here and now.[30]

It is not difficult to imagine such marginalized people responding gladly to a loud voice from the throne saying,

> See, the home (σκηνή) of God is among mortals. He will dwell with them as their God; they will be his people, and God himself will be with them; he will wipe every tear from their eyes. Death will be no more; mourning and crying and pain will be no more, for the first things have passed away (Rev. 21.3, 4).

The word for home (σκηνή) in this passage literally means tent or dwelling. It is the same word the Synoptic Gospel writers use to describe what disciples of Jesus wanted to build on a mountain top when they longed to stay indefinitely in the presence of the glorified Christ (Mk 9.5, par.). What was denied to the disciples at the transfiguration now becomes a reality on the mountain top of the New Jerusalem: permanent residence of God with his people.

Family and Household as Corollary Themes

Although political language predominates in Revelation, there also is a strain of domestic and familial imagery. The notion of home and family especially is prominent at the end of Revelation, when there is exuberant celebration at the 'marriage of the Lamb' (Rev. 19.7, 9). The bride is the church, adorned with acts of justice or righteousness (19.8; cf. Eph. 5.23-32).

---

29. J.H. Elliott, *A Home for the Homeless: A Social-Scientific Criticism of 1 Peter, its Situation and Strategy* (Philadelphia: Fortress Press, 1981), p. 134.

30. See Elliott, *A Home for the Homeless*, p. 233.

Identification of the bride as the people of God is a critical insight for interpreting New Jerusalem imagery in Revelation. The holy city comes down out of heaven 'prepared as a bride adorned for her husband' (Rev. 21.2). If the people of God are the bride, and the bride is the New Jerusalem, then the holy city is not a display of extraterrestrial architecture that suddenly drops from the sky. What comes from heaven is divine power for a people to become holy (ἅγιος 22.11), 'set apart' from the warped values and allegiances of pagan society.

In addition to describing the church as the bride of Christ, John says faithful believers will be children of God eligible for inheritance (21.7). This reinforces the domestic imagery theme, and further highlights the notion of *household* as a conceptual framework for Christian identity. Elliott draws attention to the political and social implications of family loyalties.

> The institution of the family, representing as it did time-honored relationships, roles, responsibilities, values and loyalties, served the competitive interests of Empire and Christian sect alike. Each found the concept of an all-embracing family of nations, tribes, tongues and people (cf. Rev. 14.6) a compelling model for the illustration of the universal integration of peoples which it sought. Each could use this image of the 'megafamily' to legitimate incursions into the rights of existing kinship groups. And each could appeal to the paternal implications of organizational leadership: the Emperor as *pater patriae* and the Christian elders as legitimate father figures or representatives of God the Father. For the Christian movement the household ideology provided a plausible social as well as religious rationale for the encouragement of Christian resistance to alien social pressures and even for the critique of imperial paternalistic pretensions.[31]

Christians who claimed God as Father and Jesus as Lord implicitly or explicitly rejected paternal titles held by the Emperor, and claimed status as children of God (Rom. 8.14-17).

In summarizing his life achievements, Caesar Augustus wrote that 'the Senate, the Equestrian order, and the entire Roman people gave me the title Father of his Country, and decreed that this be inscribed in the entrance-hall to my house...'[32] Subsequent Emperors did not hesitate to play the role of father. During the reign of Emperor Titus (79–81 CE) there was an eruption of Mount Vesuvius, a fire at Rome and a terrible plague. Suetonius reports that Titus showed 'not merely the concern of

31. Elliott, *A Home for the Homeless*, pp. 283-84.
32. *Res Gestae* 35.

an Emperor, but even a father's surpassing love, now offering consolation in edicts, and now lending aid so far as his means allowed'.[33]

This is paternal language that matches in tone what John says about God to suffering Christians (Rev. 21.3-4). Jesus said his followers shall 'call no one your father on earth, for you have one Father—the one in heaven' (Mt. 23.9). Although the immediate context of this statement is a discussion about Jewish religious leaders, the prohibition on calling any man 'father' as an honorary title would have extended to the Emperor as well. Some Christians who belonged to the vast network of imperial employees and servants known as the 'Emperor's household' (Phil. 4.22) must have been expected to call the Emperor 'father'. For them Jesus' warning may have had immediate implications.

5. *New Jerusalem in the Post-Apostolic Era*

John charted a course through the Mediterranean world that steered as far as possible from the corrupting influence of imperial Rome. Other Christians of the early church navigated—literally or figuratively— through the same waters, and chose their own course through the 'shallows and straits of idolatry'.[34] How widespread were John's radical notions of community and political allegiance? What lasting impact did John's teaching and example have on later Christians within the Empire?

The early church debated long and hard over whether to make Revelation part of the canon. This indecision stemmed in part from uncertainty about apostolic authorship. However, Revelation's radical critique of imperial power also may have been an issue for Christians who cherished the peace they had made with Rome.[35] Clearly some second-century Christians established a cautious *modus vivendi* with Rome that enabled them to function comfortably within social and economic structures of pagan society.

Christians Continued Relating to Rome

Thompson probably is correct in saying that already in John's day, 'the seer and his audience did not live in a world of conflict, tension,

33. Suetonius, *Titus* 8.3. Cited by Elliott, *A Home for the Homeless*, p. 176.
34. Tertullian, *De Idol.* 24.
35. Frend concludes that 'sub-apostolic Christianity [70–135 AD] was far from being a subversive cult. First, it was by now almost entirely an urban religion whose adherents accepted the very real privileges of Greco-Roman urban society'. Frend, *The Rise of Christianity*, p. 132.

and crisis. Christians lived quiet lives, not much different from other provincials'.[36] The majority of believers were satisfied to avoid both the Roman army and overt participation in pagan or imperial cults. Aside from sporadic episodes of local persecution, second-century Christians usually were able to weave their daily lives into the larger fabric of Roman society.[37] Many Christians continued to live in second-century Rome; others in the provinces had commercial or political ties with the capital city.[38]

A century after John wrote Revelation, Tertullian could tell his Roman reader,

> So, not without your forum, not without your meat-market, not without your baths, shops, factories, your inns and market days, and the rest of the life of buying and selling, we live with you—in this world. We sail ships, we as well as you, and along with you; we go to the wars, to the country, to market with you. Our arts and yours work together; our labour is openly at your service...[39]

While Tertullian may exaggerate for rhetorical effect, his comments nevertheless reflect a Christian church whose members had penetrated virtually all institutions and commercial venues of the Roman Empire.

Enduring Legacy of Radical Community
Despite signs among Christians of increasing participation in the hierarchical Roman society, some believers of John's day and subsequent generations continued to understand the faith community as a place of economic sharing and equality. Clement of Rome told believers at

36. Thompson, *The Book of Revelation*, p. 95.

37. This is not to slight the suffering of the minority who continued to resist social and political pressures. Recorded episodes of second-century persecution in Asia Minor include the trials of Christians under Pliny (*Ep.* 10.96-97); sporadic harassment in some cities during Trajan's reign (Eusebius, *Hist. Eccl.* 3.32); evidence of accusations against Christians during Hadrian's reign (Justin, *1 Apol.* 68) and mob violence against them during the reign of Antoninus Pius (*Hist. Eccl.* 4.26.10; Justin, *1 Apol.* 68). Eleven Christians were killed at the provincial games in Smyrna between 161–68 CE (*Mart. Pol.* 19), followed shortly by the execution of Polycarp, bishop of Smyrna.

38. Eusebius claims that during the reign of Commodus (180–92 CE), 'many of those who at Rome were famous for wealth and family turned to their own salvation [i.e., became Christians] with all their house and with all their kin' (*Hist. Eccl.* 5.21.1).

39. *Apol.* 42. In *Apol.* 37 Tertullian goes so far as to claim there were Christians even in the palace and among senators. Cf. *Ad Scap.* 4.

Corinth, 'Let the strong care for the weak and let the weak reverence the strong. Let the rich [person] bestow help on the poor and let the poor give thanks to God, that he gave...one to supply his needs' (1 *Clem.* 38.2). Likewise the *Didache* instructs readers, 'Do not turn away the needy, but share everything with your brother [and sister], and do not say that it is your own' (*Did.* 4.8). Hermas described the church as a place where the rich person 'provides the poor, without hesitating, with the wealth...received from the Lord' (*Sim.* 2.7). Aristides of Athens (c. 125 CE) said of Christians,

> They do not worship idols (made) in the image of [mortals]...and of the food which is consecrated to idols they do not eat...they do good to their enemies...And he, who has, gives to him who has not, without boasting... And if there is among them any that is poor and needy, and if they have no spare food, they fast two or three days in order to supply to the needy their lack of food.[40]

The anonymous author of a letter to Diognetus, also from the second century, addresses the matter of citizenship and homeland.

> The difference between Christians and the rest of [mortals] is neither in country, nor in language, nor in customs... They dwell in their own [ancestral] lands, but as temporary inhabitants. They take part in all things as citizens, while enduring the hardships of foreigners... They pass their time on earth; but their citizenship is in heaven... They love all [people]; and by all they are persecuted... They are put to death, but they gain life. They are poor, but make many rich; they are destitute, but have an abundance of everything. (*Diogn.* 5.1-6)[41]

These testimonies, from a generation or more after John wrote Revelation, illustrate how some impoverished and marginalized believers found home, material security and citizenship in a city the world could not appreciate or comprehend.

Such small-scale communal societies may seem far removed from the universal transformation depicted in John's New Jerusalem. It may be, though, that communal sharing among disciples of Jesus actually is on a

40. Aristides, *Apology* (Syriac) 15. For a similar text on fasting for the sake of philanthropy, see Hermas, *Sim.* 5.4.7. Clement reports that many believers 'have given themselves to bondage that they might ransom others' or have 'delivered themselves to slavery, and provided food for others with the price they received for themselves', *1 Clem.* 50.2.

41. *Letter to Diognetus*, from W.A. Jurgens, *The Faith of the Early Fathers*, I (Collegeville, MN: The Liturgical Press, 1970), pp. 40-42.

continuum with the eschatological hope of a Holy City. Something of the New Jerusalem becomes a physical reality when people of means give to those who beg and do not refuse those who wish to borrow (Mt. 5.42). The heavenly New Jerusalem breaks into present reality whenever people take seriously the Lord's Prayer, 'Your will be done, on earth as it is in heaven' (Mt. 6.10).[42]

6. *God as the Only Worthy Patron*

'Glory and power' belong to Christ and to Yahweh God, not to the Emperor! This *leitmotif* pervades the book of Revelation, appearing in liturgical passages throughout.[43] With his penchant for dividing humanity into two categories, John seems certain that everybody will take part in *some* patronage system—either that of the Emperor or that of Jesus. Jesus once told his followers, 'No one can serve two masters... You cannot serve God and wealth' (Mt. 6.24). Now John clarifies loyalties for his generation: no one can serve two patrons; you cannot serve God and wealth (or the Emperor who made that wealth possible).

John surveyed the hierarchical patronage system of Roman society and extrapolated beyond visible structures to the ultimate imperial patron, Satan (Rev. 13.2). In response to a society that often catalogued benefits provided by the Emperor and his subordinates, John cited benefits the followers of Jesus some day would enjoy. These included political privileges mentioned in letters to the seven churches, such as 'authority over the nations' (2.26) and a place with Christ on the throne of God (3.21; cf. 20.4). Other benefits would be of enigmatic material nature: 'permission to eat from the tree of life' (2.7), 'hidden manna' (2.17), and the 'morning star' (2.28).

Even if history delayed full realization of these benefits, Christians could honor God and the Lamb as patrons just as adherents to the imperial cult worshiped the Emperor. Participants in the imperial cult organized regional choral societies and sang praises to the Emperor. John now sees a vast choral society of people who worship God and the Lamb (Rev. 7.9-10) for their generosity, power and love.

Jesus made his people into a kingdom, into 'priests serving our God'

42. For discussion of social and political dimensions of New Testament faith communities, see G. Lohfink, *Jesus and Community* (Philadelphia: Fortress Press, 1984), pp. 75-147

43. Rev. 4.8, 11; 5.9-14; 7.15-17; 11.17-18; 12.10-12; 15.3-4; 16.5-7; 19.1-8.

(5.10)—an answer to Emperors who conferred kingdoms and authorized the Augustales. God supplied food (7.16) for his people more reliably than any Emperor ever supplied grain to cities of the Mediterranean. Whereas Rome swallowed nations and powers by dint of military might, the kingdom of God eventually would incorporate all peoples (11.15; 15.4) by means of grace and love. Any Christian tempted to share in the Roman patronage system should acknowledge God—Father, Son and Spirit—as the only worthy patron, and join the litany of praise that punctuates Revelation from start to finish.

John looks to a future when human pretensions to divinity will end and God himself will live among mortals (Rev. 21.3; cf. Zech. 2.10). Death and pain—inevitable by-products of a corrupt Empire—no longer will torment humanity in the New Jerusalem (Rev. 21.4). Far from destroying art, wealth and beauty, the holy city will be a lavish place that gives everyone equal access to resources of the earth.[44] Roman imperial society, with its pyramid of power and economic elites, will be gone forever.[45] In contrast to class-conscious and exclusive Rome, the New Jerusalem will have three gates on each side, welcoming people from all directions of the compass.[46] The gates will never be shut (21.25), and no privileged group will monopolize wealth.[47] Hope for human society redeemed, in every political, economic and social dimension, undergirds

---

44. Although he did not stress the egalitarian aspect of the millenium, Papias (c. 130 CE) apparently envisioned such material abundance in the reign of Christ as to ensure plentious supply for everyone. Bishop of the church at Hierapolis, Papias gives evidence that some second-century Christians in Asia Minor expected a very tangible kingdom. *Fragments of Papias* 4; Irenaeus, *Adv. Haer.* 5.33.3-4. See ridicule of this materialist interpretation in *Hist. Eccl.* 3.34.11-13.

45. *Sib. Or.* 2.319-24 has some parallels to Revelation in its vision of an egalitarian society after judgment: 'The earth will belong equally to all, undivided by walls or fences… Lives will be in common and wealth will have no division. For there will be no poor man there, no rich, and no tyrant, no slave…no one will be either great or small anymore. No kings, no leaders. All will be on a par together.' Cf. *Sib. Or.* 8.110-121.

46. For discussion of the missiology of Revelation, see J.N. Kraybill, 'The New Jerusalem as Paradigm for Mission', *Mission Focus Annual Review* (1994), pp. 123-131.

47. John's vision of a restored Jerusalem is the inverse of what happened after the Maccabean revolt, when the rebels 'fortified Mount Zion with high walls and strong towers, to keep the Gentiles from coming and trampling them down as they had done before' (1 Macc. 4.60).

the message of John's Apocalypse.[48] Rome will fall, and something better for humanity will take its place.

As John navigates through treacherous waters of the first-century world, it is the New Jerusalem—not Rome—for which he yearns. Having abandoned hope that Roman imperial society can be a vehicle for justice and peace, John claims citizenship in a city God himself brings into being. No longer drawn to the dazzling light of decadent Rome, he steers a course toward 'the descendant of David, the bright morning star' (Rev. 22.16). Certain of his destination, sure of God's sovereignty in history, John is willing to pay any social, political or economic price to be true to his Lord.

48. Ethicist O. O'Donovan insists that Revelation provides an ideology for political engagement rather than withdrawal. He reads the Apocalypse as presenting an *analytical* order of events rather than a *sequential* order. For example, the judgment scene of Rev. 20.4-15 represents the necessity of standing under the authority and judgment of God before one can expect to enjoy the New Jerusalem society of Revelation 21. Radical critics of Rome, such as John, 'were not acting anti-politically at all, but were confronting a false political order with the foundation of a true one', O'Donovan says. 'We must claim John for the point of view which sees criticism, when founded in truth, as genuine political engagement'. O'Donovan, 'Political Thought of Revelation', p. 90.

BIBLIOGRAPHY

Achtemeier, P.J., *Harper's Bible Dictionary* (San Francisco: Harper & Row, 1985).

Aland, K., 'The Relation Between Church and State in Early Times: A Reinterpretation', *JTS* 19 (1968), pp. 115-27.

Alexander, L. (ed.), *Images of Empire* (Sheffield: JSOT Press, 1991).

Allo, E.B., *Saint Jean: L'Apocalypse* (Paris: Gabalda, 4th edn, 1933).

Alon, G., *The Jews in their Land in the Talmudic Age (70–640 C.E.)* (trans. and ed. G. Levi; Jerusalem: Magnes Press, 1980–84).

Anderson, B.W., *Out of the Depths: The Psalms Speak for Us Today* (Philadelphia: Westminster Press, 1970).

Applebaum, S., 'The Legal Status of the Jewish Communities in the Diaspora', in Safrai and Stern (eds.), *Jewish People in the First Century*, I, pp. 420-63.

—'Economic Life in Palestine', in Safrai and Stern (eds.), *The Jewish People in the First Century*, II, pp. 631-700.

—'The Social and Economic Status of the Jews in the Diaspora', in Safrai and Stern (eds.), *The Jewish People in the First Century*, II, pp. 701-27.

Attridge, H.W., 'Hebrews', in Mays (ed.), *Harper's Bible Commentary*, pp. 1259-71.

Aubert, J., *Business Managers in Ancient Rome: A Social and Economic Study of Institores, 200 BC–AD 250* (Leiden: Brill, 1994).

Aune, D.E., 'The Social Matrix of the Apocalypse of John', *BR* 26 (1981), pp. 16-32.

—'The Influence of Roman Imperial Court Ceremonial on the Apocalypse of John', *BR* 28 (1983), pp. 5-26.

—'Revelation', in Mays (ed.), *Harper's Bible Commentary*, pp. 1300-19.

—'Hermas', in Ferguson (ed.), *Encyclopedia of Early Christianity*, pp. 421-22.

Bainton, R.H., 'The Early Church and War', *HTR* 39 (1946), pp. 189-212.

Baldwin, J.G., *Haggai, Zechariah, Malachi* (London: Tyndale Press, 1972).

Barclay, W., *The Revelation of John* (2 vols.; Philadelphia: Westminster Press, 2nd edn, 1976).

Barnes, T.D., 'Legislation against the Christians', *JRS* 58 (1968), pp. 32-50.

—*Early Christianity and the Roman Empire* (London: Variorlum Reprints, 1984).

Baron, S.W., *A Social and Religious History of the Jews* (3 vols.; New York: Columbia University Press, 2nd edn, 1952).

Barr, D., 'The Apocalypse as a Symbolic Transformation of the World', *Int* 38 (1984), pp. 39-50.

Barrett, C.K., *A Commentary on the First Epistle to the Corinthians* (New York: Harper & Row, 1968).

—*A Commentary on the Second Epistle to the Corinthians* (New York: Harper & Row, 1973).

Bauckham, R.J., *The Bible in Politics: How to Read the Bible Politically* (London: SPCK, 1989).

—*The Climax of Prophecy: Studies on the Book of Revelation* (Edinburgh: T. & T. Clark, 1992).

—'The Economic Critique of Rome in Revelation 18', in Alexander (ed.), *Images of Empire*, pp. 47-90.

—*Jude, 2 Peter* (WBC, 50; Waco, TX: Word Books, 1983).

—'2 Peter', in Mays (ed.), *Harper's Bible Commentary*, pp. 1286-89.

—'Jude', in Mays (ed.), *Harper's Bible Commentary*, pp. 1297-99.

—*The Theology of the Book of Revelation* (New Testament Theology series; Cambridge: Cambridge University Press, 1993).

Bauer, W., *Orthodoxy and Heresy in Earliest Christianity* (trans. members of Philadelphia Seminar on Christian Origins; eds. G. Strecker, R.A. Kraft and G. Krodel; Philadelphia: Fortress Press, 1971).

—*A Greek–English Lexicon of the New Testament and Other Early Christian Literature* (trans. and ed. W.F. Arndt and F.W Gingrich.; Chicago: University of Chicago Press, 4th edn, 1979).

Beagley, A.J., *The 'Sitz im Leben' of the Apocalypse with Particular Reference to the Role of the Church's Enemies* (Berlin: de Gruyter, 1987).

Beale, G.K., *The Use of Daniel in Jewish Apocalyptic Literature and in the Revelation of St. John* (Lanham, MD: University Press of America, 1984).

Beasley-Murray, G., *The Book of Revelation* (Grand Rapids: Eerdmans, 1974).

Beckwith, I.T., *The Apocalypse of John: Studies in Introduction* (New York: Macmillan, 1919).

Bell, A.A., Jr, 'The Date of John's Apocalypse: Evidence of Some Roman Historians Reconsidered', *NTS* 25 (1978-79), pp. 93-102.

Bell, H.I., 'Anti-Semitism in Alexandria', *JRS* 31 (1941), pp. 1-18.

Benko, S., 'Pagan Criticism of Christianity During the First Two Centuries AD', *ANRW* II, 23.2 (1980), pp. 1055-1118.

—*Pagan Rome and the Early Christians* (Bloomington, IN: Indiana University Press, 1984).

Boesak, A., *Comfort and Protest: Reflections on the Apocalypse of John of Patmos* (Edinburgh: St Andrew Press, 1987).

Bogaert, R. (ed.), *Texts on Bankers, Banking and Credit in the Greek World* (Leiden: Brill, 1976).

Boismard, M.E., ' "L'Apocalypse", ou "Les Apocalypses" de Saint Jean', *RB* 56 (1949), pp. 530-32.

Boring, M.E., *Revelation* (Louisville: John Knox, 1989).

Bousset, W., *Die Offenbarung Johannis* (Göttingen: Vandenhoeck & Ruprecht, 1906).

Bowe, B.E., *A Church in Crisis: Ecclesiology and Paraenesis in Clement of Rome* (Minneapolis: Fortress Press, 1988).

Bowersock, G.W., 'The Imperial Cult: Perceptions and Persistence', in B.F. Meyer and E.P. Sanders (eds.), *Jewish and Christian Self-Definition. III. Self-Definition in the Graeco-Roman World* (Philadelphia: Fortress Press, 1982), pp. 171-82.

Broughton, T.R.S., 'Asia Minor under the Empire, 27 BC-337 AD', in Frank (ed.), *An Economic Survey of Ancient Rome*, IV, pp. 593-902.

Brown, S., 'The Hour of Trial: Rev. 3:10', *JBL* 85 (1966), pp. 308-14.

Bruce, F.F., *New Testament History* (London: Nelson, 1969).

—*Commentary on the Book of Acts* (Grand Rapids: Eerdmans, 1981).

Brunt, P.A., 'The Romanization of the Local Ruling Classes in the Roman Empire', in D.M. Pippidi (ed.), *Assimilation et résistance à la culture gréco-romaine dans le monde ancien: travaux du VIe congrès international d'études classiques, Madrid, Septembre 1974* (Paris: Société d'Edition 'Les Belles Lettres', 1976), pp. 161-73.

Cadbury, H.J., 'The Basis of Early Christian Antimilitarism', *JBL* 37 (1918), pp. 66-94.

Caird, G.B., *A Commentary on the Revelation of St. John the Divine* (New York: Harper & Row, 1966).

Campenhausen, H.F. von, *Tradition und Leben Kräfte der Kirchengeschichte* (Tübingen: Mohr, 1960).

Casson, L., 'Harbour and River Boats of Ancient Rome', *JRS* 55 (1965), pp. 31-39.

—*Ancient Trade and Society* (Detroit: Wayne State University Press, 1984).

—*Ships and Seamanship in the Ancient World* (Princeton: Princeton University Press, 1971).

—'Transportation', in Grant and Kitzinger (eds.), *Civilisation of the Ancient Mediterranean*, I, pp. 353-65.

—*The Ancient Mariners* (Princeton: Princeton University Press, 2nd edn, 1991).

Charles, R.H., *A Critical and Exegetical Commentary on the Revelation of St. John* (2 vols.; ICC; Edinburgh: T. & T. Clark, 1920).

—*The Book of Enoch* (London: SPCK, 1917).

Charlesworth, J.H. (ed.), *The Old Testament Pseudepigrapha* (2 vols.; Garden City: Doubleday, 1983-85).

—'The SNTS Pseudepigrapha Seminars at Tübingen and Paris on the Books of Enoch', *NTS* 25 (1979), pp. 315-23.

Charlesworth, M.P., 'Deus noster Caesar', *CRev* 39 (1925), pp. 113-15.

—*Trade Routes and Commerce of the Roman Empire* (Cambridge: Cambridge University Press, 2nd rev. edn, 1926).

—'Some Observations on Ruler Cult, Especially in Rome', *HTR* 28 (1935), pp. 5-44.

—'*Pietas* and *Victoria*: The Emperor and the Citizen', *JRS* 33 (1943), pp. 1-10.

—'Nero: Some Aspects', *JRS* 40 (1950), pp. 69-76.

Chisholm, K., and J. Ferguson, *Rome: The Augustan Age: A Source Book* (Oxford: Oxford University Press, 1981).

Coleman-Norton, P.R., *Roman State and Christian Church* (London: SPCK, 1966).

Collins, A.Y., 'The Political Perspective of the Revelation to John', *JBL* 96 (1977), pp. 241-56.

—*The Combat Myth in the Book of Revelation* (Harvard Dissertations in Religion, 9; Missoula, MT: Scholars Press, 1976).

—'Revelation 18: Taunt Song or Dirge?' in J. Lambrecht (ed.), *L'Apocalypse johannique et l'Apocalyptique dans le Nouveau Testament* (Gembloux: Leuven University Press, 1980), pp. 185-204.

—'Dating the Apocalypse of John', *BR* 26 (1981), pp. 33-45.

—'Early Christian Apocalypticism: Genre and Social Setting', *Semeia* 36 (1986), pp. 1-12.

—'The Revelation of John: An Apocalyptic Response to a Social Crisis', *CTM* 8 (1981), pp. 4-12.

—'Persecution and Vengeance in the Book of Revelation', in D. Hellholm (ed.), *Apocalypticism in the Mediterranean World and the Near East* (Tübingen: Mohr, 1983), pp. 729-49.

—*Crisis and Catharsis: The Power of the Apocalypse* (Philadelphia: Westminster Press, 1984).

—'Insiders and Outsiders in the Book of Revelation and its Social Context', in J. Neusner and E.S. Frerichs (eds.), *To See Ourselves as Others See Us: Christians, Jews, 'Others' in Late Antiquity* (Chico, CA: Scholars Press, 1985), pp. 187-218.

—'Vilification and Self-Definition in Revelation', *HTR* 79 (1986), pp. 308-20.

Collins, J.J., *The Apocalyptic Imagination: An Introduction to the Jewish Matrix of Christianity* (New York: Crossroad Publishing, 1984).

Conzelmann, H., 'Miszelle zu Apk 18,17 'alle Kapitäne, Seekaufleute...'', *ZNW* 66 (1975), pp. 288-90.

Court, J., *Myth and History in the Book of Revelation* (Atlanta: John Knox, 1979).

Cullman, O., *The State in the New Testament* (London: SCM Press, 1957).

D'Arms, J.H., 'Puteoli in the Second Century of the Roman Empire: A Social and Economic Study', *JRS* 64 (1974), pp. 104-24.

—*Commerce and Social Standing in Ancient Rome* (Cambridge: Harvard University Press, 1981).

Daniel, J.L., 'Anti-Semitism in the Hellenistic-Roman Period', *JBL* 98 (1979), pp. 45-65.

Davies, P.R., 'Daniel in the Lions' Den', in Alexander (ed.), *Images of Empire*, pp. 160-78.

Deissmann, A., *Light from the Ancient East* (New York: George H. Doran, 1927).

Dri, R.R., 'Subversión y apocalíptica', *Servir* 19 (1983), pp. 219-50.

Eichrodt, W., *Ezekiel: A Commentary* (trans. C. Quin; OTL; Philadelphia: Westminster Press, 1970).

Eller, V., *The Most Revealing Book of the Bible* (Grand Rapids: Eerdmans, 1974).

Elliott, J.H., *A Home for the Homeless: A Social-Scientific Criticism of 1 Peter, its Situation and Strategy* (Philadelphia: Fortress Press, 1981).

Engelmann, H., and D. Knibbe, 'Das Zollgesetz der Provinz Asia: Eine neue Inschrift aus Ephesos', *Epigraphica Anatolica* 14 (1989), p. 25.

Epp, E.J., and G.W. MacRae, *The New Testament and its Modern Interpreters* (Philadelphia: Fortress Press, 1989).

Ferguson, E., *Backgrounds of Early Christianity* (Grand Rapids: Eerdmans, 1987).

—*Encyclopedia of Early Christianity* (New York: Garland Publishing, 1990).

Ferguson, J., 'Ruler Worship', in J. Wacher (ed.), *The Roman World*, II (London: Routledge & Kegan Paul, 1987), pp. 1009-1025.

—'Roman Administration', in Grant and Kitzinger (eds.), *Civilisation of the Ancient Mediterranean*, I, pp. 649-65.

Fiorenza, E.S., 'Apocalyptic and Gnosis in the Book of Revelation and Paul', *JBL* 92 (1973), pp. 565-81.

—'1 Corinthians', in Mays (ed.), *Harper's Bible Commentary*, pp. 1168-89.

—'Redemption as Liberation', *CBQ* 36 (1974), pp. 220-32.

—'Revelation', In Epp and MacRae (eds.), *The New Testament and its Modern Interpreters*, pp. 407-27.

—*The Book of Revelation: Justice and Judgment* (Philadelphia: Fortress Press, 1985).

—*Revelation: Vision of a Just World* (Minneapolis: Fortress Press, 1991).

Fischer, N.R.E., 'Roman Associations, Dinner Parties, and Clubs', in Grant and Kitzinger (eds.), *Civilisation of the Ancient Mediterranean*, II, pp. 1199-1225.

Ford, J.M., *Revelation: Introduction, Translation and Commentary* (AB; New York: Doubleday, 1975).

Fornberg, T., *An Early Church in a Pluralistic Society: A Study of 2 Peter* (Lund: Gleerup, 1977).

Fox, R.L., *Pagans and Christians* (New York: Alfred A. Knopf, 1987).

Frank, T., 'Notes on Roman Commerce', *JRS* 27 (1937), pp. 72-79.

— *A History of Rome* (New York: Henry Holt, 1923).

Frank, T. (ed.), *An Economic Survey of Ancient Rome.* IV. *Africa, Syria, Greece, Asia Minor* (4 vols.; Baltimore: Johns Hopkins Press, 1938).

Frend, W.H.C., 'The Gnostic Sects and the Roman Empire', *JEH* 5 (1954), pp. 25-37.

—*Martyrdom and Persecution in the Early Church* (Oxford: Basil Blackwell, 1965).

— 'The Persecutions: Some Links between Judaism and the Early Church', *JEH* 9 (1967), pp. 141-58.

—*The Rise of Christianity* (Philadelphia: Fortress Press, 1984).

Friesen, S.J., *Twice Neokoros: Ephesus, Asia and the Cult of the Flavian Imperial Family* (Leiden: Brill, 1993).

Fuchs, H., *Der Geistige Widerstand Gegen Rom in der Antiken Welt* (Berlin: de Gruyter, 1964).

Garnsey, P., *Social Status and Legal Privilege in the Roman Empire* (Oxford: Clarendon Press, 1970).

—'Grain for Rome', in Garnsey, Hopkins and Whittaker (eds.), *Trade in the Ancient Economy*, pp. 118-30.

Garnsey, P., K. Hopkins and C.R. Whittaker (eds.), *Trade in the Ancient Economy* (London: Chatto & Windus, 1983).

Garnsey, P., and R. Saller (eds.), *The Roman Empire: Economy, Society and Culture* (Berkeley: University of California Press, 1987).

Ginsberg, M., 'Fiscus Judaicus', *JQR* 21 (1930-31), pp. 281-91.

Goldstein, J., 'Jewish Acceptance and Rejection of Hellenism', in E.P. Sanders, A.I. Baumgarten and A. Mendelson (eds.), *Jewish and Christian Self-Definition*, II: *Aspects of Judaism in the Graeco-Roman Period* (Philadelphia: Fortress Press, 1981), pp. 64-87.

Goppelt, L., *Apostolic and Post-Apostolic Times* (Harper Torchbook; New York: Harper & Row, 1970).

Gordon, C.H., 'Tarshish', in *IDB* IV, pp. 517-18.

Gordon, M.L., 'The Freedman's Son in Municipal Life', *JRS* 21 (1931), pp. 65-77.

Grant, M., *History of Rome* (New York: Charles Scribner's Sons, 1978).

Grant, M., and R. Kitzinger (eds.), *Civilization of the Ancient Mediterranean* (3 vols.; New York: Charles Schribner's Sons, 1988).

Grant, R.M., *Augustus to Constantine: The Rise of Christianity in the Roman World* (New York: Harper & Row, 1970).

Greene, K., *The Archaeology of the Roman Economy* (London: B.T. Batsford, 1986).

Griffiths, D.R., *The New Testament and the Roman State* (Swansea: John Penry Press, 1970).

Grimsrud, T., *Triumph of the Lamb* (Scottdale, PA: Herald Press, 1987).

Gunkel, H., *Schöpfung und Chaos in Urzeit und Endzeit* (Göttingen: Vandenhoeck & Ruprecht, 1895).

Haenchen, E., *The Acts of the Apostles: A Commentary* (trans. B. Noble and G. Shinn; Philadelphia: Westminster Press, 1971).

Hammershaimb, E., *The Book of Amos: A Commentary* (trans. J. Sturdy; New York: Schocken Books, 1970).

Hannestad, N., *Roman Art and Imperial Policy* (trans. P.J. Crabb; Aarhus: Aarhus University Press, 1988).

Hanson, P.D., *The Dawn of Apocalyptic* (Philadelphia: Fortress Press, 1975).

Harnack, A. von., *Marcion: Das Evangelium vom Fremden Gott* (Darmstadt: Wissenschaftliche Buchgesellschaft, [1920] 1960).

Hauck, F., 'κοινός', in *TDNT* III, p. 805.

Helgeland, J., 'Roman Army Religion', in *ANRW* II, 16.2 (1978), pp. 1470-1505.

—'Christians and the Roman Army from Marcus Aurelius to Constantine', in *ANRW* II, 16.2 (1978), pp. 724-834.

Hellholm, D., *Apocalypticism in the Mediterranean World and the Near East: Proceedings of the International Colloquium on Apocalypticism, Uppsala, August 12-17, 1979* (Tübingen: Mohr, 1983).

Hemer, C.J., *The Book of Acts in the Setting of Hellenistic History* (Tübingen: Mohr, 1989).

—*The Letters to the Seven Churches in their Local Setting* (Sheffield: JSOT Press, 1986).

Hengel, M., 'Der Jakobusbrief als antipaulinische Polemik', in G.F. Hawthorne and O. Betz (eds.), *Tradition and Interpretation in the New Testament* (Grand Rapids: Eerdmans, 1987), pp. 248-65.

—'Hadrians Politik gegenüber Juden und Christen', *JANESCU* 16-17 (1984–85), pp. 153-82.

—*Judaism and Hellenism: Studies in their Encounter in Palestine during the Early Hellenistic Period* (2 vols.; trans. J. Bowden; London: SCM Press, 1974).

—*Property and Riches in the Early Church: Aspects of a Social History of Early Christianity* (Philadelphia: Fortress Press, 1974).

—*Studies in the Gospel of Mark* (London: SCM Press, 1985).

—*The Zealots: Investigations into the Jewish Freedom Movement in the Period from Herod I until 70 AD* (trans. D. Smith; Edinburgh: T. & T. Clark, 1989).

Hermansen, G., *Ostia: Aspects of Roman City Life* (Edmonton: University of Alberta Press, 1981).

Hopkins, K., 'Elite Mobility in the Roman Empire', *Past and Present* 32 (1965), pp. 12-26.

—*Conquerors and Slaves* (Cambridge: Cambridge University Press, 1978).

—'Taxes and Trade in the Roman Empire (200 B.C.–A.D. 400)', *JRS* 70 (1980), pp. 101-25.

—'Roman Trade, Industry, and Labor', in Grant and Kitzinger (eds.), *Civilisation of the Ancient Mediterranean*, I, pp. 753-77.

Hopkins, M., 'The Historical Perspective of Apocalypse 1–11', *CBQ* 27 (1965), pp. 42-47.

Hornus, J-M., *It Is Not Lawful for Me to Fight* (trans. A. Kreider and O. Coburn; Scottdale, PA.: Herald Press, 1980).

Horsley, G.H.R., and S.R. Llewelyn (eds.), *New Documents Illustrating Early Christianity* (6 vols.; North Ryde: Macquarrie University, 1981–92).

Horsley, R.A., and J.S. Hanson, *Bandits, Prophets, and Messiahs: Popular Movements in the Time of Jesus* (San Francisco: Harper & Row, 1985).

Janzen, E.P., 'The Jesus of the Apocalypse Wears the Emperor's Clothes', in E.H. Lovering, Jr (ed.), *Society of Biblical Literature 1994 Seminar Papers* (Atlanta: Scholars Press, 1994), pp. 637-61.

Jenks, G.C., *The Origins and Early Development of the Antichrist Myth* (Berlin: de Gruyter, 1991).

Johnson, S.E., 'Early Christianity in Asia Minor', *JBL* 77 (1958), pp. 1-17.

—'Unsolved Questions about Early Christianity in Anatolia', in D.E. Aune (ed.), *Studies in New Testament and Early Christian Literature* (Leiden: Brill: 1972).

—'Asia Minor and Early Christianity', in J. Neusner (ed.), *Christianity, Judaism and Other Greco-Roman Cults* (Leiden: Brill, 1975), pp. 77-145.

Jones, A.H.M., 'The Economic Life of the Towns of the Roman Empire', in P.A. Brunt (ed.), *The Roman Economy* (Totowa, NJ: Rowman & Littlefield, 1974).

Jones, B.W., *Domitian and the Senatorial Order* (Philadelphia: American Philosophical Society, 1979).

—*The Emperor Domitian* (London: Routledge, 1992).

Jones, D.L., 'Christianity and the Roman Imperial Cult', *ANRW* II, 23.2 (1980), pp. 1023-54.

Judge, E., 'Judaism and the Rise of Christianity: A Roman Perspective', *AJJS* 7 (1993), pp. 82-98.

—*The Social Pattern of Christian Groups in the First Century* (London: Tyndale Press, 1960)

—*The Social Setting of Pauline Christianity* (Philadelphia: Fortress Press, 1982).

Jurgens, W.A., *The Faith of the Early Fathers*, I (Collegeville, MN: Liturgical Press, 1970).

Juster, J., *Les Juifs dans l'Empire Romain: Leur Condition juridique, économique et sociale* (2 vols.; Paris: Librairie Paul Geuthner, 1914).

Kaiser, O., *Isaiah 13–39* (trans. R.A. Wilson; Philadelphia: Westminster Press, 1974).

Karris, R.J., 'The Background and Significance of the Polemic of the Pastoral Epistles', *JBL* 92 (1973), pp. 549-64.

Keresztes, P., 'The Jews, the Christians, and Emperor Domitian', *Vigiliae Christianae* 27 (1973), pp. 1-28.

—'The Imperial Roman Government and the Christian Church', *ANRW* II, 23.1 (1979), pp. 247-315.

Kimelman, R., '*Birkat Ha-Minim* and the Lack of Evidence for an Anti-Christian Jewish Prayer in Late Antiquity', in E.P. Sanders, A.I. Baumgarten and A. Mendelson (eds.), *Jewish and Christian Self-Definition*. II. *Aspects of Judaism in the Graeco-Roman Period* (Philadelphia: Fortress Press, 1981), pp. 226-44.

Klassen, W., 'Vengeance in the Apocalypse of John', *CBQ* 28 (1966), pp. 300-311.

Knibb, M.A., 'The Date of the Parables of Enoch', *NTS* 25 (1979), pp. 345-59.

Knibbe, D., and H. Engelmann, 'Das Zollgesetz der Provinz Asia: Eine neue Inschrift aus Ephesos', *Epigraphica Anatolica* 14 (1989), p. 25.

Koester, H., *Introduction to the New Testament: History, Culture and Religion of the Hellenistic Age* (New York: de Gruyter, 1987).

Kraabel, A.T., 'The Diaspora Synagogue: Archaeological and Epigraphic Evidence since Suhenik', *ANRW* II, 19.1 (1979), pp. 477-510.

Kraeling, C.H., 'The Episode of the Roman Standards at Jerusalem', *HTR* 35 (1942), pp. 263-89.

Kraybill, J.N., 'The New Jerusalem as Paradigm for Mission', *Mission Focus Annual Review* (1994), pp. 123-31.

Kreider, A.F., *Worship and Evangelism in Pre-Christendom* (Joint Liturgical Studies, 32; Cambridge: Grove Books, 1995).

Kreitzer, L.J., *Striking New Images: Studies on Roman Imperial Coinage and the New Testament World* (JSNTSup, 134; Sheffield: Sheffield Academic Press, 1996).

Kümmel, W.G., *Introduction to the New Testament* (trans. H.C. Kee; Nashville: Abingdon Press, rev. edn, 1975).

La Piana, G., 'Foreign Groups in Rome during the First Centuries of the Empire', *HTR* 20 (1927), pp. 183-403.

Lambrecht, J. (ed.), *L'Apocalypse johannique et l'apocalyptique dans le Nouveau Testament* (Gembloux: Duculot, 1980).

Lampe, P., *Die stadrömischen Christen in den ersten beiden Jahrhunderten: Undersuchungen zur Sozialgeschichte* (Tübingen: Mohr [Paul Siebeck], 1989).

Leon, H.J., *The Jews of Ancient Rome* (Philadelphia: Jewish Publication Society, 1960).

Levick, B., 'Domitian and the Provinces', *Latomus* 41 (1982), pp. 50-73.

—*The Government of the Roman Empire: A Source Book* (London: Croom Helm, 1985).

Levine, L.I., *Caesarea Under Roman Rule* (Leiden: Brill, 1975).

Lewis, N., and M. Reinhold (eds.), *Roman Civilization* (2 vols.; Harper Torchbooks; New York: Harper & Row [1951–55] 1966).

Lohmeyer, E., *Die Offenbarung des Johannes* (Tübingen: Mohr [Paul Siebeck], rev. edn, 1953).

Lohfink, G., *Jesus and Community: The Social Dimension of Christian Faith* (trans. J.P. Galvin; Philadelphia: Fortress Press, 1984).

Lüdemann, G., 'The Successors of Pre-70 Jerusalem Christianity: A Critical Evaluation of the Pella-Tradition', in E.P. Sanders (ed.), *Jewish and Christian Self-Definition*, I: *the Shaping of Christianity in the Second and Third Centuries* (Philadelphia: Fortress Press, 1980), pp. 161-73.

MacMullen, R., *Enemies of the Roman Order: Treason, Unrest and Alienation in the Empire* (Cambridge: Harvard University Press, 1966).

—*Corruption and the Decline of Rome* (New Haven: Yale University Press, 1988).

Macro, A.D., 'The Cities of Asia Minor under the Roman Imperium', *ANRW* II, 7.2 (1980), pp. 658-97.

Madden, F.W., *History of Jewish Coinage* (London: Bernard Quaritch, 1864).

Magie, D., *Roman Rule in Asia Minor* (2 vols.; Princeton: Princeton University Press, 1950).

Malherbe, A.J., *Social Aspects of Early Christianity* (Baton Rouge, LA: Louisiana State University Press, 1977).

Marx, K., *Capital: A Critique of Political Economy*, I (trans. S. Moore and E. Aveling; ed. F. Engels; London: Lawrence & Wishart, 1954).

Matthews, J.F., 'The Tax Law of Palmyra: Evidence for Economic History in a City of the Roman East', *JRS* 74 (1984), pp. 157-80.

Mattingly, H., *Coins of the Roman Empire in the British Museum*. I. *Augustus to Vitellius* (London: Trustees of the British Museum, rev. edn, 1976 [1923]); II. *Vespasian to Domitian* (London: Trustees of the British Museum, rev. edn, 1976 [1930]).

Mattingly, H., and E.A. Sydenham, *Roman Imperial Coinage*. II. *Vespasian to Hadrian* (London: Spink & Son, 1926).

Mays, J.L., *Amos* (OTL; Philadelphia: Westminster Press, 1969).

Mays, J.L. (ed.), *Harper's Bible Commentary* (San Francisco: Harper & Row, 1988).

McCrum. M., and A.G. Woodhead (eds.), *Select Documents of the Principates of the Flavian Emperors* (Cambridge: Cambridge University Press, 1961).

Mearns, L., 'Dating the Similitudes of Enoch', *NTS* 25 (1979), pp. 360-69.

Meeks, W.A., *The First Urban Christians: The Social World of the Apostle Paul* (New Haven: Yale University Press, 1983).

Meiggs, R., *Roman Ostia* (Oxford: Oxford University Press, 2nd edn, 1973).

Meijer, F., and O. van Nijf, *Trade, Transport and Society in the Ancient World: A Sourcebook* (London: Routledge, 1992).

Millar, F., 'The Emperor, the Senate and the Provinces', *JRS* 56 (1966), pp. 156-66.

—*The Emperor in the Roman World (31 BC–AD 337)* (London: Gerald Duckworth, 1977).

Mitchell, S., 'The Plancii in Asia Minor', *JRS* 64 (1974), pp. 27-39.

Momigliano, A., *On Pagans, Jews, and Christians* (Middletown, CT: Wesleyan University Press, 1987).

Morris, L., *The Revelation of St. John* (Grand Rapids: Eerdmans, 1969).

Mounce, R.T., *The Book of Revelation* (Grand Rapids: Eerdmans, 1977).

Neusner, J., *Development of a Legend: Studies on the Traditions Concerning Yohanan ben Zakkai* (Leiden: Brill, 1970).

—*Genesis Rabbah: the Judaic Commentary to the Book of Genesis* (3 vols.; Atlanta: Scholars Press, 1985).

—*The Economics of the Mishnah* (Chicago: University of Chicago Press, 1990).

Neyrey, J.H. *The Social World of Luke–Acts: Models for Interpretation* (Peabody, MA: Hendrickson, 1991).

Nock, A.D., *Conversion: The Old and the New in Religion from Alexander the Great to Augustine of Hippo* (Lanham, MD: University Press of America, [1933] 1988).

—'Seviri and Augustales', in Z. Stewart (ed.), *Essays on Religion and the Ancient World,* I (Cambridge: Harvard University Press, 1972), pp. 348-56.

—'The Roman Army and Roman Religious Year', *HTR* 45 (1952), pp. 187-252.

O'Donovan, O., 'The Political Thought of the Book of Revelation', *TynBul* 37 (1986), pp. 61-94.

O'Rourke, J.J., 'The Hymns of the Apocalypse', *CBQ* 30 (1968), pp. 399-409.

Osiek, C., *Rich and Poor in the Shepherd of Hermas* (Washington: Catholic Biblical Association of America, 1983).

Owens, E.J., *The City in the Greek and Roman World* (London: Routledge, 1991).

Parker, A.J., 'Trade Within the Empire and Beyond the Frontiers', in J. Wacher (ed.), *The Roman World*, II (New York: Routledge & Kegan Paul, 1987), pp. 635-57.

Patai, R., 'Jewish Seafaring in Ancient Times', *JQR* 32 (1941–42), pp. 1-26.

Pauly, A.F. von, and G. Wissowa (eds.), *Paulys Real-Encyclopädie der classichen Altertumswissenshaft* (33 vols.; Stuttgart: Metzlersche, 1893–1972).

Petersen, D.L., 'Zechariah', in Mays (ed.), *Harper's Bible Commentary*, pp. 747-52.

Petit, P., *Pax Romana* (trans. J. Willis; Berkeley: University of California Press, 1976).

Pleket, H.W., 'Urban Elites and Business in the Greek Part of the Roman Empire', in P. Garnsey, K. Hopkins and C.R. Whittaker (eds.), *Trade in the Ancient Economy* (London: Chatto & Windus, The Hogarth Press, 1983), pp. 131-44.

Price, S.R.F., 'Between Man and God: Sacrifice in the Roman Imperial Cult', *JRS* 70 (1980), pp. 28-43.

—*Rituals and Power: The Imperial Roman Cult in Asia Minor* (Cambridge: Cambridge University Press, 1984).

Pucci, G., 'Pottery and Trade in the Roman Period', in Garnsey, Hopkins and Whittaker (eds.), *Trade in the Ancient Economy*, pp. 105-17.

Rabello, A.M., 'The Legal Condition of the Jews in the Roman Empire', *ANRW* II, 13 (1980), pp. 662-762.

Radin, M., *The Jews Among the Greeks and Romans* (Philadelphia: Jewish Publication Society, 1915).

Rajak, T., 'Was There a Roman Charter for the Jews?' *JRS* 74 (1984), pp. 107-23.

Ramsay, W.M., *Cities and Bishoprics of Phrygia* (2 vols.; Oxford: Clarendon Press, 1895–97).

—'The Jews in the Graeco-Asiatic Cities', *The Expositor* 5 (1902), pp. 92-109.

—'The Letter to the Church in Thyatira', *The Expositor* 10 (1904), pp. 37-60.

—*The Letters to the Seven Churches of Asia* (New York: Hodder & Stoughton, 1905).

—*The Social Basis of Roman Power in Asia Minor* (Aberdeen: Aberdeen University Press, 1941).

—'Studies in the Roman Province of Galatia. VI. Some Inscriptions of Colonia Caesarea Antiochea', *JRS* 14 (1924), pp. 179-84.

Raschke, M.G., 'New Studies in Roman Commerce with the East', *ANRW* II, 9.2 (1978), pp. 605-1361.

Reese, J.M., 'Wisdom of Solomon', in Mays (ed.), *Harper's Bible Commentary*, pp. 820-35.

Richardson, L., Jr, *A New Topographical Dictionary of Ancient Rome* (Baltimore: Johns Hopkins University Press, 1992).

Rissi, M., 'The Rider on the White Horse', *Int* 18 (1964), pp. 407-18.

—*Time and History: A Study on the Revelation* (Richmond, VA: John Knox, 1966).

Robinson, J.M., *The Nag Hammadi Library* (San Francisco: Harper & Row, 1988).

Robinson, J.M., and H. Koester, *Trajectories through Early Christianity* (Philadelphia: Fortress Press, 1971).

Robinson, T.A., *The Bauer Thesis Examined: The Geography of Heresy in the Early Christian Church* (Lewiston: Edwin Mellen Press, 1988).

Rogers, R.S., 'A Group of Domitianic Treason-Trials', *Classical Philosophy* 55 (1960), pp. 19-23.

Rostovtzeff, M., *A History of the Ancient World* (2 vols.; trans. J.D. Duff; London: Oxford University Press, 1938).

—*The Social and Economic History of the Hellenistic World* (3 vols.; Oxford: Clarendon Press, 1941).

—*The Social and Economic History of the Roman Empire* (2 vols.; Oxford: Clarendon Press, 2nd edn, 1957).

Roth, C., 'An Ordinance against Images in Jerusalem', *HTR* 49 (1956), pp. 169-77.

Rowland, C., *The Open Heaven: A Study of Apocalyptic in Judaism and Early Christianity* (London: SPCK, 1982).

—*Revelation* (Epworth Commentaries; London: Epworth Press, 1993).

Ruiz, J-P., *Ezekiel in the Apocalypse: The Transformation of Prophetic Language in Revelation 16,17–19,10* (Frankfurt am Main: Peter Lang, 1989).

Russell, D.S., *The Method and Message of Jewish Apocalyptic* (Philadelphia: Westminster Press, 1964).

Safrai, S., and M. Stern (eds.), *The Jewish People in the First Century*, I (Assen: Van Gorcum, 1974); II (Philadelphia: Fortress Press, 1976).

Ste. Croix, G.E.M. de, 'Ancient Greek and Roman Maritime Loans', in H. Edey and B.S. Yamey (eds.), *Debits, Credits, Finance and Profits: Essays in Honour of William Threipland Baxter* (London: Sweet & Maxwell, 1974).

Saller, R.P., *Personal Patronage under the Early Empire* (Cambridge: Cambridge University Press, 1982).

—'Roman Class Structures and Relations', in Grant and Kitzinger (eds.), *Civilisation of the Ancient Mediterranean*, I, pp. 549-73.

Sanders, J.N., 'St. John on Patmos', *NTS* 9 (1963), pp. 75-85.

Scherrer, S.J., 'Signs and Wonders in the Imperial Cult—Rev. 13:13-15', *JBL* 103 (1984), pp. 599-610.

Schürer, E., *The History of the Jewish People in the Age of Jesus Christ (175 BC–AD 135)* (3 vols.; rev. and ed. by M. Black *et al;* Edinburgh: T. & T. Clark, 1973–87).

Scott, K., *The Imperial Cult Under the Flavians* (New York: Arno Press, [1936] 1975).

Scroggs, R., 'Woman in the NT', *IDBSup*, pp. 966-68.

Seager, A.R., 'The Building History of the Sardis Synagogue', *AJA* 76 (1972), pp. 425-35.

Shea, W.H., 'Chiasm in Theme and by Form in Revelation 18', *AUSS* 20 (1982), pp. 249-56.

Sheppard, A.R., 'Jews, Christians and Heretics in Acmonia and Eumeneia', *Anatolian Studies* 29 (1979), pp. 169-80.

Sherk, R.K. (ed. and trans.), *The Roman Empire: Augustus to Hadrian* (Translated Documents of Greece and Rome, VI; Cambridge: Cambridge University Press, 1988).

Sherwin-White, A.N., *Roman Society and Roman Law in the New Testament* (Oxford: Oxford University Press, 1963).

—*The Letters of Pliny: A Historical and Social Commentary* (Oxford: Clarendon Press, 1966).

—'Domitian's Attitude towards the Jews and Judaism', *Classical Philosophy* 51 (1956), pp. 1-13.

Smallwood, E.M., *The Jews Under Roman Rule: From Pompey to Diocletian* (Studies in Judaism in Late Antiquity, 20; Leiden: Brill, 1976).

Sordi, M., *The Christians and the Roman Empire* (trans. A. Bedini; London: Croom Helm, 1983).

Stambaugh, J.E., and D.L. Balch, *The New Testament in its Social Environment* (Library of Early Christianity; Philadelphia: Westminster Press, 1986).

Stauffer, E., *Christ and the Caesars* (trans. K. Smith and R.G. Smith; London: SCM Press, 1955).

Stern, M., 'The Jewish Diaspora', in Safrai and Stern (eds.), *The Jewish People in the First Century*, I, pp. 117-83.

Stoeckle, 'Navicularii', PW, XVI.II, cols. 1899-1932.

Strand, K., 'Two Aspects of Babylon's Judgment in Revelation 18', *AUSS* 20 (1982), pp. 53-60.

—'Some Modalities of Symbolic Usage in Revelation 18', *AUSS* 24 (1986), pp. 37-46.

—'The Eight Basic Visions in the Book of Revelation', *AUSS* 25 (1987), pp. 107-21.

Sutherland, C.H.V., *Roman Coins* (London: Barrie & Jenkins, 1974).

Sweet, J.P.M., *Revelation* (Philadelphia: Westminster Press, 1979).

Swete, H.B., *The Apocalypse of St. John* (London: Macmillan, 3rd edn, 1911).

Swift, L.J., 'War and the Christian Conscience I: The Early Years', *ANRW* II, 23.1 (1979), pp. 835-68.

—*The Early Fathers on War and Military Service* (Wilmington, DE: Michael Glazier, 1983).

Tamari, M., *'With All Your Possessions': Jewish Ethics and Economic Life* (New York: The Free Press, 1987).

Taylor, L.R., *The Divinity of the Roman Emperor* (Middletown, CT: American Philological Association, 1931).

Tcherikover, V., *Hellenistic Civilization and the Jews* (trans. S. Applebaum; Philadelphia: Jewish Publication Society, 1959).

Temporini, H., *et al.* (eds.), *Aufstieg und Niedergang der römischen Welt* (Berlin: de Gruyter, 1972–79).

Theissen, G., *The Social Setting of Pauline Christianity* (trans. J.H. Schütz; Philadelphia: Fortress Press, 1982).

Thompson, L., 'Cult and Eschatology in the Apocalypse of John', *JR* 49 (1969), pp. 330-50.

—*The Book of Revelation: Apocalypse and Empire* (Oxford: Oxford University Press, 1990).

Thompson, S., *The Apocalypse and Semitic Syntax* (Cambridge: Cambridge University Press, 1985).

Thompson, W.E., 'Insurance and Banking', in Grant and Kitzinger (eds.), *Civilisation of the Ancient Mediterranean*, II, pp. 829-36.

Trebilco, P.R., *Jewish Communities in Asia Minor* (SNTSMS, 69; Cambridge: Cambridge University Press, 1991).

Van Henten, J., 'Dragon Myth and Imperial Ideology in Rev 12–13', in E.H. Lovering, Jr (ed.), *Society of Biblical Literature 1994 Seminar Papers* (Atlanta: Scholars Press, 1994), pp. 496-515.

Vermes, G., *The Dead Sea Scrolls in English* (Harmondsworth: Penguin Books, 3rd edn, 1987).

—'Dead Sea Scrolls', *IDBSup*, pp. 210-19.

Vogelgesang, J.M., *The Interpretation of Ezekiel in the Book of Revelation* (Ann Arbor: University Microfilms International, 1986).

Wacher, J., *The Roman World* (New York: Routledge & Kegan Paul, 1987).

Waelkens, M., 'Phrygian Votives and Tombstones as Sources of the Social and Economic Life in Roman Antiquity', *Ancient Society* 8 (1977), pp. 277-315.

Walbank, F.W., 'Plutarch', in *Encyclopaedia Britannica*, XIV (15th edn, 1978), pp. 578-80.

Waltzing, J.P., *Etude historique sur les corporations professionelles chez les romains* (Louvain: 1895–1900).

Watson, G.R., *The Roman Soldier* (Ithaca: Cornell University Press, 1969).

Wengst, K., *Pax Romana and the Peace of Jesus Christ* (trans. J. Bowden; Philadelphia: Fortress Press, 1987).

Whedbee, J.W., 'Joel', in Mays (ed.), *Harper's Bible Commentary*, pp. 716-19.

Wilken, R.L., 'The Christians as the Romans (and Greeks) Saw Them', in E.P. Sanders (ed.), *Jewish and Christian Self-Definition*. I. *The Shaping of Christianity in the Second and Third Centuries* (Philadelphia: Fortress Press, 1980), pp. 100-125.

Wink, W., *Engaging the Powers: Discernment and Resistance in a World of Domination* (Minneapolis: Fortress Press, 1992).

Wolterstorff, N., *Until Justice and Peace Embrace* (Grand Rapids: Eerdmanns, 1983).

Yadin, Y., *The Scroll of the War of the Sons of Light Against the Sons of Darkness* (Oxford: Oxford University Press, 1962).

Yamauchi, E.M., *New Testament Cities in Western Asia Minor* (Grand Rapids: Baker Book House, 1980).

Yoder, J.H., *The Politics of Jesus* (Grand Rapids: Eerdmans, 1972).

Zanker, P., *The Power of Images in the Age of Augustus* (trans. A. Shapiro; Ann Arbor: University of Michigan Press, 1988).

Zimmerli, W., *A Commentary on the Book of the Prophet Ezekiel* (2 vols.; trans. J.D. Martin; Philadelphia: Fortress Press, 1983).

INDEXES

INDEX OF REFERENCES

OLD TESTAMENT

NEW TESTAMENT

OTHER ANCIENT REFERENCES

INDEX OF SUBJECTS